Prussian Schoolteachers

𝕻𝖗𝖚𝖘𝖘𝖎𝖆𝖓 𝕾𝖈𝖍𝖔𝖔𝖑𝖙𝖊𝖆𝖈𝖍𝖊𝖗𝖘

PROFESSION AND OFFICE, 1763–1848

ANTHONY J. LA VOPA

THE UNIVERSITY OF NORTH CAROLINA PRESS

Chapel Hill

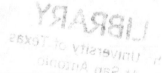

© 1980 The University of North Carolina Press
All rights reserved
Manufactured in the United States of America
ISBN 0-8078-1426-1
Library of Congress Catalog Card Number 79-24873

Library of Congress Cataloging in Publication Data

La Vopa, Anthony J   1945–
Prussian schoolteachers.

Bibliography: p.
Includes index.
 1. Teachers—Prussia—History.   I. Title.
LA721.5.L38   371.1'00943   79-24873
ISBN 0-8078-1426-1

To my mother,
and to the memory of my father

CONTENTS

Contents

ACKNOWLEDGMENTS

A fellowship for the academic year 1971–72 from the German Academic Exchange Service (DAAD) allowed me to spend a semester at the Universität Köln and another at the Freie Universität in West Berlin, where I continued work on this book begun at Cornell University. My second research trip to Germany in the summer of 1977 was made possible by a grant from the Faculty Research and Development Fund at North Carolina State University.

Unfortunately I can mention only a few of the many people whose friendship and ideas helped shape the book. Among them are David Crew, Mary Nolan, James E. Crisp, Robert M. Collins, Gordon D. Newby, and Nancy Ketchiff. My fascination with German history dates back to undergraduate years; it was instilled and guided by the teaching of John L. Heineman. Bernard W. Wishy has been generous with both encouragement and sound advice. In recent years Joan W. Scott has greatly enriched my understanding of social history and its potential. Fritz K. Ringer kindly read a long dissertation and encouraged me to fashion it into a short book. Aside from his superb readings of my work, Donald M. Scott helped focus it by sharing his insights on the history of the professions in the United States. Likewise the contribution of Stanley Suval goes well beyond specific criticisms and suggestions; like so many others, I have benefited immeasurably from his friendship, his intellectual rigor, and his infectious commitment to the discipline of history and the life of the mind. As a student of Mack Walker I have had special reason to appreciate his scholarly integrity and imagination. He guided my dissertation through several shoals and has remained a patient mentor.

The research for the book took me to several German archives, and to more libraries than I can list here. I am particularly grateful to the staffs of the Hauptstaatsarchiv Düsseldorf, Abteilung Kalkum; the Geheimes Staatsarchiv, Berlin-Dahlem; the Staatsarchiv Münster; the Universitäts- und Stadtbibliothek Köln; the Universitätsbibliothek der Freien Universität Berlin; and die Pädagogische Zentralbücherei des Landes Nordrhein-Westfalen in Dortmund. I would like to extend a special word of thanks to the Pädagogische Zentralbibliothek in the Haus des Lehrers, East Berlin, where I found many of my most cherished sources. The cooperation of the staff made my work there both pleasant and fruitful.

A portion of this work appeared in an article entitled "Status and Ideology: Rural Schoolteachers in Pre-March and Revolutionary Prussia" in the March 1979 issue of the *Journal of Social History*.

My wife, Patricia Gwaltney, was not interested in history when we met, and I may stop trying to convert her. She knows that the book owes a great deal to her tolerance and love.

Prussian Schoolteachers

INTRODUCTION

Schoolmasters survived on the margins of rural and urban life in eighteenth-century Germany. Most of them worked in the "lower" schools to supplement other meager livelihoods and lacked training or other qualifications for teaching. The title "master" (*Meister*) was misleading; it suggested a degree of skill and prestige that the practitioners of the occupation did not possess. In the popular stereotype "the poor little schoolmaster" was more a tragicomic figure—a caricature of servility and impotence—than a target of hostility. But he was tolerable only so long as he accepted markedly humble terms of employment and minimal, precarious compensation.

The stereotype persisted well into the nineteenth century, but particularly in Prussia, the largest German state, it was based on a vanishing breed. By the 1840s the Prussian elementary school system was the envy of foreign educators. The majority of its younger instructors were schoolteachers, or *Volksschullehrer*, who had been trained for two or three years in state normal schools known as seminars (*Seminarien*). The difference between the generations lay more in self-image and expectations than in working conditions. In the 1830s a handful of seminar graduates began to articulate a new "professional consciousness" (*Standesbewusstsein*) and launched a movement to "emancipate" their profession. Repressed in the mid-1840s, the movement resurfaced and spread through most regions of Prussia in the Revolution of 1848. Like the revolution, it failed; but it had combined a detailed program for the emancipation of the teaching corps with an outspoken defense of the revolution and its ideals.[1]

This study examines the transition from schoolmasters to schoolteachers and focuses on the emancipation movement. It may be read as a case history of incomplete or abortive "professionalization," but I have deliberately avoided that term. At least in this case my attachment to historical particularism is neither blind nor perverse. Too often, professionalization substitutes a descriptive rubric, detached from time and place, for an explanation of a process. The so-

ciological literature on the subject is only beginning to confront national variations, and its application to nineteenth-century Europe
is limited by its reliance on recent and contemporary examples.
Rather than test models at this stage, the historian's task is to explain a sequence of causes and effects with close attention to national context.

German models for *Professionalisierung* are usually hybrids,
combining native and Anglo-American sociological traditions.[2] The
term is borrowed from and remains rooted in another historical and
linguistic context. *Profession* entered German usage in the seventeenth century; in Germany, unlike England, it came to refer primarily and sometimes exclusively to the crafts and manual trades.
The more appropriate designation for an intellectual or educated
profession in the English sense was, and still is, *Berufsstand.* Both
nouns in that compound have a complicated lineage. To historians
the *Stände* usually refer to the legally constituted estates (or orders),
each with its peculiar rights in a fixed hierarchy, which acceded to
modern classes in the nineteenth century. That is a precise but restricted usage. The twentieth-century editors who continued the
Grimm brothers' *Deutsches Wörterbuch* devoted nearly eleven col-
umns of small print to *Stand* as "the social pattern of civil society
according to social rank [*rangordnung*] and occupational classes [*be-
rufsclassen*]." They noted that *Stand* depends partly on birth, but is
also "determined by occupation and office and to that extent is subject to change and the will of the individual and other men." Particularly since the French revolution the *Hauptstände* usually have
included "many more *stände* . . . distinguished without definite
number or firm principle" and these "refer to the various *berufs-
classen* with which the *bürgerstand* is numerously membered."[3]

The latter usage—*Berufsstand* as a subcategory—is central here,
but again there are levels or, more precisely, concentric circles of
meaning. By the eighteenth century it was common to link *Beruf*
not only with social rank or "station" but also with office (*Amt*) and
its public responsibilities. It speaks volumes for the evolution of
Germany that the latter association has survived into the modern
era. Depending on the context, the collective *Berufsstand* may en-
compass much less or much more than "profession." The word,
which can simply denote an occupational group without implying
anything about its members' relationship to each other, or their
position in society, or the nature of their work, is also rich in connotations that defy a one-word translation. "Professional corporation" may not suffice, but at least suggests that both objective characteristics and group solidarity, or "consciousness," are intended.

At the close of the eighteenth century schoolmastery hardly constituted a *Berufsstand* in the narrowest sense. With the emancipation movement the first generation of trained schoolteachers sought recognition as a professional corporation in the public service. Spokesmen aired their grievances and aspirations, often with remarkable candor, in their own journals and the general press, in petitions to their official superiors and the national assembly of 1848, and at the numerous teachers' assemblies of that year. To say that their goal was the professionalization of an occupation may be correct, but is historically trivial. The approach here is to locate the constituents of the emancipation movement in the social and institutional structure of Prussia, to explain how its reform program had been shaped, and to assess the kind of professional status and corporate organization it pursued. The movement's social vision is particularly intriguing because the great majority of seminar graduates, like the schoolmasters who preceded them, had been raised in uneducated families among the "lower orders." Integral to the emancipation appeal was a claim to upward mobility. To understand why mobility became an issue and how it was perceived, the study suggests, neither a national nor a local framework will suffice. It was necessary to operate on both levels and keep them in tandem. Despite state intervention the elementary school was still primarily a communal institution in the mid-nineteenth century. Its teachers were communal employees, and most of them lived and worked in villages and small towns that were still largely agrarian in structure. The emancipation movement represented men who had been denied recognition by their pupils' parents, by the neighbors with whom they were in daily contact, and by the local officials who were their immediate superiors. To emancipate the *Lehrerstand* meant not only to lift its members into a national elite, but also to liberate them from the communities they had to serve.

An important article on the "middle class" in the nineteenth century contrasts England with continental Europe, where the state created a middle-class core that combined professional and bureaucratic characteristics.[4] Again an English term becomes problematic in the German context. One of my purposes is to explain how the middle class, in a loose sense, was conceived by an excluded group. More precisely, I have tried to identify the criteria by which that group defined and subdivided a *Bürgertum*, a hierarchy of *Mittelstände*, that had been in the process of change since the eighteenth century. The state played a critical role in the process, and the early history of Prussian elementary schools and teachers is an ambiguous but instructive case in point. From the Enlightenment through the Reform

Era and Pre-March, the Prussian state administration was not only the prime mover in their creation but also one of the brakes on their development.

There is now a bulk of literature on the intellectual and political evolution of state policy, its translation into laws and ordinances, and their implementation in the scattered regions of Prussia from the late eighteenth century onward. The many local and regional studies are particularly valuable; even those bordering on antiquarianism offer glimpses into archival records that have been destroyed or are not available to western scholars. With this literature it is possible to study the Prussian teaching corps on a national scale while noting regional variations. The archival research for this study was limited to the Rhine Province, Westphalia, and Brandenburg, and was concentrated on government districts (*Regierungsbezirke*) Düsseldorf (Rhine Province), Arnsberg (Westphalia), and Potsdam (Brandenburg).[5] These were only three of the twenty-five districts in Prussia. Since the school records for many other districts were destroyed or are inaccessible, selectivity was unavoidable. But the chosen three seemed particularly relevant to the subject. In school reform none of them was particularly backward; Düsseldorf, in fact, was quite advanced. But all three were centers of the emancipation movement in its initial phase, during Pre-March, and resumed that role in 1848. They also exemplify the socioeconomic and legal-institutional differences between west-Elbian and east-Elbian Prussia, and above all between the agrarian societies on both sides of the river.

The school records include the internal policy memoranda of provincial and district officials, inspection reports by superintendents and pastors, and, in Westphalia and Brandenburg, rolls of the graduating classes of the seminars. Most interesting are the local files that the district governments kept from the early nineteenth century onward. Aside from documenting the implementation of state policy, they often are an invaluable entry into the communal context of this study. The bombing in World War II reduced the files for the Potsdam district to a fairly small and manageable number. For the other two districts it was necessary to choose at random from a great bulk of files. The resulting case studies and anecdotes cannot be considered typical of teachers' experiences and are not offered as proof of my interpretation. It was not uncommon to pore through a file only to conclude, reluctantly, that it contained nothing but routine matters, or at least that more interesting matters had remained beneath the written record. But the files used here do illustrate, in a very concrete way, the conditions that underlay the emancipation movement and the grievances it articulated.

What emerges from this research is a variation on an old but still timely theme of Prussian and German historiography—the relationship between state and society. Reform from above created elementary school teaching and imposed it on an indifferent, and occasionally hostile, public. However, practical obstacles combined with policy considerations to prevent a clean break with schoolmastery. It was this mixed legacy—this balance of ambition and restraint—that produced the emancipation movement and shaped its goals.

Part II ends with the Revolution of 1848 and reevaluates the political credentials of the emancipation movement in the light of its social profile. Two recent studies fix the movement solidly in the liberal camp, but judge it from opposite ends of an ideological spectrum. A West German historian concludes that the "new *Lehrerschaft*," formed by the state but faced with a radical discrepancy between self-image and socioeconomic position, was "disposed to revolution in its majority" by 1848.[6] To an East German historian the teachers' movement in Westphalia was one product of the "relatively high development" of capitalist industry. He hails the teachers' "progressive" ideal of the *Volksschule*, but regrets that in 1848 they threw in their lot with the "bourgeoisie" rather than with the "proletariat" and "the laboring classes [*Schichten*] united with it."[7] Both verdicts lack a detailed analysis of, first, the occupational and social experience that produced the emancipation movement and, second, its stance on specific social and political issues. As a result, neither adequately explains the relationship between status and ideology. In this study the spokesmen for the emancipation movement are not characterized as revolutionaries, pure and simple, or as a potential vanguard who went astray. They were formulating a *Standespolitik*—an ideological rationale for group self-interest—and appropriated liberalism as a very pliable medium.

Part One

TOWARD A NEW PROFESSION

One

SCHOOLMASTERY

"Lower" or "German" schools originated in the medieval towns. They proliferated through the countryside in the sixteenth century, when it became urgent to Protestant sects and a defensive Catholic church to insure doctrinal orthodoxy among the rural masses. Protestant clergymen also hoped to spread literacy for scripture reading and neat penmanship on the parish scrolls and perhaps to improve the Sunday services with children's choirs. These tasks had originally fallen to the pastors, who were the farthest extensions of orthodoxy in the vast countryside. By the seventeenth century most pastors had delegated the instruction of children to their sextons (*Küster*) and other lay schoolmasters. The survival of lower schools in many parish centers during the Thirty Years' War, despite the hardships and dislocations caused by that conflict, testified to the energy of clergymen and to the underlying strength of literary and liturgical traditions in popular religion. But in the early eighteenth century many rural settlements, and particularly those without their own churches, had not yet introduced schools. In others "school" still meant simply instruction in catechism and scripture after the Sunday service. Even where instruction was more frequent, it often did not merit a special building; the children gathered in the church, in the sexton's lodging, or in the schoolmaster's private dwelling. In winter school was held only a few days a week, and parents sent their children if and when they pleased. In "summer," that is, the long season of planting and harvesting from spring to fall, it was standard practice for the schoolmaster to close shop. For most rural children a visit to the schoolhouse was an occasional event, breaking up the routine of household chores and farming.[1]

King Frederick William I of Prussia had devoted considerable attention to the rural lower schools in the early eighteenth century. In 1763 they figured in Frederick II's plan to promote domestic recovery at the close of the Seven Years' War. At his command, eccle-

siastical officials in Berlin hurriedly revised the draft law prepared
for Minden-Ravensburg over thirty years earlier and issued it as a
General-Land-Schul-Reglement for the entire kingdom, except the
newly acquired province of Silesia. The "school system" in the
countryside, its preamble stated, had "fallen into extreme decay."
Now it must become the "solid foundation" for "the true welfare of
all the estates [*Stände*] in our lands" by providing "a reasonable as
well as a Christian instruction of youth to true piety and other useful things." The language echoed a Pietist ideal, so dear to Frederick's father, but also struck the more secular and practical keynotes
of the Enlightenment. In keeping with this duality, a detailed lesson
plan allotted daily hours to singing, prayer, catechism, and the three
Rs. More striking were the accompanying obligations. Parents had
to send their children to school from age five to thirteen or fourteen,
and indeed for thirty hours per week (Monday through Saturday) in
winter. Summer sessions were shortened to three hours per day, but
vacations were expressly forbidden "even during the harvests." The
instructors, the schoolmasters, were owed a weekly fee (*Schulgeld*),
graded from early instruction to writing and arithmetic and lowered
by one-third in summer.[2]

The *Reglement* was one of several new laws with which the German states began to draw popular education into their jurisdiction.
Though six thousand copies were distributed and presumably read
from village pulpits, it became another reminder of the enormous
gap between the pretensions of "absolute" monarchy and the reality
of its power in the second half of the eighteenth century. In 1768,
when Frederick ordered an inspection of all rural schools and a report on their progress, the president of the High Consistory noted
considerable improvement in the Kurmark; but that politic response
did not do justice to the reports of local pastors and diocesan superintendents. Throughout Prussia consistorial and judicial (*Regierung*)
councillors, echoing those reports, stressed persistent obstacles and
saw little prospect for their removal. Officials in Prussia and other
German states were citing the same obstacles at the turn of the century.[3] The development of a recognizably modern school in rural
communities—the kind of school the *Reglement* had blueprinted—
required either internal changes, producing new needs and resources, or imposition from above. The former were not in evidence,
and the latter presupposed a degree of state enforcement that was
still impossible. In the absence of both, the rural school remained
what it had been for several centuries: a local institution adapted to
and severely restricted by its natural setting.

To stipulate regular, year-round attendance was to indulge in wishful thinking. The physical obstacles were more or less imposing, depending on the settlement pattern and the terrain. Sheer distance was a factor where villages consisted of scattered farmsteads (as in the Münster region) or where one parish school served a number of settlements (as in East Prussia). A walk of two or three miles was hard on younger children and virtually precluded their attendance in severe winter weather, particularly in hill country like the Trier region in the middle Rhineland.[4] The more serious problem, even under more favorable conditions, was that children stayed at home to work. So long as crops had to be planted and harvested without machinery, child labor was an integral feature of the rural household economy. In some ways it was a mere convenience to the peasant who was a relatively secure tenant, owing rents but no labor services to his landlord. He could devote full attention to his holdings and might be prosperous enough to dispense with a younger son's work in the barn or the fields. But a teenage son, and indeed a ten year old, could spare him wages for a hired hand and in any case was indispensable during the peak periods of planting and harvesting. Younger children who lacked the strength for heavy field work could tend the livestock all day; that was an essential task in villages without fenced-in grazing areas or communal herdsmen.[5] During the harvest the six or seven year old who stayed at home, minding the younger siblings and doing chores, made it possible for his (or her) mother to work in the fields.

Services that were more or less a convenience for prosperous landholders were a dire necessity for other rural families. In east-Elbian Prussia peasants owed labor services, perhaps three or four days a week, to the estate lords and in some cases their teenage sons had to serve as domestics (*Gesinde*). Under those circumstances it was impossible to farm the family holdings unless a younger son worked in the landlord's fields or filled in at home. Throughout Prussia (and Germany) school absenteeism was most frequent among the dwarfholders and landless laborers, often lumped together as the "slight countrymen" or simply the "poor." In their case the child—even the five or six year old—was another wage earner, and his earnings were essential to his family's hand-to-mouth survival. In 1787 the school commission in Stift Essen, like Prussian officials in the late 1760s, had to face these realities and saw no way to circumvent them. Its recent school ordinance had stipulated daily attendance for the entire year except the harvest, but in response to protests by the villages it suspended the law from Easter to the end of October for the "day laborers and other poor countryfolk as well as peasants who lack the means to keep hired hands and cow herders."[6]

Clergymen and state officials often attributed the failure of school laws to the countrymen's "ignorance" or "superstition" or even "perversity." Though those loaded terms distilled the contemptuous stereotypes of outsiders, they point to the underlying conflict between a meddling state and its tradition-bound subjects. Aside from the practical needs of the household and the farm, parents responded to the new school and its requirements as unwanted intrusions on their cultural and social values. "Superstition" meant a religious tradition that was based on literal faith rather than a "reasonable" grasp of doctrine and included a host of unorthodox beliefs in the supernatural. The school remained limited because parents persisted in conceiving of the family as a working unit in which children, even if they were not essential wage earners, had to earn their sustenance from an early age. As for the "other useful things" cited in the *Reglement*, they were not relevant to a semiliterate population that simply passed on agricultural practices and lore from one generation to the next. Children learned them best, and in the process acquired familial virtues, by working with their parents at home.[7]

The instructor remained shaped to the institution and its marginal, strictly circumscribed role. In the hiring of schoolmasters, intellectual qualifications and pedagogical skills, if they were considered at all, had to accede to the capacities and needs of communities with limited occupational differentiation. Schoolmastery survived in marriages of convenience with other local services, offering each partner a bit more living space than it could command alone. The most typical union, the sexton-schoolmaster, was also the most workable. Though instruction merited a special fee, it was hardly distinguishable from the sexton's other responsibilities toward the local children. He taught them catechism and scripture during the week, led them into church on Sunday, and accompanied their hymns on the organ or kept them quiet and alert during the service. What had allowed the extension of lower schools from the parish centers to outlying villages since the mid-seventeenth century was the overcrowding of the trades (*Handwerk*). Artisans excluded from the town guilds had to eke out a living in the countryside, where markets were very limited. They could supplement their trades with some farming and—if they had acquired the rudiments of reading and writing, or at least could claim to have mastered those skills— some schoolmastery. In 1722 a royal ordinance in Prussia respected guild prerogatives by restricting schoolmastery to those exceptional trades already tolerated legally in the countryside. Tailoring was suitable for the simple reason that it was quiet; its rural practitioner could supervise the children's lessons while sewing at his table. In 1735 rural schoolmasters were allowed to practice tailoring without the approval of a town guild so long as they did not accept apprentices and journeymen. A year earlier schoolmastery had been made a requirement for the rural tailor; thus the state tried to limit the spillover of the trade from town to country but at the same time enlist it for the lower schools. But the ordinances only encouraged the inevitable; sheer overcrowding explains why the tailor was the most frequent artisan-schoolmaster in the late eighteenth century, particularly in the outlying villages of east-Elbian parishes.[8]

During the long farming season, when children stopped attending school and parents stopped paying a fee, an artisan-schoolmaster could put more time into his trade or work in the fields. In small settlements with scattered farmsteads and poor traveling conditions the cheaper and more efficient arrangement was a "winter" or "mobile" school. Its instructor was usually the local herdsman, who offered no particular qualifications but needed something to tide him through the winter. For several months he simply went from farmstead to farmstead (as he perhaps was already wont to do), adding instruction to the domestic activities and receiving lodging, food, and perhaps a small fee. That eliminated the need to provide a schoolhouse, spared the children long walks, and kept the cost of supporting a schoolmaster to a bare minimum. By the late eighteenth century these winter schools seem to have been dying out in the lower Rhineland, but they were still common in the hill country to the south and in the poorer east-Elbian regions.[9]

Sextons, artisans, and herdsmen were the most common schoolmasters, but the wide variety of local conditions allowed for a host of other occupational unions. In lieu of the herdsman one of the local field hands, likewise free in winter, could make the rounds. To judge by school laws some schoolmasters ran brandy or beer concessions, despite the bad example to the children, and others encouraged the peasants' passion for litigation by serving as notaries. In Prussia, where those practices were officially discouraged, both Frederick William I and Frederick II saw no reason why the lower schools should not offer a means of survival to their invalid soldiers.[10] The choice was appropriate; it confirmed that schoolmastery tended to be a refuge for men without other prospects. Some men may have preferred it to other work, but they entered an occupation that seldom offered enough income to support a family and often needed several supports. In Taplacken (East Prussia) the schoolmaster was also the shoemaker and could serve as joiner, cooper, and turner "in a pinch."[11]

In 1814, Josef Görres, serving as a Prussian school commissioner in the middle Rhineland, summed up his impressions of rural schoolmasters in a report on a recent inspection tour. "Since the teacher is dependent on the peasants, like any of the other hands [*Knechte*], they exercise their rule [over him] as they would over a serf [*Leibeignen*] and he must conform to their will in everything. . . . The teacher cannot use discipline; if he tries the children run away, the mothers approve their behavior, and the father holds back his portion of the wage [*bedungenen Geldes*]."[12]

It was obvious to Görres and other officials that the rural schoolmaster, despite his educative function, belonged to the uneducated "lower orders." What scandalized them was his lowly place in local rural society among the laboring masses of German villages and agrotowns. Comparisons with field hands and even beggars generalized from the more extreme cases, but the point was well taken. The schoolmaster's relationship to his neighbors at once reflected and confirmed his lack of "station." In the language of the eighteenth century he was "without property" (*eigentumslos*) and hence "without *Stand*" (*standlos*). Lacking either physical property or an established profession, he belonged outside, and below, a society of estates.[13]

Schoolmastery was an extension of the pastorate, but hardly bore comparison with it. By the eighteenth century the standard route to a pastorate was the university, where the candidate studied academic theology, or a seminary. The rural pastor was the local guardian of faith and morals, the presiding figure at the major (and perhaps only) cultural events, the official record keeper and link with higher ecclesiastical and civil administrations. He was a communal employee, not a salaried state official; but in recognition of his vital services he occupied an endowed office in the parish. In contrast, schoolmastery was a part-time, marginal service that did not require distinctive educational credentials. Despite the title *Schulmeister*, in fact, it lacked the specific training requirements and other marks of self-regulating trades. Occasionally a young man would apprentice for a few years with his father or a nearby schoolmaster. And there was a kind of trade lore on the proper methods of exercising children's memories and keeping them in line (largely with a healthy use of the rod). For the most part, however, sextons, artisans, and lesser residents practiced schoolmastery not as an independent livelihood but as a financial crutch or refuge from unemployment. Most of them had received, at best, perfunctory tutoring from pastors, and some had not spent enough time in a lower school to master writing.[14]

Annual income was the most obvious index of the schoolmaster's local status. Unfortunately contemporary estimates did not include earnings from trades and other outside sources, and their cash valuations of noncash incomes—the farm plot or lodging attached to a position, for example, or deliveries in kind—were made by local officials or the schoolmasters themselves. In gross terms, though, the figures leave no doubt that schoolmasters were seldom prosperous, even by rural standards, and often dirt poor. In a rural region of Cleve, 17 of the 69 schoolmasters had an "official income" of 100 thaler or more in 1802–3. Another 39 ranged from 50 to 100 thaler, and 13 fell under 50 thaler.[15] In the Kurmark the lower ranks were far more crowded: according to the official figures compiled in 1806 only 195 of the 1,648 schoolmasters had over 100 thaler and 1,142 had under 60 thaler.[16] Most of the higher figures in both regions included income from the sextonship. As for herdsmen, day laborers, and many of the artisans, they needed the school fee for hand-to-mouth survival. Comparable figures are hard to come by, but a day laborer made 50 to 100 thaler per year in the late eighteenth century, and the sexton-schoolmaster's official income, even in a better-endowed position, was rarely half that of his pastor.

If rural schoolmastery was at the bottom of Prussian society, it differed from many higher occupations only by degree. In the eighteenth century men who lived entirely off cash salaries were still the exceptions to the rule, and even in the state bureaucracies and the academic schools annual incomes often were markedly low. Schoolmasters lacked "station" primarily because their terms of employment involved extreme dependence on their neighbors. In the village pecking order elite status was reserved for families with secure and sizable landholdings; they supplied the civic and church officials and occupied the front pews at Sunday services. In his various functions, and particularly in his capacity as instructor, the schoolmaster was at the opposite pole. Even if he enjoyed use of land, it was usually a small parish or communal plot attached to the sextonship, not a family patrimony. Though the arrangements for school support were makeshift and varied from place to place, their common effect was to define the schoolmaster as a "communal servant" (*Gemeindebedienter*) and make him dependent on the cooperation, and in some cases the largesse, of individual residents for the bulk of his livelihood. A preference for face-to-face relations over formal institutions is typical of small agrarian communities. In this case, however, informality and personal contact were used primarily to exact deference from a servant and keep him vulnerable to sanctions—not to express neighborly affection or esteem.

It is striking that the "winter" schoolmaster, even when he was not a herdsman or day laborer, received the same treatment. He was a rotating servant, hired from year to year and taking what lodging and food each family cared to offer. In some villages the schoolmaster, like the other landless help, was allowed to glean the remains from the fields at the end of the harvest, a custom most expressive of the landholders' charity. In 1794 a pastor recalled that his father, a village schoolmaster in Waitzenrode (Silesia), had been "directed to a part of the fields from which the grain had just been taken to rake together the sheaves that had been left lying, bundle them and bring them back home." School was suspended for four or five weeks, he noted, while the instructor and his family "played the day laborer."[17]

As a parish "office," modeled on the pastorate to some extent, the sextonship offered more security. In some villages the pastor and church elders presided over a vesting ceremony in which the community promised cooperation if the appointee fulfilled his oath of office and led an exemplary Christian life. Informal custom had evolved into written contract, which stipulated the sexton's rights as well as his duties. Since the sextonship shared in the parish endowment, its occupant normally received a small portion of the church lands and a yearly payment in money or kind from the treasury. Like the pastor, the sexton received token payments from local families for his services at baptisms, weddings, and funerals. These *Akzidenzien* originally had been customary gifts, but had often become obligatory fees. Their careful definition in contracts suggests that the communities, or at least their officials, had learned that moral obligations did not suffice in such matters.[18]

But the contracts also spelled out, often in great detail, the host of chores with which the sextonship had been burdened over centuries. In addition to assisting at liturgical services and perhaps ennobling them with organ or choir music, the sexton served as parish custodian. That meant, to cite the most common duties, that he had to ring the bells that woke the village and brought it to church, keep the church in good repair and clean its pews, and shovel the snow from its entryway. In these and other ways he was a kind of servant-at-large, in attendance on parishioners as well as the pastor. Even with written contracts his neighbors had ample means to underscore and enforce that status. In some Rhineland villages, in fact, enforcement had become ritualized. On a certain Sunday each year, before the assembled parish, the sexton had to hand over the church keys to the pastor or elders; they were returned to him only after those present had aired their complaints and he had promised to mend his ways.[19] Like the pastor the sexton usually received a significant portion of his income in kind (bushels of rye, baskets of eggs, loaves of bread, and so forth), with the contributions either limited to the larger landholders or distributed proportionately through the community. These contributions were to be expected in a semimonetary economy and were a great advantage to the recipient when bad harvests brought high prices. But the advantage to the donor was that, even when fixed in written contracts, payments in kind were by nature more flexible than a fixed number of thaler. A bushel of rye might not be quite as full as it should be. The peasants could distinguish between eggs that would bring a good price or were fit for home consumption and those fit for the sexton—particularly when they bore a grudge against him.[20]

The sexton's vulnerability was particularly obvious in a gift-giving custom known as the "circuit" (*Umgang*), by no means universal but still frequent in the Rhineland and several other regions in the late eighteenth century. At Christmas or Easter the sexton had to go from farmstead to farmstead, paying his respects and in return receiving donations in money or kind. In some communities he made the rounds alone; in others he led a group of choirboys who entertained at each stop and shared in the proceeds. Though the custom had become a right of office it was still a form of charity, or, as a schoolmaster in the Bergland recalled, an occupational right to beg.[21] When local families chose to trim their contributions to their economic fortunes, the yield could sink very low. In 1810, when the Bergland was suffering the brunt of French occupation, a mayor reported that the schoolmasters in his area, who had formerly received thirty to forty stuben from each family on the circuit, were now receiving only two—and were left waiting fifteen minutes at the door.[22] Even in good times, of course, the schoolmaster's appearance offered residents an opportunity to approve his performance with hospitality and a generous gift or settle accounts by making him feel the unwanted beggar. In 1802 an indignant schoolmaster in Könitz, an agrotown in West Prussia, described a particularly virulent use of the circuit for the latter purpose; "parents whose prejudices we [i.e., he and his assistant] violate with our instruction . . . either do not give us any gift at all or make us wait, complaining all the while, and finally give us a small gift sourly."[23]

The school fee was payment for services rendered, not a gift. In fact the *Reglement* of 1763 had elevated it to a head tax, payable whether or not children attended school, and had threatened negligent parents with forced collections (*Exekutionen*) and fines.[24] But in 1801 thirty schoolmasters in Inspection Zossen (Kurmark) reminded the consistory that the *Reglement* was a dead letter and that the fee remained a very precarious day wage. As their petition noted, the schoolmaster could hardly enjoy the proceeds of a public tax so long as he had to make the collection rounds himself.[25] Most parents paid only for days attended (i.e., when they could do without their children's labor) and some—if they wanted to spite the schoolmaster for disciplining their children too harshly, nursed some other grudge against him, or simply could not afford it—refused to pay at all. The local poor were least likely to pay regularly, but more prosperous parents were hardly more cooperative. Residents did not persist in these habits simply out of stinginess or poverty; to treat the schoolmaster cavalierly was to impress on him that his service could not upset familial and communal priorities. In 1814, Emmanuel Kriegskotte, a young instructor in Schwelm (Westphalia), summed up the helplessness of the wage earner in the face of "indifference" and "poverty."

> Thus in places where the school fee is paid weekly one hears the common man saying on Monday, when his children ask him for the fee, "I have other uses for my money, stay out of school again this week," and so it goes for many weeks until staying at home becomes the habit. . . . Where the fee is paid monthly one can always figure that only two-fifths of the school-age children attend. The teacher is always left waiting for a quarter of the fees from those attending and he can't even complain about it so as not to lose favor; the second quarter is paid to him reluctantly, and he only receives half without grievances.[26]

Not all schoolmasters endured this kind of treatment with passive resignation. But it was integral to their dilemma that protests were not likely to succeed and might very well backfire. In the absence of effective support from local or outside officials the schoolmaster who insisted on his due was, in the words of a pastor in Nassau-Saarbrücken, "the most preposterous and superfluous person on God's earth."[27] Even with official support he could not afford to "lose favor"; he was entangled in too many dependencies at once, and thus his neighbors had too many opportunities to "make his life sour."[28] Parents did not have to refuse outright to pay the school fee; they could deprive him of fees by sending their children to a neighboring school, even if the children had to walk several miles to get there. The schoolhouse—where one existed—was also the "service lodging," and its repair depended on local goodwill. A land endowment involved fewer tribulations than contributions in kind, but was not invulnerable. In 1799 a superintendent in Lienen (Westphalia) reported that his schoolmasters could not demand the legal fee because they needed the peasants' equipment to farm their holdings.[29]

The underlying problem was that the schoolmaster had neither impressive educational credentials nor official authority with which to counter local spite. Far from respecting his expertise, his neighbors could easily dismiss him as an incompetent and, if that did not work, resort to more personal and venomous attacks. The escalating feud between Schoolmaster Julius Fetting and the village of Marwitz in Prussian Pomerania was an instructive case in point. Marwitz was a small "filial" village of modest landholders (*Kossäten*) whose school was under the jurisdiction of the magistrate in Glatz. Like his father, Fetting was a tailor-schoolmaster; by the standards of the late eighteenth century he seems to have been fairly well trained and competent. In 1798 the villagers, eager to lure him from a position nearby, had added six bushels of rye and a few other bonuses to the official income. But the schoolhouse, which was supposed to serve as Fetting's lodging, was being used to house the communal herdsman. Despite the consistory's order the herdsman was not removed, and Fetting's complaints provoked a full-scale feud.[30]

Parents' initial response was to send their children to a retired schoolmaster in a village four and a half kilometers away. In late 1802, after the magistrate had forbidden that tactic, several residents suddenly evinced concern that Fetting could not instruct their older children in arithmetic. The magistrate dismissed this complaint as "mere chicanery." Likewise the pastor attributed it "solely to Fetting's insistence on the rights and incomes attached to his very humble position" and mocked "the unfair demand of many members of the community that Fetting bring their children, who are stupid by nature, as far as he could bring others with a better mental capacity [*glücklicherem Genie*]." But Fetting was hauled before the local court and informed that if he did not allow parents to use another school he would be deprived of the six bushels of rye and other "advantages." At a meeting with the magistrate the mayor (*Schulze*) and jurymen (*Gerichtsleute*), pressed on the subject of Fetting's competence in arithmetic, raised the more scandalous issues of domestic strife and excesses in discipline. Following a battle with his wife, they charged, Fetting had struck the mayor's daughter so hard

that "the stripes had been seen on her hips."[31] After five years of recalcitrance and harassment, the village may finally have mended its
ways, but only because outside officials had offered the schoolmaster a degree of support that was rarely forthcoming. Significant improvement of Fetting's position did not begin until 1811—in a new
era of state intervention.

To an extent the pastor likewise could not afford to violate his parishioners' standards or demand too much of them. However, he represented academic learning, and though supported by the parish, his
office was the final link in the chain of command that constituted
church and state. With the new school laws state officials tried to
deepen their penetration of rural life, but their legal reach exceeded
their grasp. Schoolmastery remained imbedded in the culture and
power structure of local society.

TOWN MARKETS

In the eighteenth century the focus of school laws acknowledged the
demographic and economic preponderance of the countryside, or
"flat land" (*plattes Land*), over the towns. Even by a very liberal definition of *Stadt*, only a small minority of Prussian subjects—roughly
20 percent—were townsmen. Those who lived in small agrotowns
combined trades and other urban occupations with seasonal farming
or field labor in the surrounding countryside. Likewise their schoolmasters derived a good deal of support from land endowments and
contributions in kind attached to the sextonship. Their incomes
were usually higher than those of the surrounding countryside because the sexton endowments were more generous and they often
received extra compensation for their services as cantors.[32]

In the late eighteenth century several *Gymnasien* in Berlin and
other large Prussian towns were in the process of reform. Their directors were constructing blueprints for urban school systems, with
curriculum tracks and examinations designed to channel pupils into
commercial as well as academic and official careers. What prevailed
in most towns was institutional stagnation and confusion. Only a
few nonclassical high schools, known as *Realschule* or *Bürgerschule*, concentrated on preparation for occupations that did not
require university study. To reformers most of the academic high
schools, the so-called Latin schools, were backwaters of rote learning. They combined classical scholarship, which was essential for
university study, with a hodgepodge of subjects for pupils who
stayed only a few years. Though sometimes loosely attached to

these institutions, the "lower" or "German" schools hardly differed from their rural counterparts. Their main purpose was to provide rudimentary instruction, above all in catechism and scripture, to the children of artisans and apprentices, small shopkeepers, resident soldiers, and lesser members of the urban "lower orders." For the most part the lower schools were extensions of the neighborhood parishes; they were "municipal" only in the sense that the magistrate reserved the right to license their schoolmasters and might provide token aid from the public treasury, usually to subsidize free instruction for the children of public paupers.[33]

In towns of all sizes school attendance and fee payment were highly sporadic. Urban concentration allowed more competition than the sprawling countryside. In the villages parents who wanted to use a neighboring school were hindered by distance and poor traveling conditions, but the towns were open school markets. Children usually were not assigned to districts, and in any case their parents were free to shop around for the schoolmaster whose fee was lowest, whose instruction seemed most appropriate, or whose disciplinary methods best suited their tastes. It was all the more necessary for licensed schoolmasters to please parents because they had to compete with unlicensed practitioners known as *Winkelschulmeister* or *Klipschulmeister*. These included all sorts of urban dwellers who lacked a secure livelihood or had not yet entered one: struggling artisans and apprentices, widows (including schoolmasters' widows), retired and invalid soldiers, high school students from poor families, theology graduates waiting for pastorates and unable to find private tutoring. Though limited to only four quarters of the city, an inspection in Berlin uncovered 102 unlicensed schoolmasters in 1788; as an official report complained, "Virtually anyone who has no other resources opens a new position, without inner vocation [*Beruf*] or training, and without examination or authorization."[34] Even Dortmund, an agrotown with four small parishes, had ten *Winkelschulmeister* in the mid-eighteenth century.[35] In response to schoolmasters' complaints, church officials and magistrates occasionally tried to root out the unlicensed instructors, but their licensing ordinances were rarely enforced.

Though schoolmasters in the towns lived and worked in close proximity, their circumstances precluded the development of corporate self-regulation and self-protection, even in a rudimentary form. The problem was not simply that they were a heterogeneous lot. Like their counterparts in the countryside, they offered a marginal service that did not require the kind of skill attributed to established trades. In fact, far from boasting academic learning, most schoolmasters in the towns had not received any formal training. Both the licensed and the unlicensed had no choice but to accept their neighbors' terms, and the less fortunate among the latter—those who could not escape to better livelihoods—survived on the outer fringe of urban life.

Two

REFORM FROM ABOVE

THE NEW MISSIONARIES

The rural schoolmasters of eighteenth-century Germany were homegrown products, satisfying local needs without straining local capacity. Their successors were products of a state-sponsored reform from above that finally began to have an impact in the early nineteenth century. In Prussia the Reform Era added dimensions to a profile of the new schoolteacher (*Schullehrer*) that had emerged in that broad, eclectic intellectual movement known as the German Enlightenment. Schoolteaching as it was originally conceived was missionary work among the rural natives; that assignment shaped its identity as a new profession in the public service.

The German Enlightenment may have lacked brilliance and originality, but by the close of the century its standards and ambitions had permeated the public discourse of the educated and official elite. Eberhard von Rochow, one of the more famous contributors, was an estate lord who had been shocked by his peasants' ignorance and helplessness in the face of an epidemic. More typical was Baron Karl Abraham von Zedlitz, a Prussian state minister and head of the Lutheran department; he was one of many enlightened higher officials in the civil and ecclesiastical administrations of the German states. The rank-and-file enthusiasts included university professors, publicists, and a scattering of pastors. They were all "friends of man" (*Menschenfreunde*), exchanging ideas and bolstering each other's morale in periodicals, essay contests, and lecture societies like the *Mittwochsgesellschaft* in Berlin. The philanthropic impulse made most of them "friends of the school" (*Schulfreunde*) as well.[1]

The ultimate objective was "popular enlightenment" (*Volksaufklärung*), which required the transmission of new knowledge and behavioral norms to the uneducated lower orders. At center stage was the "countryman" (*Landmann*) or "peasant" (*Bauer*)—the latter term properly referring only to a particular category of non-noble landholders, but often used to designate the entire population engaged in agriculture (except, of course, the estate lords). At mid-century cameralist recognition of the countrymen's economic potential was already supplanting Pietist concern for their religious welfare. In their efforts to improve agriculture by disseminating scientific information and methods, the cameralists profiled the peasant estate (*Bauernstand*) as a distinct occupational group, and indeed the crucial one for a productive economy. The peasant assumed a new importance and dignity to the measure that his work required intelligent, efficient application of specialized knowledge. With the importation of Enlightenment thought the image of an expert husbandman expanded into a multifaceted ideal of the peasant as the embodiment of a new morality (*Sittlichkeit*). Though long stereotyped as a benighted, brutish, slothful creature, more beast than man, he was now assumed to share with all other men an innate human capacity for rational understanding (what the French called *bon sens*). Among his new virtues were those which, while "rational" and therefore noble in themselves, also promised economic progress—frugality in household and farm management, a never-waste-a-minute industriousness, and the "cleverness" (*Klugheit*) to exploit new opportunities. The peasant could become a more "reasonable" believer, freed from popular "superstitions" as well as the theological niceties that cluttered Protestant and Catholic orthodoxy and following the simple, eminently rational dictates of Christian ethics. Once he understood the laws of his state, it was assumed, he would be more able and willing to conform to them.[2]

As its advocates liked to remind each other, the enlightenment of the countrymen was an eminently humanitarian end in itself. But the end loomed so important and found expression in numerous school laws because of its potential benefits to the German dynastic states. Like the members of other estates, the peasant was encouraged to advance his self-interest only so long as it did not degenerate into selfish privatism. The hallmark of the truly enlightened *Staatsbürger* was voluntary, intelligent dedication to the public welfare. That was what Johann Bernhard Basedow, the founder of an experimental school in Dessau, meant by "public virtue." Rochow used the term "national spirit" and hoped to instill that spirit in the isolated, apathetic peasantry of Prussia with a "national education."[3] Though "public" and "national" had different connotations, they both referred to society as it had been organized into a governmental and administrative unity. An enlightened peasantry seemed critical because, in addition to promoting economic development and expanding the tax base, it could contribute more than any other socioeconomic group to the moral and ultimately political strength of the state.

In the late eighteenth century interest in popular school reform derived from and focused on this nexus of peasant enlightenment and state interest. The multiplication of books and periodicals on the subject was marked by increasing tension between ambition and caution, and by increasing disagreement on ends and means. In 1786, Heinrich Gottlieb Zerrenner, the editor of *Der Deutsche Schulfreund*, limited enlightenment to "making [the people] rational and good to the degree necessary for them to become useful to the state as well as in every circumstance and relationship with other men, to be happier with their own lives, and to be more satisfied with their estate."[4] Contemporaries who were willing to transcend this limitation posited a fund of "general education" as the foundation for a national school system. Several reform plans spelled out the most radical implication: the new elementary school should include all children and apply the criteria of natural aptitude and performance, regardless of social origins, in supplying pupils to the higher school levels. But the more common tendency was to envision a new breed of countrymen without accepting any major consequences for the social and political structure. If the estate hierarchy could not survive in pristine purity, it should at least retain its basic divisions and lines of authority. Rather than join the attack on manorial obligations, in fact, many contributors argued that a safe dosage of enlightenment, guaranteed not to "overeducate" or "miseducate," would allow the peasants to better their lot despite their inherited legal status. By improving itself, the peasant estate would shed its pariah status without aping the life-styles of the higher estates or abandoning the land in a futile quest for fame and fortune in the towns. The peasant-*Bürger* would acquire some familiarity with the state constitution, but only to enhance his traditional political role as a passive and obedient subject. If the rural school was not to transgress these limits it had to be the lowest of several disconnected school types, each gearing its education to its pupils' inherited social circumstances and occupational needs. An enlightened but still rudimentary instruction in religion and the three Rs, supplemented by some practical instruction directly relevant to agriculture, would suffice to make peasant youth at once more "useful" and more "satisfied."

At issue here was not simply the threshold of political danger in the education of the rural masses. While some reformers emphasized inheritance of stations in an estate society, others projected a social hierarchy that would reward talent and achievement. The other issue was what role, if any, the state should play in school reform. In the early 1790s, Joachim Heinrich Campe and Ernst Christian Trapp, two of the more prominent reformers, argued against state-regulated schools and in favor of free competition in the private sphere. But Campe and Trapp were apostates, and even they considered it essential that the state subsidize the instruction of poor children. In mainstream opinion state intervention was the *sine qua non* of reform, but neither could nor should sweep aside the traditional guardians of education.

For the most pressing reforms—the introduction of a standard school curriculum, insurance of teaching standards with examinations and licenses, enforcement of compulsory attendance and overhaul of school support—the state had to issue new laws and oversee them from the highest administrative level. But the parishes could not be deprived of certain historic rights over their schools. Aside from their rights, the Protestant and Catholic hierarchies—the provincial consistories, diocesan superintendents, and pastors—had long functioned as arms of the state and supplied a disproportionate number of reform enthusiasts who, far from seeing a conflict between throne and altar, believed that an enlightened faith was essential to the welfare of both. In any case clergymen were indispensable; there were neither men nor funds to establish a separate administrative apparatus for the lower schools.[5]

The differences of opinion presaged ideological camps in school reform, but were still largely academic at the turn of the century. The practical dilemma, how to make a start somehow with popular enlightenment, continued to defy solution. Little was accomplished with simplified farm journals and edifying storybooks about model peasants like "William the Thinker" and "Sebastian the Clever," who represented the virtues of enlightened behavior as well as its concrete pecuniary rewards. Though printed in surprisingly large numbers, few of these found their way into peasant homes.[6] Since the 1760s the failure of the Prussian *Reglement* and other school laws had made it painfully obvious that, however vast their potential, the countrymen were both intractable and inaccessible. A population dispersed over the vast countryside and encased in its thousands of villages and small towns seemed virtually immune to influence from the urban centers of administration and academic learning. Nonetheless, in its efforts to bridge this gap, the educated and official elite persisted in assigning an awesome role to the pastorate and the school. Both were local conduits, already well dispersed through rural society and capable of a direct, continuous impact on its inhabitants. Since the rural pastor was an educated man with official authority, he was acclaimed as the "popular educator" (*Volkserzieher*) par excellence and was expected to use his sermons, his house calls, and indeed his entire range of contacts with parishioners to spread secular and religious improvement.[7] The school and its instructor would remain subordinate to the pastor, but offered a peculiar advantage. Although adult parishioners were perhaps already beyond enlightened salvation, the school could convert their children despite them.

In this estimation of the strategic importance of the rural school the traditional schoolmaster became a preposterous figure, a foil to the true "teacher" (*Lehrer*). This part-time occupation, on the fringe of rural life, had to accede to a genuine profession (*Beruf*) with a modest but secure station. Some authors inflated the schoolteacher's mission to absurdity and thus blurred his professional identity. Gotthilf Samuel Steinbart, a consistorial councillor in Brandenburg, envisioned an "entirely new breed of men" who would "fill in the great gaps between the theorizing academicians and the rural and town laboring populations" by holding school, dispensing agricultural expertise and emergency medical aid, promoting domestic industry, settling legal disputes, and—if he still had any spare time—conducting surveying projects.[8] Others, though more realistic, hoped that he would spur the countrymen to more industrious use of their spare time by introducing fruit tree culture, raising bees, or cultivating that talisman of cameralism, the silkworm. But the focus was on the schoolhouse, and in the typical curriculum proposals instruction in diet, hygiene, geography, and other practical subjects was secondary. The core subjects, religion and the three Rs, would form the younger generation and predispose it to moral and material improvement in virtually all areas of rural life.[9]

It was obvious that, unlike schoolmastery, schoolteaching had to stand on its own two feet as a virtually full-time occupation. Instruction in the new curriculum would occupy several hours a day for the entire year, including most of the farming season, and required preparation of lessons at home as well. These new demands were beyond herdsmen and field hands, and also precluded regular practice of a craft or farming beyond a very modest scale. But the independence of a new profession also derived from the nature of enlightened instruction. To be sure, schoolteaching was not to be compared with an academic profession. Though its practitioner must have a "capable head," Bernhard Overberg wrote in his *Guide to Purposeful School Instruction*, he need not be a "great academic" with "very broad knowledge and insight into scholarly disciplines."[10] To judge by what he had to know, in fact, he was a dilettantish mediator rather than a master of a new discipline. His assignment was simply to purvey material that had been packaged for popular consumption. But Overberg and others also found it absurd that the typical schoolmaster was on a par with his pupils' semiliterate, ignorant parents. Their missionary had to be a good deal more literate and knowledgeable, and to that extent would be distinguished from the vast majority of his neighbors as an "educated" (*gebildeter*) man.

What the schoolteacher taught was less important than why and how he taught it. In Rochow's words his task was to "stop the spirit-deadening parroting which teaching usually has amounted to until now and educate the growing youth to think more and more."[11] Few of Rochow's contemporaries had such an open-ended notion of the rational purpose of the rural school, but most agreed that, aside from its informational value, the curriculum should exercise the child in mental skills and moral habits so as to make them operative throughout his life. To that end Rochow, Overberg, and several other reformers translated the abstractions of Enlightenment philosophy into the systematic precepts and methods of "pedagogy." To them the schoolmaster's reliance on memory drills and physical punishment was a *Schlendrian*—rote work that reflected the tradition-bound, irrational world in which it had developed and thus mistook the child for a kind of deficient adult. Their discovery was that childhood was a unique formative period, the stage in which the human being's "natural" intellectual capacities and moral tendencies had not yet been corrupted by his environment. In that light even the peasant son, though born into a distinctly unenlightened world, was peculiarly educable. What the new pedagogy offered was a way to improve on—or, better, promote—nature. The older generation was proof enough that children, and particularly the countrymen's children, would not become reasonable men if left to themselves. And the more the theorists turned to practice, the more they were impressed by the sheer difficulty of teaching young children to think and behave properly. Though the child had an innate desire to learn he also was easily distracted. Though predisposed to be good he was also given to mischief and even malice; his moral tendencies had not yet developed into a conscience.

The state of childhood, when the light of reason shone pure but was in grave danger of flickering out, posed both an opportunity and a challenge to the new schoolteacher. His work became a highly conscious and purposeful art (*Kunst*) of cultivation, accepting the child as he was, in all his weakness, so as to tap his latent potential.[12] In the rural schoolhouse cultivation had to be as efficient as possible, since one man had to teach the entire new curriculum to a large number of children of different ages. With these objectives, so typical of Enlightenment thought, the teaching handbooks of the late eighteenth century projected the physical setup and procedures of a recognizably modern classroom. The schoolmaster had one pupil or a few pupils recite their lessons from memory and left the rest to work (or play) at their seats. To cover the curriculum efficiently the teacher had to instruct all his pupils—or at least the younger or older half—at the same time, as an audience who sat facing him in rows for hours on end. To keep their attention he had to arrange the daily lessons in the most advantageous order, illustrate their content with striking examples, and pose salient, eye-opening questions. At the same time he had to develop the pupils' reasoning powers and ground their consciences in understanding by building inductively from concrete, familiar objects in nature and in the schoolhouse to more abstract concepts and principles. The same fusion of purposefulness and efficiency characterized a "good discipline," which was all the more necessary now that the teacher had to keep an entire class quiet and orderly and which, beyond that practical purpose, was integral to moral education. The schoolmaster seemed an arbitrary, irrational despot; his inconsistent, often brutal punishments controlled by fear rather than by reason, and their effect diminished with repetition. If discipline was to develop the pupil's conscience, the schoolteacher had to be an enlightened monarch, stern but understanding, and indeed one steeped in psychological insight. He would use the rod or the hand only as a last resort, not as an all-purpose crutch. Nonphysical punishments were far more purposeful, particularly if they escalated with the gravity of the offenses and were designed to make the child realize why his behavior was wrong and feel shame for it.[13]

Even as a pedagogue the schoolteacher stood well below an academic; he was expected to master the praxis of a new discipline, not to understand its theoretical scaffolding. But the crucial, if obvious, implication of teaching handbooks was that teaching belonged among the "intellectual" (*geistige*) professions. Its practitioner could not be equated with a *Professionist* who plied a manual trade, since the enlightened schoolhouse was fundamentally different from a workshop. In 1794 one author, defending the "honor" of the title *Schulmeister*, reminded his readers that it evoked the skill expected of a *Handwerkmeister*. In fact, he continued, the teacher's "art" was far more demanding than that of the kitchenmaster or stablemaster, since his raw material was "reasonable men." However, the same logic led Pastor Meyer in Halberstadt to compare school work "merely with the lungs, mouth, rod and hand," even if performed by a "*Bac-calaureus* and the master of seven arts," with "the uselessness of a thoughtless artisan."[14]

In 1793, Georg Krünitz included a lengthy discussion of the rural school in his *Economic-Technological Encyclopedia*. Like anyone else with "an important office in the state," Krünitz noted, the village schoolmaster needed "external honor" to insure his loyalty and integrity. If he was now "practically the most disdained man in the village," he should be "in union with the pastor, the most honored."[15] Ten years later Josef Schram, in his book on popular education "from a moral, political, pedagogical and administrative standpoint," was more specific about the honor projected for a new profession: "Schoolmen who fulfill their duty with integrity and dedicate their knowledge and talents to the common weal, like all other officials about which the same can be claimed, deserve a distinctive rank and sufficient income so that they can meet the demands of their taxing profession with dignity and satisfaction."[16]

Schram assumed an equation between profession (*Beruf*) and office (*Amt*) that had been quite common in school reform literature and central to its objectives since the mid-eighteenth century. With it elite status was extended, in modified form, to missionary outposts. By the eighteenth century the primary function of German universities was to supply personnel for the most extensive state bureaucracies in Europe. The nexus between state office and academic education (*Bildung*) was perhaps tightest in Prussia; its General Legal Code of 1794 confirmed that the members of a new elite, the *Staatsbürgertum*, enjoyed social and legal preeminence by virtue of their degrees and the offices to which those degrees entitled them.[17] Most advocates of popular education who were not higher civil and ecclesiastical officials with full membership in the new estate were at least "state servants" on its bottom edge. From their standpoint the lower school instructor—that is, the new schoolteacher—seemed a very distant kinsman. His lower educational level and his more direct, familiar relationship with the lower orders precluded ascent to their own lofty rank. But even attenuated kinship drew the teacher across the basic status divide between manual and intellectual labor. To call the teacher a "state servant" or "official" was simply to acknowledge his public role. At the turn of the century, as in earlier decades, it was unrealistic to expect the German states to match their enthusiasm for school reform with a willingness to salary thousands of new officials from their own treasuries.[18] But reformers never tired of stressing that the schoolteacher would make vital contributions to his community and ultimately to his state. For that reason the community must award him, like the pastor, with a public office scaled to local proportions.[19]

Public security and prestige were not simply occupational rights of schoolteaching. They were also tools of reform, essential to recruit for the new profession and guarantee its effectiveness in the field. As Schram put it, "Can we really expect that . . . men who consider themselves only modestly able to find a more respectable livelihood in another field will enthusiastically enter a station [*Stand*] in which they see themselves constantly reduced to the class of hirelings [*Miethlinge*] and have to be masters of the art of economy to make it through hard times?"[20] Only the rewards of office would attract and hold a new generation of "better men," distinguished by talent and dedication from the struggling artisans and "ne'er-do-wells" who drifted into schoolmastery. These men were to be instruments of a kind of cultural imperialism; they were entering a mission territory considered inferior as well as alien and had to erase many of its traditions and values rather than grant them relative merit. The problem was that the new school would not overpower the natives simply by the force of its rationality or usefulness. Popular enlightenment required a mediator, but one who would command respect, and thus make an impact, as the emissary of a superior world. In 1781, Johann Friedrich Prenninger offered this typical advice in his *Rural School Library*: "The skillful and pious school servant . . . will neglect nothing in his entire outer appearance to acquire and maintain the respect he deserves for himself and his office. I do not want to exaggerate the matter, or to demand from all of you what only some, who are better prepared, can achieve. But a certain personal respectability in your speech, in the company you keep, in your dress, etc., must at least distinguish all of you from the peasant. He must be left with no doubt that you have advantages over him, and that his children can learn something from you."[21]

Prenninger was not alone in laying the main burden of "respectability" on the man rather than the office. Often enough, in fact, the incumbent schoolmasters were consoled with reminders that teaching was a selfless calling in the traditional religious sense and with assurances that faithful service to God and Caesar would bring an "eternal reward" as well as the "inner satisfaction of a good conscience." Even the poorly paid schoolmaster need not descend to the natives' level—to what Krünitz called "the dirty, paltry life-style of the peasantry"—if he practiced frugality and used his farm plots cleverly.[22] Reformers offered this advice, however, because they realized that there was little hope for improvement in the immediate future. In the long run, it was generally recognized, even the educated and devoted schoolteacher could not command respect without certain props. By the turn of the century it was an axiom of reform thought that the income from teaching alone must attain a "decent" or "respectable" level. In 1773, Zedlitz cited a minimum of 100–120 thaler per year, but Rochow wanted to raise the figure to 200 thaler.[23] The various estimates were calculated to award an educated official with a modest livelihood, scaled to the simple living standards of the countryside but allowing him to maintain the appearances appropriate to his station. The schoolmaster's dependence on individual residents for his livelihood seemed as shameful as his poverty and as detrimental to the new assignment of the school. A public income was, by definition, "secure" (*fest*), and the winter school and circuit obviously did not meet that requirement. The school fee and other traditional endowments could survive only as taxlike communal levies, payable to the local mayor or tax collector rather than to the schoolteacher himself.[24]

Though proposed as the bare minimum these reforms aimed at a radical overhaul of teacher-community relations in the countryside. Their purpose was not simply to insure an appropriate standard of living but also to disentangle a new profession from the local social fabric and its terms of employment. In Schram's words, collection of the school fee by a local official was an unfortunate but necessary "detour"; it would end the "unbearable behavior" of many parents who "instead of honoring their children's teacher as one of their best friends . . . regard him as a tradesman they have contracted and expect him to adjust his behavior to the wage."[25] An "independent" teaching office—one with secure, circuitous, and largely impersonal support—would allow its occupant to educate children despite their parents' recalcitrance. Ultimately, the prestige of office would rest on local appreciation; that was the purpose of an annual school examination, with local dignitaries presiding and proud parents (it was hoped) in attendance. But the immediate problem was to clear a space and fence it in. In several school laws, for example, parents were required to take their complaints to the pastor or mayor, rather than confront the teacher directly and subject him to personal abuse before the children. Like the church the schoolhouse was now to assume a special sanctity in the community—as an inviolable professional domain.[26]

At the turn of the century these reforms, including those sponsored in state law, existed only on paper. It remained an open question whether the critical ones could be funded in the absence of an enormous state expenditure. The school fee was at least a cash compensation, and in Prussia it had the legal status of a head tax. But even if a local official mediated, the teacher would be enjoying a better living at the expense of individual parents with school-age children rather than of the community as a whole. In the many smaller settlements his income would necessarily be very low, and distance and poor traveling conditions often made it impossible to combine them into larger "school communities."[27] The more serious problem, even in larger communities, was that the yield from the fee was often limited by the landless and near-landless poor, who seemed to multiply at an alarming rate with the population increase of the late eighteenth century. According to the inspection reports of the late 1760s, an annual rate of one or two thaler per child was an onerous burden for parents who maintained a household on the edge of subsistence and below it in hard times, and particularly for those with large broods. Advocates of school reform were well aware of rural poverty, and in fact argued that, by teaching poor children manual skills and good work habits, the new school would enable them to become valuable members of the work force.[28] However, the fact remained that the families who would benefit most from enlightened instruction were least able to afford it. Dwarfholders, day laborers, and the like, Councillor Heilsberg reported from East Prussia in 1787, could not be blamed if "their concern for their children's bodily nourishment takes precedence over concern for their spiritual life, and if they prefer to provide for their own brood rather than for [the schoolmaster's]table."[29] The school fee, in other words, put the poor at odds with a man who was practically one of them.

One way to satisfy both parties, or at least to ease their conflict, was to allow fee exemptions to families enrolled as public paupers and to compensate the schoolmaster from local relief funds. But in the late eighteenth century poor relief was still a parish affair; outside officials could neither elicit local funds for fee compensation nor, in their absence, prevent a very liberal definition of poverty in the case of school parents. The *Reglement* of 1763 had acknowledged this dilemma without confronting it head-on; only "when no other way is available," it stipulated, should the fee for public paupers be paid from the Sunday collection, the poor chest, or the communal treasury (in that order). Despite the loopholes this provision provoked numerous complaints in the Kurmark. In response to them two ordinances of 1771 in effect allowed the villages to continue arranging matters internally at the expense of their schoolmasters.[30]

In 1768, Ignaz von Felbiger, the author of the Catholic *Reglement* for Silesia, had tried to replace the school fee with a communal tax that assessed all residents, including those without school-age children, and varied according to wealth. That was an obvious way to fund a public office and circumvent local poverty. Though Felbiger may have prevailed over stiff opposition in his own parishes,[31] it should not be surprising that officials elsewhere in Prussia had not taken up his scheme or anything similar by the 1790s. So long as the landed wealth of the estate lords was exempt from direct taxation, the full weight of any new burden would fall on the peasants and other non-noble landholders. While shouldering the great bulk of royal taxation, they also paid rents in cash or kind and, in east-Elbian regions, still owed labor services that left them with little time to farm their own holdings. It was this double burden—and not just the plight of the landless poor—that had led Councillor Wilhelm Abraham Teller to reject a new tax for the schoolmasters in 1768; instead, he had advised his colleagues, the High Consistory should be trying to alleviate the "almost universal indigence" so that the peasant would have "the capacity and the time to realize that he is a human being."[32] The underlying question was whether reform from above could enlighten the countryman, and thereby improve his lot, without tampering with the *Ständestaat* erected on his labor.

Against this backdrop of mounting ambitions and persistent obstacles, the promulgation of the Prussian General Legal Code in 1794 marked a significant, though very tentative, step forward. Its authors put the seal of approval of the state on several decades of reform literature by including the lower schools among "state institutions" (*Veranstaltungen des Staates*) but also reflected the prevailing moderation of opinion. While teachers in the academic high schools were declared "officials of the state" with an "exempted" legal status, the "common schoolteacher" was explicitly subject to the local judiciary and thus excluded—if there had been any doubt about it—from the privileged *Staatsbürgertum*. In keeping with the code's respect for traditional privileges, the estate lords were made responsible only for the school contributions of subjects who were "permanently or temporarily" unable to pay. But the code also stipulated that "where no special endowments [*Stiftungen*] are available . . . the teacher is to be supported by all heads of households [*Hausväter*] in each locality, whether or not they have school-age children" and "in proportion to their properties and livelihoods." With those provisions the ambitions of school reform finally prevailed over doubts about the financial capacity of its intended beneficiaries.[33]

The General Code merely provided guidelines for future legislation, without overriding existing law at the provincial and local level, but its school tax endowed a new profession with an official status corresponding to its mission. In the legal anatomy of the Prussian *Ständestaat* the schoolteacher remained a communal employee but now merited the public support of a tax-based office. Whether the Prussian state administration could erect that office in rural communities, despite their incapacity and resistance, remained to be seen.

THE REFORM ERA

By the close of the eighteenth century popular school reform, which had begun as one of the halfhearted projects of the Prussian state administration, was one of the more pressing items on its agenda. The lower school had merited attention in the General Code because of its strategic importance to economic development, religious and moral improvement, and the creation of an enlightened *Bürger*. In the Reform Era of the early nineteenth century, however, school reform finally got underway in the spirit of a radically new departure. To Baron Karl vom Stein and his collaborators the military collapse of Prussia in 1806 confirmed the moral bankruptcy of the traditional *Ständestaat*. Under the stifling tutelage of an absolutist bureaucracy the society of estates had ossified into a caste system, each caste selfishly pursuing its interests without regard for the public welfare and the fate of the monarchy. The task at hand was to resurrect this corpse and fuse its parts into a modern nation-state by dismantling the legal privileges of the estates, breaking down the social and cultural barriers between them, and stimulating their cooperation.

To the post-1806 reformers the "national community" promised political as well as cultural salvation. Their goal was to transform a rigid hierarchy of subjects into a community of citizens who shared a common national identity and participated actively in public life. Although bureaucratic absolutism was blamed for the decay of the old regime, reform from above seemed all the more urgent. The imperatives of national renewal required a revitalized, dynamic state administration, distinguished from the officialdom of the old regime not only by its organic union with the nation but also by its more centralized, efficient structure. The "development [*Bildung*] of a nation," Hardenberg wrote in his Riga Memorandum in 1807, must go hand in hand with a "doubling of the powers of the state."[34]

Both purposes informed the new departure in school policy but, as in so many other areas, the post-1806 regime could neither remove nor bypass longstanding obstacles. In 1811, K. H. Neumann, a pastor in Brandenburg, described how earlier school legislation had miscarried for want of "powerful support from above": "In fact in many places the schoolmasters did not receive support even when their complaints were about continual arrears in their well-earned pay. If they or their pastors went further and appealed to higher officials the matter came back to the *Justiziarien* [royal judicial officials] and the latter did whatever they pleased. Under these circumstances the common man very soon realized that there was neither force nor earnestness behind all the ordinances, arrangements and complaints [and] . . . was guided merely by his caprice, his arbitrary will and his selfishness."[35]

The overhaul of school administration was most successful at the top, where it was easiest. The consistories had been ineffective partly because the schools were one of their tangential concerns and partly because they had gotten bogged down in jurisdictional morasses. In 1808, Wilhelm von Humboldt was summoned from his diplomatic post in Rome to Königsberg, where the government had transferred after the defeat, to head a section for religion and public instruction in the new Ministry of the Interior.[36] Though still formally church institutions the lower schools now became the responsibility of full-time, expert councillors. Humboldt's lack of experience with domestic administration was more an advantage than a handicap. He brought several younger, reformist officials and clergymen into the section and tried to avoid bureaucratic myopia in the formulation of policy by appointing prominent academics and intellectuals, including Friedrich Schleiermacher, to the newly created Scholarly Deputation (*Wissenschaftliche Deputation*). In 1817 the king elevated the section to a separate Ministry of Culture—a step he had denied Humboldt—and entrusted it to Baron Karl von Altenstein, a veteran bureaucratic infighter. Meanwhile, most affairs of the lower schools—their curriculum, financial support, and so forth—were removed from the provincial consistories and assigned to church and school sections in the twenty-five new district governments (*Bezirksregierunge*), which were to serve as the major administrative channels between the Berlin ministries and the localities.[37]

But the full-time, expert councillors in Berlin and the district centers could only monitor and occasionally lecture thousands of communities on paper. For enforcement of new laws they had to rely on the same personnel the consistories had found wanting. Rochow was not typical of the estate lords; as a whole they had been conspicuous by their indifference or opposition to earlier reform efforts. The new regime could neither curtail their patronal rights nor supplement them with new responsibilities. In 1811, Neumann expected a new spirit of cooperation, but Ludwig Natorp, one of his superiors in the new Potsdam section, had already concluded that the lords were still "the single crucial obstacle" to rural school reform.[38] The diocesan superintendents were expected to serve as state inspectors without financial compensation for their new duties or even for travel expenses. Natorp was perhaps too harsh when he complained that many of the superintendents in Brandenberg were "weak-headed men who can be used only as postmen," and indeed that some would be "very lazy and worn-out postmen."[39] But aside from lack of interest and expertise ecclesiastical officials lacked the time for more than sporadic, cursory visitations of the many village schools scattered across their dioceses. Like the consistories, the district sections pinned their hopes for effective local supervision primarily on the pastorate. The pastor, after all, was in a unique position to shepherd the countrymen into reform by virtue of his higher education and official authority. But it was the ideal pastor who had long been hailed as an agent of enlightenment; there was little reason to expect the typical theology graduate, settling into the intellectual isolation of a rural outpost, to become an avid reformer. In any case it was as much a handicap as an advantage that he was a local official on the scene; his parishioners could dampen his enthusiasm for unpopular measures by absenting themselves from church functions or skimping on the contributions that composed so much of his income. The new regime could neither transform the incumbent clergymen into school zealots nor insulate them from local reprisals. Yet, for want of alternatives the pastor had to serve as local school inspector; as such, he was responsible for his parishioners' and schoolmaster's diligent compliance with new laws and obligated to submit detailed reports on both to the sections.[40]

The heightened ambitions for rural school reform made these weaknesses of administrative grasp all the more glaring. At the turn of the century Eberhard von Massow, the last head of the Lutheran department, had drafted a state school law squarely in the mainstream of Enlightenment thought. His school divisions had matched inherited stations, and his rural curriculum had been designed merely to train cooperative subjects and efficient producers.[41] But now the integration of the great mass of the peasantry into a national community seemed the single most urgent step toward the moral and political regeneration of Prussia. To that end Wilhelm von Humboldt and other post-1806 reformers insisted on excluding "mechanical" occupational instruction from all school levels. They planned the elementary school, or *Volksschule*, as the foundation of a new system, in "organic" unity with academic institutions. Their formula was a "general education" (*allgemeine Bildung*) to develop the innate human potential for intellectual life and transmit the cultural traditions shared by all Prussians (and Germans). Only by transcending (but not, of course, eliminating) occupational and social distinctions would the school system equip all children to participate in public life.[42]

In the rhetoric accompanying this educational ideal the missionary-schoolteacher ceased to be a mere agent of enlightenment. Reinhold Bernhard Jachmann, one of the more ambitious advocates of a "general German national education," called for a new corps of "nation-builders." To Wilhelm Harnisch, a young pastor, capable *Volksschullehrer* would be "jewels of the people," reawakening their "slumbering power" and thereby insuring an "unbreakable" state structure.[43] At the close of the War of Liberation Emmanuel Kriegskotte, a young instructor in the small town of Schwelm in Westphalia, carried this ideal of a new profession to a logical, though naive, conclusion. His petition to the Berlin section proposed a 10 percent increase in state taxes so that all schoolteachers, like "all other educational officials," could enjoy fixed salaries scaled to local conditions. With the return of Prussian administration to the western Mark, Kriegskotte expected that "popular education [would] be given a direction appropriate to the spirit of the age [*Zeitgeist*]." He was addressing officials who had taken it upon themselves to emancipate society and create a nation because they already constituted a national *Stand* and their offices allowed them to stand above narrow local interests and prejudices. With a state salary the schoolteacher, profiled for decades as a public servant and now as a nation-builder, would represent the independent, emancipatory state bureaucracy at the very center of local society. Most schoolmasters, Kriegskotte wrote, "come from the common orders," and the school fee made them "fawning, subservient and dependent on every member of the community." But in the new era "only a free man with pure sentiments can educate a free people; a slave is not capable of any enthusiasm and produces a slave mentality."[44] To put that another way, the schoolteacher could educate his community in national freedom only if he stood above and beyond it, as an arm of the state operating free of local control.

It is a measure of the centralizing impulse of the Reform Era that Kriegskotte's proposal received the support of Baron Ludwig von Vincke, the provincial president of Westphalia.[45] However, the more likely route to a public teaching office was a communal tax. Though that legacy of the old regime might exclude the estate lords from school support, it at least had the imprimatur of the General Code. More important, the code tax suited the plans of the Stein-Hardenberg ministries to offset centralization with a measure of communal "self-administration" (*Selbstverwaltung*) and thus avoid a relapse into bureaucratic absolutism. In 1810, in fact, Humboldt considered a state school tax only as an emergency measure; he preferred to look forward to "the time when the section will have fulfilled its purpose and will transfer its business entirely into the hands of the nation."[46] It was primarily through the community—through the initiative and sense of responsibility citizens brought to their local affairs—that the nation was to become, in Stein's words, an "educational institution." The school was a prime tool for this kind of civic training; a glaring example of local neglect could become a monument to self-administration and imbue future generations with a communal-national spirit that would permeate every area of public life. In the teens the district sections required rural communities, like the towns, to establish school committees. The instructions for the committees left no doubt that in the immediate future they would serve as instruments of reform from above; the pastors, mayors, and other local notables who sat on them were responsible for implementing measures they had had no part in formulating. But in the long view the committees were intended to embody and stimulate public responsibility and thus allow outside officials to keep their direct meddling and punitive measures to a minimum. Aside from managing school funds and enforcing attendance, they were expected to arbitrate disputes between parents and teachers and protect the latter from local spite.[47]

But the rural school committees anticipated a framework that did not materialize. The Municipal Law (*Städteordnung*) was not extended, even in modified form, to the countryside. In 1807, Pastor Ferdinand Hasenklever, a school commissioner in the Prussian Mark, tried to introduce a communal school tax in Schwelm and its neighboring villages but found that the national spirit had not erased an older mentality. Indeed the village councils were several decades behind; they protested that the "philanthropic [*philanthropinis-*

tische] method of education," associated with Basedow and his fol-
lowers in the late eighteenth century, would require parents to pay
for all sorts of instruction that would be useless to their children in
later life. Their main grievance against the tax was that it would produce "an inflated notion of [the schoolmasters'] worth, egotism and
its common result, laziness." With existing arrangements, on the
other hand, "each man, following the fourth commandment of the
Lutheran catechism, will strive to make a living and take pains to
win the approval of parents as well as the love and trust of the children with skill, kindness and an understanding, liberal treatment."
Rebuffed by the War and Domain Chamber, the councils spelled out
this latter point in a second petition. They could not fathom why
the schoolmasters alone should be "protected and supported at the
cost of the starving classes" and added:

> If all schoolmasters were ideal in morality, skill and behavior,
> or indeed if we could hope that they would remain what they
> have been to this point, or at least what the candidates pretend
> to be until they are hired, we would consider alleviating their
> difficulties in making a living in this way [with a tax]. But who
> guarantees that? As soon as they cease to be dependent on
> parents and children we will have nothing with which to re-
> mind them of their duty but the mere ideal of it. As for the
> effect of that on most people, one need only observe the daily
> example of many officials [*Beamten*] of all classes.[48]

Though the councils pleaded poverty, like so many countrymen
before them, they also recognized that a communal school tax
meant a jolting institutional and social intrusion. To replace the
school fee with a fixed salary was to burden their villages with
teachers whose instruction they could not control and whose social
pretensions they could not curb. They had equated an "independent" teacher with "them"—with the arbitrary power of officialdom—and were defending the schoolmasters' dependence on parents, with its opportunities for economic and social sanction, as a
right of accountability.

Most Prussian villages did not have to articulate that right.
Though Humboldt pressed for royal approval of a communal tax in
1810, shortly before leaving office,[49] the section (later ministry) did
not adopt it as a policy and the district sections would only recom-
mend it to exceptional communities. Part of the problem was that
the incumbent schoolmasters seemed too poorly educated and incompetent to merit public salaries. But that only strengthened the
overriding objection that a school tax was neither politically ad-

visable nor fiscally realistic. In 1809 the new district section of the Littau (East Prussia) had countered Humboldt's plans with the warning that any new tax imposition would make the lower schools "unpopular."[50] Five years later Kaspar Friedrich von Schuckmann, Humboldt's successor, pointed out that there could not be a worse time to impose new obligations on the peasantry.[51] The Emancipation Edict of 1807 offered no help in the immediate future; its implementary legislation excluded the smallholders and required the more prosperous peasants to sacrifice a portion of their holdings for free proprietorship. The state administration also had to consider the impact of war and occupation for the past two decades. In 1800, with an eye to recent French invasions, the War and Domain Chamber of the Prussian Mark had predicted that implementation of the code tax would produce "anger and dissatisfaction in the bulk of the popular classes."[52] The War of Liberation in 1813 rid Prussia of Napoleon and his occupation levies, but brought costs and levies of its own. Seen against this backdrop, the fate of the tax underscores the irony of the entire Reform Era; the circumstances that produced and nourished its ideals also made its reform from above, in hard fiscal terms, very ill timed.

With the return to peacetime conditions in the late teens an inter-ministerial commission finally drafted a state school law. The guiding figure on the commission was Councillor Johann Wilhelm Süvern, a post-1806 reformer in the Ministry of Culture who had survived Humboldt's departure. In the preamble to the draft Süvern reaffirmed the Prussian commitment to a "national" system of education whose elementary schools would guarantee a fund of "general education" to all children. The commission had tackled the fiscal problem by authorizing provincial authorities to set minimum teaching incomes. To meet the minimum, school communities might retain most traditional endowments, including the school fee—though the fee was awarded "the priorities of a general state levy," and poor parents were at least partially exempted. If that did not suffice, however, the communities had to levy a school tax on "all landholders, residents and other heads of households." In its report the commission made it clear that, unlike the code tax, this provision was intended to draw the landed property of the estate lords into school support.[53]

This school tax was a state dictum, camouflaged within a maze of less daring provisions but promising a solid, expandable base for rural teaching incomes. But the draft law did not survive the gauntlet of official opinion in the early 1820s. By then Frederick William III, prodded by Metternich, was presiding over a political reaction that had already extended to the universities. In a memorandum to the king, Ludolph Beckedorff, the ministerial councillor for the elementary schools, distilled the new climate into a principled attack on the educational ideals of the Reform Era. Süvern's draft, he protested, rode roughshod over the traditional, still valid rights of the churches, the communities, and parents. His more disturbing objection was that a national education would undermine the "natural inequality" between the estates by stuffing rural children with all sorts of abstract principles and useless knowledge.[54] Despite his reactionary tone Beckedorff was simply calling for a return to the more cautious reform tradition of the old regime. But his kind of alarmism joined continuing fiscal scruples to prevent the promulgation of a state law. Without it a modern teaching office remained what it had been for decades: an obvious public need that seemed to require too great a public sacrifice.

BETWEEN COMMUNITY AND STATE

In a decree of June 12, 1826, the Prussian Ministry of Culture warned against burdening communities with new costs for their schools "merely because [such] an arrangement is better than the previous one." Only in rare cases, it instructed the sections, was it necessary "to impose an arrangement prescribed in the law." As a rule the sections should proceed "only in agreement with the communities," since experience proved that "forced measures" could not produce true "inner" improvement.[55]

The language of the decree barely disguised a strategic retreat, and the experience to which it appealed held a very different lesson. In 1820, a decade or so after the sections had launched their reform drive, they measured its pace with statistics on the incomes of teaching positions. Though income from the sextonship was included, two-thirds of the rural positions were valued at less than 100 thaler and one-third at less than 60 thaler. The rural average was about 85 thaler for all of Prussia.[56] The reform process behind these figures had been marked by initial caution and ensuing attrition. Most sections had refrained from tapping public funds, and all of them had relied primarily on patchwork measures to enforce fee collection and improve other traditional endowments. At the same time, to be sure, rural schools had finally been subjected to regular, detailed bureaucratic surveillance. By the 1820s each school had a file in the district office, including inspection reports, schoolmasters' contracts, and, in some districts, annual school budgets. But the councillors were limited to paper work; in the absence of full-time inspectors and reliable local agents it often was impossible to enforce unpopular measures.

In 1809, Ludwig Natorp was called from the western Mark to the Potsdam section and had an eye-opening encounter with the east-Elbian countryside. An inspection tour convinced him that the rural schools still bore "the stamp of the most common triviality," and left him appalled by the "depth of *Uncultur*" to which the rural population had sunk. The Westphalian countrymen, he wrote to Baron von Vincke, were at least "free men"; there were thousands in Brandenburg who, as the estate lords' "serfs" and day laborers, had been reduced to "the most miserable animal life."[57] Natorp had primary responsibility for the school policy of the Potsdam section, which acknowledged these conditions by postponing the introduction of a tax and trying to work miracles with lesser measures. An ordinance in 1810 improved on the *Reglement* merely by fixing a fee rate of one thaler / eight groschen per year—the rate that had been set for advanced instruction—for all pupils. As for poor children, the section reiterated the vague, long-unworkable provisions of the *Reglement*—fully expecting that attrition from the poor would, by Natorp's estimate, reduce the yield from the fee to about one thaler per child. But the fee alone was to fund a local "school treasury" for a fixed teaching salary, periodic raises for a job well done, and the children's school materials.[58]

Even a slightly revised *Reglement* posed a threat to the Brandenburg countrymen, who were accustomed to ignoring its provisions and were suffering the brunt of French occupation. They reacted, Pastor Neumann recalled, with a "cry" almost everywhere and "stubborn opposition" in some places.[59] Natorp dismissed their complaints as "no different from those to be found in the archives from the year 1763 and the most fortunate years before the war" and wanted to "push this good matter through with solid consequence."[60] But the section had to make concessions long after he returned to the greener pastures of Westphalia in 1816. In the village of Wandlitz, north of Berlin, reform was relatively successful because Pastor Felgentreber was an unusually conscientious local inspector. In 1810 his predecessor, Pastor Johann Wilhelm Mielisch, had reported that only eighteen of the forty-four "heads of households" were full "peasants." Mielisch had entertained little hope that fee collection or attendance could be improved, and the section seems to have largely ignored the village until 1819. In that year, while admitting to the section that Schoolmaster Hermann Tietz was a mediocre instructor, Felgentreber supported his complaints about the fee arrears that had accumulated over the past few years. The new pastor had no patience with "ignorant parents" who "presume to pass judgement on [Tietz's] instruction" when "no single one of them can measure up [to him] in arithmetic or other school subjects." As for the demand that Tietz drop his tailoring, it was hardly possible so long as he could not collect most of his teaching income.[61]

But Felgentreber's reports to the section from 1819 to 1821 dramatize the pastors' inability to extricate reform from a vicious circle. In 1819 he noted that the school committee "fulfills its duty as much as it can be combined with the work of the countrymen, but like the pastor is unable to remove the many local obstacles which arise from the poverty of the people and the resulting irregularity of school attendance." A year later he submitted the following grim but realistic plaint:

> When parents keep their children at home for a day or several days, or indeed for weeks at a time, they never lack excuses: "I have to pay my contributions and taxes," it is said, "and I even have to pay a head tax for my child from age twelve on. How can I manage all that if the child does not help me make a living? I cannot send my children to school regularly because I cannot do without them at home." And how is this abuse to be eliminated? I have often pondered that question, but in vain. Should the parents be fined? The result would surely be long lists of arrears in fines to be collected, which would surpass the arrears in monthly fees. And would you want to collect them when the fee can be collected only with great effort and trouble?[62]

The irony of the story is that the annual fee collection in Wandlitz had reached a staggering 92 thaler for eighty-six school-age children by 1830. That was possible only because the two lay members of the school committee had become exasperated with Tietz's demands for fee arrears, and had persuaded Felgentreber to assume management of the school treasury.[63] Briest, a village in *Kreis* Prenzlau, is a more instructive case. In 1810, Pastor Nernst had listed thirteen of the fifty-eight families as *Bauer* and another ten as smaller landholders (*Cossäthe* and *Büdner*). The nineteen families listed as "laborers" (*Arbeitsmänner*) contributed twenty-four of the sixty-three school-age children. Schoolmaster Schiffmann, an invalid soldier who had returned to Briest to succeed his father, managed to earn about 20 thaler per year with linen weaving. Most of his relatively high "official income" of 121 thaler was in sexton fees and contributions. He received only 25 thaler annually in school fees, and parents made his life difficult on the collection rounds, Nernst reported, "partly because of their poverty and partly because of their lack of understanding."[64]

In September 1810, Superintendent Hoffmann swore in three peasants as school committeemen and reported to the section that the "community" wanted to limit Schiffmann's fixed salary temporarily to thirty-six thaler. Within a few months a local feud had surfaced. The Briest school district, it had turned out, included fourteen school-age children whose parents were day laborers for the local estate lord and lived in one of his settlements, the Wendemark. Supported by the headman, the committee had proposed to compensate Schiffmann for them by collecting a small sum from each farm. But the rest of the landholders had opposed this scheme and now hoped to spite the committee by refusing to pay any fee at all. At this point Hoffmann appealed to the section for help. He was one of Natorp's "worn-out postmen" and indeed was more than willing to admit that the time-consuming duties of school inspection were beyond him. Barraged with "undeserved attacks," he could not counteract "the error on the part of all communities" that he and his pastors had undertaken the reform on their own initiative. To make matters worse, he complained to the section, the *Kreis* director in Prenzlau felt that the school committee in Briest had overstepped its authority. In a letter to the director Natorp requested that he "not encourage the community's recalcitrance by stalling on school fee collection," but also slapped down the committee's distribution scheme. Only in the most pressing cases could fee losses be covered with a general levy, and Briest was apparently not one of those cases. Natorp recommended charitable collections at "blessed occasions like weddings and baptisms." When Schiffmann retired in 1816 the annual fee collection for eighty school-age children was only about sixty-six thaler and the Wendemark laborers, pleading extreme poverty, were still refusing to pay. In 1831, a new teacher had a fixed teaching salary of fifty thaler; lacking a trade or other side-job, he requested one thaler per child so that his income would at least "keep step with the times."[65]

In Schönewalde, a community near Wandlitz, poverty combined with much bolder resistance to paralyze the section. Though considered a village, Schönewalde had been founded in 1756 to provide yarn for the shops in Berlin and other towns. Its original settlers had been a few of the many "colonists" who had been attracted to Brandenburg by small land grants and freedom from the usual obligations of tenantry. By 1810, according to Pastor Voigt's report, only 6 of the

127 "heads of households" were cotton weavers (although many more may have done domestic weaving). In addition to the 25 carpenter's and mason's apprentices, who presumably found construction work in the area, there were 58 "day laborers"—a tag that does not specify whether they worked in the trades or in agriculture, but leaves no doubt that a sizable portion of the residents had very meager livings. The laborers contributed about 40 percent of the 121 school-age children.

Voigt stressed that recent "hard times" had only strengthened the community's basic indifference toward its school. "If their livings do not improve soon," he predicted, "one colonist position after another will be abandoned." Natorp responded with a point-by-point condemnation of prevailing school conditions in Brandenburg. Now that school support had become a public responsibility, he wrote, parents could no longer treat the schoolmaster "like a day laborer whom they provide with bread and work only at certain times of the year and then dismiss with a 'thanks a lot.'" But at a meeting in May 1811 the residents informed the new pastor, Felgentreber, that they were willing to raise only 60 thaler per year—though they legally owed 160 thaler in school fees. When Felgentreber threatened forced collection, several of those present retorted that "an entire community cannot be saddled with it." He concluded that "certain cryers" nursed a vendetta against Schoolmaster Christian Felber and were "decidedly against doing anything to benefit him." In July 1811 a local deputation to _Amt_ Mühlenbeck explained the opposition of the village in somewhat different terms. What bothered them was that, in addition to enjoying the use of twice as much land as the other colonists, Felber was receiving 50 thaler annually from the royal treasury. He was "in a better situation than many schoolteachers in the peasant villages."[66]

This egalitarian approach lay behind the villagers' sudden complaints that their children were not learning reading and writing. Natorp and his colleagues might doubt their sincerity, but could hardly claim that Felber had more knowledge or pedagogical skill than most schoolmasters. "A very mediocre teacher," his superintendent had reported in 1804, and one who would never become a "magnus Apollo" (!). In August 1812 the section made its first concession by lowering the required sum of fees to ninety thaler and limiting Felber's share to sixty until he proved his worth. However, parents now concluded that they no longer owed a fee for their older children, since a head tax had been levied on them to help finance the War of Liberation. The school treasurer, Felgentreber noted, "has accepted this assumption for a long time without asking me about it." The section feared that neighboring villages might follow the lead of Schönewalde, but the pastor counselled against forced collections for such a "trivial matter" now that the village was "making sacrifices for the fatherland." The War of Liberation aside, Felgentreber had come to his wits' end with his parishioners.

The section agreed to sixty thaler for the next two years and might have given no further attention to Schönewalde if Felber had not complained in 1817. Since 1813 the headman had received fee payments in his office every month without bothering to record those in arrears. According to Felber's record, older pupils were still exempt and many of the others—most of them belonging to parents with two or more school-age children—were also going free. By January 1818, when Superintendent Hoppe finally returned to settle the issue, schoolmaster-community relations had grown very rancorous indeed. Felber, who had led the hymns at Sunday service for more than twenty years, now had to admit that his ear was faulty and his voice somewhat weak. But he denied the more serious charge that he was "venting his anger against parents who insulted him" by thrashing the children too much. Hoppe was able to report a compromise settlement, with the school committee promising to raise the seventy-two thaler needed to grant Felber a twelve thaler raise. The section councillor scribbled a curt approval on the margin of the report; after nearly eight years he had to settle for less than half of the legal total in school fees.[67]

Schönewalde and other recent colonies may have been unusually poor or at least unusually stubborn in their opposition to reform. But the surviving budgets for local school treasuries in the Potsdam district—a few of the many which the superintendents had to submit to the section every year—chart the slow and spotty improvement of rural teaching incomes. In Superintendency Angermünde a majority of the rural communities—thirteen out of twenty—were collecting one thaler or more for each school-age child by 1825. But the superintendent attributed his success largely to persistent forced collections and had the advantage that his district was rather small. In Superintendency Zehdenick a less draconian superintendent had had similar success with only eleven of his fifty-one villages by 1830. Another nine were, like Schönewalde, still collecting one-half or less of the legal fee.[68]

Rural school reform had better prospects in the newly organized Rhine Province, where French officials had already carried state intervention well beyond the *Reglement* by dictating minimum teaching incomes and new collection procedures to their mayoralties. In the Grand Duchy of Berg the school instruction of 1812 retained a fee but required compensation for poor children from the local "welfare institutions." More important, every community had to recognize its schoolmaster as a communal official, at least partially, by providing a minimum annual salary of 250 francs (about 65 thaler) from its public treasury.[69] In 1814, Johann August Sack, the head of the Prussian occupation government, concluded from his school commissioners' reports that "the French government put little worth on this subject [i.e., improving teaching incomes], so unimportant or even contradictory to its interest, and in any case had only bothered with it when there was absolutely nothing else to support." Sack wanted school support to be given "top priority" in communal budgets and in 1816 appealed for local cooperation to effect a "radical improvement."[70] But without a state law the sections merely tried to enforce regular fee collection and tighten other traditional support arrangements. Only the Düsseldorf section went further by maintaining the minimum salary of the Berg instruction.

Thanks to this innovation, Düsseldorf stood high above all the other districts in the official income statistics for 1820. But its rural average was still only 152 thaler for Protestant schools and 120 thaler for Catholic schools. Unable to apply the General Code to newly acquired territories, the section had let school attendance and fee collection slide. In 1825 the ministry filled the breach with a separate decree, and the section, having elicited opinions from its inspectors and local officials, issued a new school ordinance. Its lengthy, tortuous "explanations" reveal that school support had become a very sensitive issue in the lower Rhineland. The section had rejected proposals to replace the school fee with a larger communal salary, primarily because of "the heavy burdens now weighing on the landowners." Now it had to defend a shoestring budget against local encroachments. It dismissed complaints that a fee rate of three groschen per month was too high, particularly for "unpropertied residents," and that fee compensation for poor children would overburden most communal treasuries. While insisting that the teachers could not afford any losses, however, the section also left local officials with a gaping loophole by requiring compensation *only* for the days on which poor children actually attended school.[71]

The loophole was significant because nascent industrialism in the lower Rhineland was already exacerbating the old conflict between poverty and rural school reform. Many children of "unpropertied residents" continued to be hired out for farm labor, particularly in the summer months; others were now working year-round in the textile "factories" that had proliferated through the countryside as well as the towns. By the mid-1820s, the section itself estimated in response to a ministerial inquiry, there were about 5300 "factory children," most of them below fourteen years of age, and most working ten to sixteen hours a day.[72] Industrialism posed a new obstacle to school reform, but also strengthened the national economy and offered new employment opportunities to an already overpopulated region. For those reasons the ministerial regulation of 1827 only threatened enforcement of regular attendance, and counselled solicitude for "hard-pressed parents" as well as "the existing factories, which cannot do without this cheap labor if they are to flourish." It was sufficient that children who were not "too young" and did not suffer moral or physical harm in the factories receive instruction only for a few days per week, or hours per day, or in special evening or Sunday schools. They might, in fact, be dispensed from it entirely.

In the Düsseldorf and Potsdam districts the preference of the sections for minimal improvements instead of sweeping changes had entangled reform in local poverty and opposition tactics. In other provinces, east and west, similar measures encountered the same process of attrition. The official income statistics for 1820 measured, in a deceptively neat way, the impact of a limited, makeshift kind of state intervention. Behind their cash figures lay the sextonship, the school fee, and other survivals that were, at best, semipublic arrangements. Rural school reform had finally been launched, but had hardly begun to travel a long, hard road.

Three

THE SEMINARS AND THEIR GRADUATES

By the early nineteenth century the recruitment and training of a new *Lehrerstand* was long overdue. New teaching handbooks and school primers were futile as long as schoolmastery remained an occupational crutch or refuge, perpetuating rote, senseless methods instead of promoting an enlightened pedagogy. Sons who followed in their fathers' footsteps inherited a kind of trade without necessarily bringing interest or talent to it. An apprenticeship was not required, and in any case the apprentice simply mimicked his master's time-honored *Schlendrian*. Most schoolmasters lacked any formal training beyond a rudimentary lower school instruction, perhaps supplemented by a pastor's tutoring in catechism and scripture.

If the incumbent schoolmasters could not enlighten children, they also could not win over adults. In the sporadic reform efforts since the mid-eighteenth century they had proven to be poor ground troops, too exposed and vulnerable to overcome the countrymen's entrenched resistance. Part of the problem was that outside officials often found it difficult to distinguish well-founded gripes about the schoolmasters' misconduct or neglect of office from spiteful charges fabricated to settle personal scores or counter the demands of the moment. But even the man whose personal life was irreproachable and who was willing to hold school regularly could not claim to be the countrymen's "better" in a social or intellectual sense. He had not acquired the polish and other marks of an educated man, and in fact was hardly more educated than his village neighbors. Why should such a man, the countrymen were prone to ask, merit new sacrifices of their money or their children's time?

In the early nineteenth century Prussian school officials were only too well aware of these handicaps. In 1814 a school commissioner in the lower Rhineland listed 317 of his 900 schoolmasters as particularly "weak" and another 67 as "useless." Natorp even considered pensioning several hundred of the most hopeless cases in the Potsdam district.[1] Despite the incumbents, improvement of teaching positions could not be postponed; the only way to attract "better" men was to offer higher financial and social rewards. However, the very assumptions of school reform led officials to expect that well-trained missionaries would convert the natives. Ignorance and prejudice aside, the countrymen were rational human beings; they would eventually reward deserving teachers who demonstrated that the school could benefit them and their children. If reform from above was to make headway, local improvement and teacher training had to reinforce each other. New men had to help make their offices.[2]

With new procedures for recruiting and licensing candidates, a state-regulated apprenticeship required a minimum of new personnel and money. But even if the typical schoolmaster was willing to devote sufficient attention to his charge, he was likely to shape the boy in his own image, with precisely the social attributes and schoolhouse methods that had to be eradicated. Though certainly better qualified, the pastors could not carry the burden; too many of them were neither interested in school reform nor familiar with the new pedagogy.[3] In the second half of the eighteenth century several German states, including Prussia, had experimented with another route: the regional centralization of training in special schools known as seminars (Seminarien). Their disadvantage was that they required a significant investment to provide facilities, pay a teaching staff, and perhaps help support candidates who otherwise could not attend. Because the states had been so niggardly, the early seminars had been small, makeshift affairs, supplying their regions with no more than a trickle of new teachers and relying largely on part-time clergymen for their teaching staffs. The seminar established in Berlin in 1756 was still relegated to inadequate space in the Realschule in 1814. Most of its pupils had been artisan apprentices who lived scattered through Berlin and attended the one-year course part-time while supporting themselves with their trades.[4]

If institutional centralization was expensive, it was also efficient. With it the state could extricate large numbers of teaching candidates from the local treadmill of schoolmastery and submit them to intensive, well-supervised training, complete with classrooms and competent instructors. These advantages explain why, despite the reluctance to incur new expenses in a wartime fiscal crisis and its immediate aftermath, the Prussian state administration endowed a network of new seminars from 1806 onward and remained committed to them. By 1834 there were thirty main seminars (Haupt-Seminarien), most of them accommodating fifty to one hundred pupils and all offering two- or three-year courses. Each province had at least two, and Silesia, the most populous province, had five. In addition there were eleven smaller, "auxiliary" seminars. The annual seminar budget in 1831 was about 110,000 thaler, and of that over 80,000 thaler came directly from the state treasury.[5]

The Altenstein ministry had been quick to insure a full return on this investment by incorporating the seminars into the administrative structure and regulating their procedures. Though the confessional division had survived in the lower schools, Catholic as well as Protestant seminars were entrusted to provincial school colleges rather than to the sections so that recruitment and training could be coordinated throughout each province. Preference was given to younger men, in their late teens and early twenties, whose pastors and schoolmasters could testify to their character and performance in the lower school. To attract qualified candidates and facilitate their entry into teaching positions the crown not only allowed seminar pupils to postpone their military service until after graduation but also reduced their active duty from the usual two years to six months. The graduates were bound to repay this generosity by accepting any assignment during their first three teaching years—on pain of recompensing the state for the entire cost of seminar instruction. Where an apprenticeship survived it was to serve largely as an interim preparation between graduation from a lower school and acceptance by a seminar. Two ministerial ordinances in 1826 requiring outside candidates to take the same licensing examination as seminar pupils and obliging communities to give preference to the latter in hiring insured that the seminars would assume a virtual monopoly over training.[6]

In at least one regard the ministry overestimated its achievement in teaching training. Despite its projections the influx of seminar graduates did not keep pace with the rapidly growing school-age population of the 1830s and 1840s. Even with a one-year course for some of their pupils, in fact, the seminars in a few provinces could not replace all the retiring and deceased schoolmasters. But by the 1840s the majority of younger instructors in most provinces were state-trained professionals.[7]

A CONTROLLED EXPERIMENT

In 1807, Johann Anton Küpper, a clergyman and school commissioner in the lower Rhineland, accompanied his appeal for state-financed seminars with a warning that, unlike their eighteenth-century predecessors, the new institutions must avoid the mistake of treating their pupils like university students. There were two unavoidable facts: most seminar recruits would come from the "lower orders," and most would have to enter rural teaching positions. The typical student, Küpper reminded his readers, had been raised in an "educated family," and thus was prepared to absorb an academic education. But to cram "lower," uneducated youth with a similarly broad and theoretical education during their brief stay in the seminar was to court disaster. The result would be half-baked, insufferably conceited intellectuals, who disdained elementary schoolchildren and their parents as too "small" and "common." If allowed a student lifestyle, the recruits would acquire a "sense of freedom, a pride, a contempt for all small, restrictive conditions of civilian life." It was hard enough for the student, Küpper noted (perhaps recalling his own experience as a young pastor), to reintegrate into "civilian life"; but he could put off a career for a few years after graduation (presumably because his parents could support him), and if he ended up a pastor, doctor, or government official in a "desolate island" in the countryside, he would at least enjoy a superior status and have enough time to pursue leisure interests.[8] Küpper evoked another fate for the seminar graduate who was assigned to a rural outpost after a university-like training:

> Not seldom the *Seminarist* is suddenly transferred from this
> paradise to a world in which he is in contact almost ex-
> clusively with crude countryfolk and artisans who deny him
> the respect to which he has become accustomed, in which his
> superior is a boorish peasant Church *Scholarch*, in which he
> has to make his living with bitter sweat, submit to the yoke of
> civilian convention [*bürgerlichen Convenienz*], and find
> scope for his academic freedom and pleasures in the cramped
> schoolhouse, in intercourse with uneducated and uncouth
> children. Should we be surprised if this lightning stroke, which
> destroys his previous freedom, likewise shatters his sense of
> contentment, and if he becomes dissatisfied with his profes-
> sion [*Stande*], his circumstances, his neighbors, his superiors?[9]

Küpper's warning came when a new state institution promised to equip its pupils with the methods and precepts of school reform and thus lift an occupation from the margin of rural society into the ranks of educated, public professions. But at least in the foreseeable future the new profession could not compete with older, more attractive ones for the sons of propertied and educated families. The seminars would be more selective than schoolmastery had been, but would not significantly raise the upper social limit of recruitment.

Most recruits would be sons of artisan, peasant, and lesser families, and the schoolmasters themselves were expected to contribute a healthy share.

Under these circumstances the seminars complicated a question that had accompanied the formulation of state educational policy for several decades. Should a reformed school system help preserve an estate society, based on inheritance of occupations and social positions? Or should it institutionalize equality of opportunity and thus promote intergenerational mobility? In the late eighteenth century state policy had waffled between these alternatives: while confirming the rule of inherited stations, it had allowed exemptions from military service for sons of peasant and other lower families who seemed particularly capable of university study. By the turn of the century the more radical reformers, including several gymnasium directors and higher officials in Prussia, were proposing structural reforms based on "general education" and using a series of examinations to select pupils for various kinds of higher schools. In their view the vitality of the state as well as the welfare of its subjects required that talent replace or at least supplement birth in recruitment for the higher occupations. To allow individuals, regardless of their origins, to develop their potential was to create and continually reproduce a competent, dedicated body of public servants.[10]

The recruitment and training of a new elementary teaching corps represented a very modest step in opening a new career to talent. Rather than include elementary school teaching among the occupational choices for university graduates, the seminars created a segregated, considerably lower career route. But the fact remained that the state was sanctioning and indeed financing an exception for a group of young men who, by the nature of their profession, would be highly visible to and influential among the lower orders. Not surprisingly, Küpper and other post-1806 officials, while accepting that prospect, were markedly uneasy about it. Their cultural and political ideal of the nation was posed against the castelike divisions of the old regime; it did not deny the legitimacy of a hierarchy in which individuals and groups knew, and accepted, their proper station. In the seminars crude raw material—young men from uneducated families, and in most cases from villages and small towns whose cultural horizons were particularly narrow—were to be molded into self-consciously educated public servants in two or three years. The problem, in the language of the early nineteenth century, was to shape their "inner" transformation to their "objective circumstances" (*äussere Lage*). In modern terms the subjective

experience of mobility, with its cluster of expectations about future
role and rewards, had to be fastened somehow to its objective possibilities, to the more or less narrow limits that the pace and ultimately the purpose of state-sponsored reform imposed.

In this perspective the new seminars represent the tight, delicate
nexus between state policy and social change in Pre-March Prussia.
Though unwilling to impose a uniform policy, the administration
approached the seminars as hazardous instruments and tried to fashion them into a controlled experiment. In keeping with a long-
standing stereotype and with decades of reform literature, Küpper
fixed his sights on the "crude countryfolk" and their "desolate islands." Rural Prussia was the "flat land" (*plattes Land*)—a term referring more to its sociocultural topography than to its physical
landscape, and still evoking a primitive, brutish peasant life at the
turn of the century. In the Enlightenment the countryman's "simple" and "natural" ways had been extolled and even declared his peculiar virtues. This positive language was another way of stating the
fact of the matter: his world was much more austere and confining
than that of the townsman. The small service elite that rural Prussia
had long supported—Küpper's pastors, doctors, and officials—occupied a peculiar station in the social hierarchy. Rural pastors in particular, the conventional wisdom had it, must strike a balance in
their posture toward the crude countryfolk, never forgetting that
they represented a "higher" culture and society, but at the same
time, for want of alternative satisfactions, learning to appreciate the
natural beauty and simple, homespun ways of the countryside.

In one sense, then, seminar graduates faced a problem of adjustment that was neither new nor unique. What struck Küpper and others and made them regard the seminar as a peculiarly hazardous
instrument was the peculiar degree to which the graduates would
have to adjust. Their relationship with the uneducated mass was
necessarily more delicate than that of established members of the
service elite, including the pastors. Even in the more optimistic projections for income reform their positions remained well below
well-endowed pastorates, and were hardly comparable with higher
government posts. More important, a respectable, secure public office was still a distant ideal in the early nineteenth century. In the
immediate future seminar graduates would have to accept the countrymen's timetable. Facing that reality in 1806, Küpper speculated
that it might be more prudent to postpone the seminars. Later most
rural positions would offer a "respectable" standard of living and
thus attract recruits from the "educated *Stände*."[11] In 1823, Ludolph
Beckedorff drew the standard conclusion from over a decade of re-

form: the task at hand, he informed the director of the new Potsdam seminar, was to "educate a large number of rural teachers whose demands on their future schoolchildren and on their objective situation are no greater than the present state of things justifies."[12] Beckedorff's point was that, by their very success in training a new generation of schoolteachers, the seminars might outstrip the pace of local reform. Unable to drive rural communities forward, the state had to keep a tight brake on its training experiment.

To restrain the seminars meant to locate them emphatically less than halfway between a schoolmaster's apprenticeship and a university education, though as professional schools they might be considered more analogous to the latter. What underlay Küpper's warning was the enormous experiential difference between the two. Under a schoolmaster the local boy had received a kind of *Handwerk* training, limited to mastering the rudimentary curriculum of the lower school and practicing the traditional schoolhouse methods. His social experience was likewise confined; he lived at home or with a nearby schoolmaster, assisted in the instruction of the local children, and remained subordinate to the pastor and other local authorities. Imagine that the same boy or a neighbor's son had gone off to a university, thanks to an ambitious father or, more likely, a wealthy benefactor. He would be intellectual and social worlds apart, absorbing the "higher" culture of academic learning and shaking off the fetters of family life and native community. Within the university town, students formed a distinct, privileged corporation, beyond the yoke of "civilian convention." Free to "cultivate" themselves in a unique hiatus between family upbringing and career demands, they were known to spend more time brawling and sampling the variegated life of the towns than attending lectures.

Post-1806 officials differed on matters of seminar curriculum, but were in virtually unanimous agreement that the new social initiation into teaching, so different from a local apprenticeship, required a tight brake. Küpper's warning was a variation on an old theme; seminar graduates trained in Berlin and other towns had already been stereotyped as a troublesome lot, too "pretentious" for their rural outposts. In their case, as in the case of university students, the problem had been traced back to *Luxus*. That term distilled an ancient prejudice against the sinful vanity and frivolous amusements of urban life and enriched it with the moralistic glorification of "sobriety" and "industry" in Enlightenment thought. The moral contrast between country and town pointed to the more sophisticated culture and greater material comforts of the latter—the theaters and cafés, fancy clothing, and fine foods. Within the framework of an estate society these were seen to imperil the future rural schoolteacher's fate in this world as well as in the next. Spoiled by *Luxus*, he ended up a malcontent and misfit in the countryside, where life was wholesome but also primitive.[13]

A sure way to avoid this fate, often recommended in the late eighteenth century, was to locate the seminars in rural settings or at least to keep them out of the larger, temptation-ridden towns. The recommendation, and the specter of "spoiled" seminar graduates that lay behind it, survived through the Reform Era, side by side with its heightened ambitions for teacher training. Whenever possible, Süvern's draft law stipulated in 1819, the new seminars should be located in places that were "not too large." Thus they could protect their pupils from "distraction, corruption and habituation to a way of life unsuitable to their future situations" without resorting to "strict isolation."[14] Following that advice, school officials in the Rhine Province passed up Cologne, Koblenz, and other large urban centers for two sleepy provincial towns, Brühl and Meurs.[15] Other provincial administrations probably had similar intentions, but seminar locations were sometimes chosen more for their practical advantages than for their moral environment. The school colleges and sections were concerned above all to avoid the expense of new buildings by converting existing facilities—a secularized cloister, for example, or an old seminar—and so proceeded rather haphazardly, taking whatever was available. As a result nine of the main seminars did end up in middle-sized and larger towns (in six cases using the facilities of older seminars).[16]

But alarmism about the early town seminars obscured their reality. In 1794, Councillor Streithorst explained why and how the seminar in Halberstadt compensated for a perilous environment. Like every other *Stand*, rural schoolmasters required a kind of "moral education" fitted to their peculiar way of life. To insure happiness and usefulness in a rural position the seminar must not only isolate its pupils from urban *Luxus* but also condition them to limit their wants to the bare essentials, to enjoy the pure joys of nature, to accept the less dignified duties of their offices, and to honor mankind "even in the coarsest dress, at the lowest level of social contact."[17] For these purposes the early seminars, at least as they were organized on paper, had submitted their boarding pupils to a markedly strict and austere regimen. As another observer argued at the turn of the century, the town-trained graduate would not consider his village assignment an "exile" if seminar life had been conducted "with the same moderation, simplicity and industry as in a village."[18] Properly organized, in other words, the institution could simulate the conditions its pupils would later have to face.

Both Humboldt and the commission that drafted the school law of 1819 recommended this alternative form of social restraint.[19] In the teens and twenties provincial officials applied it to most seminars with the *Internat*, or boarding school organization. Whenever the proper facilities were available (and they were lacking in some cases), most pupils were housed in the seminar itself. There a resident director and his staff could hold them to a tight, "industrious" schedule, keep their living conditions sufficiently modest, and limit their contacts with the surrounding town to a minimum. In the "auxiliary" seminars simulation of rural hardships was particularly blatant, since they were established specifically to supply teachers for the poorer rural positions in their provinces. In Pyritz, the director explained in 1824, strict discipline and an extremely frugal household were necessary so that the pupils, "who belong to the poorer classes, and whose destiny it is to be the teachers of the poor, may willingly continue in that condition and not learn to know wants which they will not and should not be able to satisfy."[20] The main seminars were larger, more ambitious affairs, supplying teachers for the better rural positions. Typically, however, there were no private quarters; the pupils slept and studied in large common rooms, and where facilities allowed they also took their meals in a common dining hall. Their day was long and thoroughly supervised, with religious services at five or six in the morning and again in the evening. Housekeepers, Beckedorff informed the Potsdam director, were both unnecessary and ill advised; once on the job the graduates would have to make their own beds and wash their own clothes, at least until they could marry.[21] In 1832, Victor Cousin observed this organization on a visit to the Potsdam seminar and was struck by "the perfect order and austere discipline which prevail there, as in a Prussian barracks."[22]

Seminars that were located in larger towns, the 1819 draft law stipulated, were to hold their pupils "in strictest possible isolation."[23] Most directors respected that dictum by limiting free time to one or two afternoons a week and by declaring theaters, cafés, and other urban entertainments off-limits. In Breslau, the largest of the seminar towns, Acting Director Wilhelm Harnisch hoped to accomplish the same purpose with more circumspection. Harnisch considered the provincial capital "very educational" for his country-bred pupils, though he felt that a rural setting would have been preferable "in a moral sense." But in a memorandum on disciplinary problems in 1821 he drew his staff's attention to an alarming shift from thievery, uncleanliness, and crudity to arrogance, sham, and a "craving for material pleasure," particularly among "the best heads." The challenge, it seems, was no longer to polish the rough edges off country bumpkins but to bridle city slickers. Harnisch was particularly alarmed about his pupils' tendency to imitate Breslau's university students "in laughable ways." To his mind, though, the solution was neither to allow the pupils the freedom of students nor to subject them to a cloistered discipline. He proposed to steer a middle course by intensifying religious instruction and by arranging more musical entertainments in the seminar so as to insulate the pupils from "the evil of the big city" without their realizing it. [24]

Though the *Internat* was designed to curb expectations, the seminars should not be reduced to a cold, calculated experiment in environmental control. Indeed state officials and directors justified the *Internat* not as an artificial contrivance but, paradoxically enough, as an attempt to minimize the artificiality of institutional life. They were paternalistic by instinct and wanted a kind of efficiency that would not "spoil" the natural process of family upbringing. Though roughly the same age as students, young men in their late teens and early twenties were still *Knaben*, in their formative years. To keep a small, manageable group under the supervision of a resident director and his staff was to provide them with something of the familial warmth from which they had been abruptly removed. In that sense the new institution would, like the guild master, serve *in loco parentis* while insuring a far more efficient training than the old apprenticeship. Here the key figure was the director; he must not only set a professional example but also serve as resident patriarch, insuring the pupils' moral education by softening a strict regimen with personal concern. [25] As for the simplicity of the *Internat*, the need for social restraint coincided nicely with financial expediency. The families of most pupils would find it difficult, if not impossible, to pay for living quarters and other expenses outside the seminar. With an *Internat* free of *Luxus* the state was able to eliminate or at least limit parental sacrifices without undue expense to itself. Despite their skimpy budgets, in fact, most seminars managed to provide completely free room and board for one-third to one-half of their pupils. [26] That in turn made seminar training possible for many poorer youths and thus allowed the state to choose its candidates from a more competitive field of applicants.

In the final analysis the *Internat* is a measure of the ambition as well as the restraint that the state administration brought to its seminar experiment. It allowed the full-time, concentrated effort without which raw recruits could not be whipped into intellectual shape and rid of rough manners in the brief span of two or three years. In 1827 the ministry itself struck the proper balance in a circular on gymnastic exercises. Less than a decade earlier gymnastics, tainted by its association with nationalist "demagogues," had been banned from the entire school system. By 1827 it seemed politically safe and otherwise useful to encourage physical fitness among future rural schoolteachers. If the schoolteacher was to command the proper respect among rural parents, the circular explained, he must avoid "awkward and embarrassed manners," which "usually prove that a man is coarse and ignorant, or at least ill-assured in the use of his faculties." Gymnastics would give him the social poise appropriate to an educated man. It would also, however, prevent the "air of grandeur or retirement" that often resulted from an overly sedentary education and was "incompatible with the position of a rural schoolteacher, who is usually forced to perform hard physical labor to support his family."[27] Seminar pupils, in other words, had to be conditioned for hardships that most educated men did not have to face.

The balance of ambition and restraint was more precarious in the curriculum planning for the new seminars. On the one hand two or three years of classroom instruction hardly sufficed to equip the recruits with the fund of enlightened knowledge and new pedagogical methods that had thus far failed to penetrate most rural schools. But the seminars had to compensate for brevity without losing sight of their pupils' background and destiny. Juxtaposing the two, Küpper and others tended to exaggerate the impact of formal education on a young man's self-image and corresponding expectations of social reward. Might not seminar instruction be too heady an intellectual dosage for sons of the lower orders? Might it not inflate their expectations to an absurd degree—beyond what was possible in the "flat land," and well beyond the "objective circumstances" of most rural teaching positions? What threatened was a "half-educated" parvenu who disdained his crude neighbors and envied the truly educated elite.

Küpper's major concern was to spare the graduates this personal tragedy, but the more disturbing prospect was that their pretensions would become contagious. After all, seminar graduates would be in a unique position to shape basic attitudes among the mass of rural children—attitudes toward their inherited station, toward the agricultural labor for which most of them were destined, and toward the state itself. Aside from setting a bad example, malcontents might very well try to compensate for their lack of recognition by becoming subversives, "overeducating" or—what amounted to the same thing—"miseducating" future generations of countrymen. This kind of politically-charged alarmism, already common in the late eighteenth century, accompanied the new seminars from their birth. It posed far-reaching questions about the proper role of the *Volksschule* in a new system of public education and, in more general terms, about the proper relationship between the masses, represented overwhelmingly by the countrymen, and the sociocultural elite.

Again complaints about the early seminars had not done justice to their policies. In the eighteenth century the Berlin seminar and others had tapered their instruction to the minimal needs of the lower orders. Professional training was confined to a narrow, practice-oriented sphere that differed in nature—not just degree—from a university education. To be sure, the courses had included more "useful" material than the typical schoolmaster could teach, and had provided an "enlightened" introduction to religion and ethics. But they had not ventured into "higher" learning, since the school-teacher needed only to master those rudimentary subjects that future countrymen could safely absorb in the schoolhouse. As for pedagogy, its foundation in the Enlightenment's ideal of man, and its assumptions about human psychology and childhood, had shaped the purpose of the seminars without receiving explicit attention in their curricula. The pupils were to absorb the spirit of the new school without exploring its theoretical origins. For the most part they had learned by doing, by practicing the new methods in a neighboring schoolhouse or one attached to the seminar itself. That kind of training sufficed to produce competent, well-equipped missionaries while keeping the lid on popular enlightenment.[28]

From 1806 onward the imperatives of national renewal loosened that lid and opened new vistas, at least in theory, for the training of elementary schoolteachers. The very commitment of the administration to the seminars was a decision against sending teaching candidates to the regular academic institutions, which were to remain limited to a small elite. But the neo-humanistic ideal that now prevailed was a "general human education" (*allgemeine Menschenbildung*), and Humboldt was determined not to compromise on it. To Humboldt the goal of education was the well-developed personality, which would insure, by definition, an active and responsible citizenry. That goal required that elementary and academic education be integrated stages of one system. Neither the new *Volksschule* nor the new gymnasium, he insisted, could include specialized training that would frustrate the pupils' potential by determining their occupations prematurely. Likewise, Humboldt wanted a strict institutional separation between the stages; if the *Gymnasien* were allowed to introduce elementary instruction, the *Volksschulen* would be reduced to "popular schools in the denigrating sense of the term."[29] The implication was that the *Volksschullehrerstand* would form one branch of a teaching corps that differed in function at its various levels but shared a common fund of cultivation (*Bildung*) and scholarship (*Wissenschaft*). If the *Volksschule* was to be the foundation of a national system, its teacher could no longer get along with arithmetic, geography, and a few other enlightened but rudimentary subjects; he had to be a truly educated bearer of the national spirit, thoroughly familiar with a cultural and literary tradition. Although the instruction of young children required peculiar methods, his pedagogy was to be informed with the same spirit and purpose as that of academic teachers. Humboldt and his councillors were so attracted to the Pestalozzian method because it promised to replace rote learning with "self-activity" and understanding at all school levels and thus provide an ongoing training in national citizenship.

Humboldt left office in 1810 before he could translate his ideal into a plan for the entire school system. Outside the section enthusiasts of "general human education" took divergent paths and exhibited varying degrees of realism. In his Berlin addresses, for example, Johann Gottlieb Fichte wrote off his contemporaries as hopelessly apathetic and self-interested and unveiled a harsh but logical scheme for a "universal national education." The only way to overcome the past was to isolate children from their parents and entrust them to a democratically recruited corps of schoolteachers. These were to be true scholars, introducing Pestalozzi's "self-activity" primarily by exercising their pupils in the national language.[30] In his essays on a "general German national education" (1812), Reinhold Bernhard Jachmann echoed Fichte's tribute to language as the most noble expression of human rationality and the peculiar achievement of national character without sharing his preference for German syllables and syntax. Like Humboldt, Jachmann was a neo-humanist who reserved the preeminent place in German culture for ancient Greek and Latin. Whereas most neo-humanists were content to make classical studies the core of the new gymnasium as preparation for the university, he wanted his "nation-builders" to extend them to all children. Therein lay his extremism, but it proceeded from standard assumptions about the potential contribution of classical languages and literature to the national renewal. The peculiar value of Greek, Jachmann argued, was that it offered "the most complete model" for the "national virtues"; precisely because the clas-

sics were not "useful"—because they could not be justified as preparation for particular occupations—they were the best solvent for the
rigid estate divisions in the school system and the society at large.
As the core of a national education at the elementary level they
would serve as a universal, integrating property.[31]

Post-1806 officials were not likely to pursue Jachmann's vision of
thousands of schoolteacher-philologists descending upon town and
country to groom many more thousands of Prussian (and German)
school children in their Homer and Cicero. But there was still a considerable range of possibilities for teacher training. In official circles
the issue was not whether elementary school teachers should master Greek and Latin but whether their nonclassical education should
nonetheless be, at least in a minimal sense, scholarly and cultivated.
In that regard the Pestalozzian method proved ambiguous. Under
Humboldt the Berlin section placed great hopes in an experiment
undertaken by Karl August Zeller, a Pestalozzian from Württem-
berg. Zeller's strategy was to turn the royal orphanage in Königsberg
into a "normal institute" combining the training of teaching candidates with the continued education of men in the field. Groomed in
the master's method from early childhood, the orphans would form
the nucleus of a new *Lehrerstand* and spread the method to older
colleagues through "model schools." To the section the normal institute was attractive not as an alternative to seminars but as a
cheap, efficient way to produce immediate results among the incumbent schoolmasters. Nonetheless, Ludwig Natorp, another
Pestalozzian, regarded the experiment as objectionable in principle.
Zeller's enlistment of very young children and his concentration on
practical skills to the exclusion of broader educational influences reduced training to a kind of group apprenticeship. Zeller would produce "good *Routiniers*," Natorp warned the section, but the new
school needed "educated" (*gebildete*) men. It was imperative, first,
that the actual training of teaching candidates follow a general elementary education and, second, that it take place in a seminar offering broad, theoretical "education" (*Bildung*) as well as practice.[32]
Asked to submit a new curriculum plan for the Berlin seminar,
Natorp included a full semester course on "pedagogy, didactics and
elementary school materials," beginning with the "principles from
which education in general and elementary education in particular
proceed." Further—and here is the more startling measure of his
ambition—seminar pupils were to study the classics of German literature with formal lectures and written exercises, as in the study of
the "old classics" in the academic high schools.[33]

Though the section became disillusioned with the normal institute, largely because of Zeller's personal idiosyncrasies, it did not embrace Natorp's alternative. The response to his seminar plan was drafted by Friedrich Schleiermacher as acting director of the Scholarly Deputation and was signed by, among others, Süvern. It stated categorically that elementary school teaching must operate "in and through practice"; its practitioners "do not belong in those classes which attain their education in a truly literary way with lectures and critical studies . . . nor in those who can isolate and proceed from the theory behind their work as a system of general principles."[34] That was an opinion rather than a hard-and-fast policy; but it marks the tension between ideal and policy that was so characteristic of the Reform Era and helps explain why the official commitment to "general human education" did not preclude the development of a castelike educational hierarchy. Although the prescription for the lower schools had changed, policymakers were unwilling to risk a radical dosage. Instead they hoped to fuse a splintered society into a national community without erasing the traditional distinction between popular and academic culture.

In 1810, when the section was still enamored of Zeller, it required an elaborate qualifying examination for teachers in the academic high schools. Two years later—just before rejecting Natorp's seminar plan—it introduced a new "maturity" examination (*Abitur*) for high school pupils seeking admission to the universities. Those two measures laid the basis for the development of a professional corps of gymnasium teachers, dominated by classical philologists and controlling the route to academic and official careers. The irony is that pedagogical practice—the kind of training the seminars concentrated on—was conspicuously absent from the training of gymnasium teachers. But what mattered was that they became exemplars of cultivation and scholarship by virtue of their university study of the classics, whereas seminar graduates were not comparable to them in either respect. By the 1820s the result was obvious: the graduates stood below the status line that had been drawn in the General Legal Code and survived, with adjustments, in the Reform Era. They were not granted the privilege of "exempted" legal status that gymnasium teachers already enjoyed. Indeed they were judged inferior to gymnasium pupils, including those who did not achieve the *Abitur*, in the military regulations that replaced exemptions from canton duty. Education was the principle qualification for active service in a special corps of "one-year volunteers," which in turn led to *Landwehr* service as an officer. But young men who reached the *Untertertia* class formed the bottom line for that privilege; seminar graduates merited only a reduction of active service to six months. Though made an exception in view of their public function, they were deprived of one of the prerequisites for membership in the educated *Bürgertum*.[35]

The marked downswing in seminar policy came in the wake of the Reform Era. In March 1822 a royal ordinance censured the misguided "enthusiasm" in popular education and above all in teacher training.[36] Again the key figure in the ministry was Beckedorff, who had recently found much to criticize on his tour of the new seminars. His role was to confirm state sponsorship of a new institution while adjusting it to clearly circumscribed goals for rural education. The state, he argued in his critique of Süvern's draft law, must not only respect the traditional hierarchy of estates and occupations but also use the schools to strengthen their ties of sentiment and mutual obligation. Süvern had in fact minimized the implications of "general education" by emphasizing direct observation and practice, not theory, in his curriculum guidelines for the seminars and by omitting literary studies, classical or German. To Beckedorff the draft law nonetheless threatened to turn the seminars into "schoolmaster universities." Their "scarcely half-educated" graduates will produce only "quarter- or eighth-educated" subjects, he prophesied, and if the lower orders are "swamped" with such men "arrogance and demands of all sorts, hostility to subordinate occupations, and the most unfortunate discontent will soon gain the upper hand."[37]

This antidote to the Reform Era did not bode well for the reputation of the new seminars, but Beckedorff intended it only for internal consumption. The only public statement by the ministry, the 1822 ordinance, was a general warning to keep teacher training within modest limits, not an explicit repudiation of "general education." In the twenties and thirties the seminars were left to develop in a rather loose administrative framework. Survivors of the Reform Era in the provincial school colleges and district sections buffered them against ministerial interference, and in any case the more anxious councillors in Berlin were too wary of bureaucratic centralization to impose state-wide regulations.[38] The school colleges enjoyed some leeway in the appointment of directors and to an extent each director could chart his own course. He could not, of course, proceed arbitrarily; for any important changes in the original charter of the seminar he needed the approval of the ministry as well as his provincial superiors. More important than the paper organization, however, and less susceptible to supervision, was the spirit with which each director presided over his domain. Usually entrusted with less than one hundred pupils, most of them boarders, he could put his personal stamp on virtually all aspects of seminar life.

In 1822, on the recommendation of Rhineland officials, Adolph Diesterweg was appointed first director of the Meurs seminar in the Düsseldorf district. The ministry probably was unaware of Diesterweg's more radical views and could not have suspected that he would end up an outspoken liberal maverick in its own jurisdiction. In the late 1820s he was already arguing that the seminars should be thoroughly academic professional schools, avoiding slavish imitation of the universities but offering courses in a "national" theory of pedagogy as well as in modern psychology, linguistics, and literature. But in 1832 the ministry conveniently removed Diesterweg from rural education by appointing him director of the new Berlin seminar, which had the special and exclusive assignment of training schoolteachers for the towns.[39] Schweitzer in Brühl, Ferdinand Stiehl in Neuwied, Ferdinand Striez in Potsdam, and Franz Ludwig Zahn, Diesterweg's successor in Meurs, were more representative of Pre-March directors. All of them eschewed literary studies and included very little pedagogical theory in their curricula.[40] Wilhelm Harnisch, who transferred from Breslau to Merseburg in 1822, tried to keep his curriculum, like his *Internat* policy, on a tortuous middle course in the 1820s and 1830s. Though he had shed his youthful radicalism, he consistently defended the "intellectual" status of the teaching profession and thus insisted that seminar pupils be truly "educated," not just crammed with facts and drilled in methods. But Harnisch was equally insistent that rural schoolteachers not be "overeducated," because their professional mission, unlike that of academics, was to instruct young rural children and because their peculiar fate was to live on close terms with the countrymen. As a professional school with special demands the seminar could not be a "university for *Volksschullehrer.*"[41]

THE ROOTS OF DISCONTENT

From the mid-1830s onward Prussian school officials faced mounting evidence that their seminar experiment had backfired. In journal articles and collective petitions seminar graduates announced that the teaching corps had attained, or at least was in the process of attaining, "professional consciousness" (*Standesbewusstsein*). Their goal was the "emancipation" of a new profession from anachronistic conditions and above all from the surviving shackles of the countryside.

In late December 1845, Dietrich Wilhelm Landfermann, the school councillor in Koblenz, tried to explain the emancipation movement by looking back down "the road traveled so long." Since the Reform Era, he reminded his provincial president, the administration had shown a "most unfortunate, one-sided preference" for "higher education" in seminars, without bothering to provide their graduates with "a corresponding position in life or suitable supervisory officials." The inevitable result was that the *Lehrerstand* became "malcontent" wherever teachers were not "insulated . . . by stupidity or a lack of education, or by a measure of resignation not to be expected as a rule." Like Diesterweg, Landfermann was a liberal partisan among school officials; he exaggerated the Prussian commitment to "general education" so as to persuade his superiors to "progress to its final goal."[42] His memorandum, however, cut through the alarmist stereotypes that surrounded the new seminars and explained the emancipation movement on its own terms. What produced the movement and shaped its goals was the "one-sided preference" in state policy or, more precisely, the glaring discrepancy between two kinds of reform from above.

The emancipation movement attests to the emergence of a new consciousness without allowing quantitative measurement of its breadth and depth among the nearly twenty-nine thousand elementary school teachers scattered through Prussian communities by 1848. Teachers began to publicize their grievances in the *Preussische Volks-Schul-Zeiting*, launched in Berlin under the editorship of Doctor J. G. Kobitz in 1833. Yet until the early 1840s, it should be stressed, there was hardly a movement at all. Teachers' activity was limited to literary forays by self-appointed spokesmen like Karl Böhm and several other Berlin teachers and Wilhelm Nehm in the small Westphalian town of Werl. It was concentrated in the lower Rhineland, Westphalia, and Brandenburg, where the influence of Adolph Diesterweg was strongest. In the late 1830s two other journals—Diesterweg's *Rheinische Blätter* and *Der Sprecher*—became popular forums. They were joined by the *Schlesische Schullehrerzeitung*, edited by a seminar teacher in Breslau, in 1843. Nehm died in 1840, and for the next few years Böhm, the most impressive spokesman, was eclipsed by Wilhelm Wander, an outspoken radical in Silesia. The more important development was that a genuine movement was beginning to take shape; teachers in the Rhineland, Westphalia, Brandenburg, and Silesia submitted collective petitions to their official superiors and the provincial *Landtagen* and were organizing, or at least planning, provincial associations.

In the mid-1840s the movement was stifled, though not entirely, by the Ministry of Culture and its district sections. The "March Days" allowed it not only to revive in the Pre-March centers but also to spread to provinces where teachers had been relatively quiet. Assemblies were held throughout Prussia in the spring of 1848, and those in Berlin, Breslau, and several other provincial centers attracted hundreds of teachers. Virtually everywhere the activists drew up petitions and tried to launch associations. In the summer teachers were granted a unique opportunity for a collective expression of opinion; the new Ministry of Culture sponsored provincial conferences, with delegates elected at the *Kreis* level, to advise it on the draft of a school law.

Even when the movement became a national phenomenon, its active participants were limited to a small minority of the teaching corps. Most of those participated indirectly by providing sympathetic audiences at the spring assemblies and electing delegates to the provincial conferences. The implication is not that the spokesmen for the movement, whether self-appointed or elected, were atypical. They were willing and able to articulate reactions to prevailing conditions, and in that sense were the vanguard of a profession-in-the-making. Most of them—from Wilhelm Nehm, the first to attract widespread attention, to the 1848 activists—were seminar graduates representing classmates who made the same demands on teaching. As for their many colleagues who remained beyond the pale of professional consciousness, they were to be found primarily among the older generation of schoolmasters—the men who had entered teaching via a traditional apprenticeship or without any special training and who had come to take its hardships for granted long before the emancipation movement got underway.

But the seminars were not uniform processing plants. They varied too much among themselves, and, more important, they did not receive a standard material. In both Protestant and Catholic seminars the pupils had a variety of religious backgrounds which conditioned their experience of training and helped shape their perspectives. Graduates with an orthodox religious upbringing, particularly in a Catholic family and community, could be remarkably patient about subordination to the pastors and other teaching conditions that so many found intolerable.[43] The fathers' occupations listed on the surviving annual rolls of graduating classes for four seminars—Potsdam and Alt-Döbern in Brandenburg, Soest and Büren in Westphalia—are often vague but suffice to indicate the important social distinctions. A small minority of graduates were not sons of the lower orders; their fathers were pastors and officials at the lower levels of state and municipal administration.[44] Presumably the sons turned to teaching because the fathers could not afford to prepare them for careers equal or superior to their own (most likely in the case of

	Total Graduates	School-masters' Sons	Percentage
Potsdam (1827–30, 1834–35, 1837, 1847)	186	67	36.0
Alt-Döbern (1819–49)	670	220	32.9
Soest (1826–45)	567	156	27.5
Büren (1828–35)	307	81	26.4

younger sons), or because they had failed to meet the standards of academic education. Although some may have resigned themselves to a regrettable but unavoidable fate, others probably tended to make extreme demands on teaching to avoid, or at least limit, social descent.

Admission policy in all four seminars favored schoolmasters' sons, and as a result they constituted roughly one-quarter to one-third of the graduates for the available years. One explanation for these figures is that schoolmasters' sons had few alternatives; there was little or no property to inherit and an academic education was too costly. But in view of the reform efforts since 1806 necessity probably was reinforced by a certain optimism. Schoolmasters had reason to hope that, endowed with new credentials from a state institution, their sons would enjoy a better livelihood and higher status.[45]

Aside from schoolmasters' sons most seminar graduates were from artisan and agricultural families. The rolls are a reminder that population growth and economic change was making those sectors of the lower orders increasingly heterogeneous. About 11 percent (20) of the fathers of Potsdam graduates for the available years were in agriculture. They represented all levels of rural landholding and status and included 5 *Schulze* and 7 *Bauer* as well as 3 *Kossäte* and 2 *Pächter*. Agricultural occupations constituted 25.4 percent (144) of the total for the Soest seminar from 1826 to 1845 and 28 percent (86) of the total for the Büren seminar from 1828 to 1835. The more precise designations include 1 *Meier*, 10 *Bauer*, 2 *Kötter*, 3 *Heuerlinge*, and 27 *Tagelöhner*. The sons of *Schulzen*, *Meier*, and the more prosperous *Bauer* probably were younger brothers who could not inherit land; they came from prestigious local families and, like pastors' and officials' sons, may have had to accept teaching for want of better prospects. But even under the conditions of Pre-March, teaching could be far more attractive, and indeed offer an escape route, to the son of a smallholder in Brandenburg or a *Heuerlinger* or *Tagelöhner* in Westphalia. Like the fathers with little or no land, some of those in the trades belonged in the growing "proletariat" or were at least on its edge. On the Potsdam rolls 27 percent (50) were listed as tradesmen and, of those, 28 were designated *Meister*. Most of the others, one suspects, were village artisans, or in any case were not prosperous enough to have apprentices. Of the 245 trades on the Soest and Büren rolls—28 percent of their combined total—there were 7 "towel makers," 23 "weavers" (including 12 linen weavers), and 18 "smiths." Most of these were probably not independent artisans but domestic workers in the expanding textile and metal industries of Westphalia.

The rolls suggest that fathers made an occupational choice for their sons, or accepted the sons' choice, for a variety of reasons. Unfortunately they do not yield a set of equations between the graduates' family backgrounds and their expectations about teaching. Despite the variety of occupational and social circumstances, however, the great majority, including the schoolmasters' sons, had a common heritage. They had been raised in uneducated families among the rural and urban masses and, in that fundamental sense, came from the lower orders. In the countryside, where most graduates began their careers, disillusionment could easily lead to passive resignation. Yet those who participated in or at least supported the emancipation movement left no doubt that seminar training had been the crucible. What they derived from it was the conviction that their professional grievances were legitimate and, as important, the rationale for translating those grievances into a coherent reform program.

Although makeshift facilities, an austere boarding life, and small town locations may have had some inhibiting effect, they could not negate the obvious: the Prussian state administration had assumed direct responsibility for a new profession. What mattered to the graduates was their recruitment and licensing and their daily supervision and instruction in a state-financed institution. Older schoolmasters might sympathize with their younger colleagues' complaints, but were grateful for the new presence of the state and impressed by the results. In 1834 a retired Westphalian schoolmaster ended his reminiscences with thanks to the higher administration which "protects and supports us, and thus . . . sees that the teacher's sweat never goes unrewarded."[46] But when seminar graduates compared their training with their fate as teachers, they found a radical difference in the degree and ultimately the nature of reform at each end. All the inadequacies they paraded through petitions and journal articles stood as proof that higher officials remained unwilling to match their eagerness to train a new profession with effective intervention at the local level. From the distance of rural outposts, in fact, seminar training seemed a brief and cruel form of adoption. In 1843, Karl Böhm, a graduate speaking for rural teachers as well as his colleagues in Berlin, summed up their sense of abandonment: the district sections, he wrote, "have given their teachers a higher education, but they have placed them . . . in the midst of a world whose intellectual improvement has been only apparent, and they say, 'Fend for yourselves!'"[47]

The emancipation movement served notice that seminar graduates could not and should not have to fend for themselves. Its spokesmen posed as self-righteous creditors, badgering state officials to honor the debt they had incurred by training a new profession and showing little patience with those who reproached them for ingratitude. To Louis Balster, a graduate of the Soest seminar (Westphalia), curtailment of military service and other "favors" seemed a kind of bait with which he and other unsuspecting recruits had been lured into teaching. In view of the later "disadvantages," he wrote, "it would be difficult to induce a sufficient number of candidates to dedicate themselves to the profession of elementary school teaching— if the tragedy did not begin with such a show of favor."[48] Disillusionment was intensified by the awareness that seminar training was a circular track, leading back to—and only to—the lower schools. In 1839, Wilhelm Nehm, the son of a joiner, pointed out that most graduates were already too old to learn a trade when they completed their obligation to accept any assignment.[49] More important, they could not move up; a seminar diploma did not qualify them for an academic education and the more attractive careers that education made possible.

Conservatives and alarmed officials pinned the blame for the graduates' "tragedy" on a misguided "overeducation." In their view the seminars were pseudouniversities. Their graduates had been too puffed up by a quick dosage of pedagogical abstractions, and had become too enamored of literary pursuits, to find satisfaction in a rural schoolhouse.[50] That stereotype distorts the tensions between a professional ethos and the realities of the Pre-March countryside. The graduates were not misplaced academics but working missionaries, trying to "enlighten" the rural natives in the modest sense of eighteenth-century school reform. In part their professional ethos was based on mastery of the officially sponsored curriculum, which included a smattering of geography, history, and natural science as well as religion and the three Rs. More important, the stress on training over scholarship in the seminars was designed to produce skilled practitioners of pedagogy. In the practice schools attached to the seminars, candidates had been groomed to replace the schoolmasters' *Schlendrian* with "rational" and "purposeful" methods— with new approaches to reading and writing, for example, and with a "good discipline" stressing moral suasion over physical punishment. And the seminars had to dispatch public servants impressed with the dignity and importance of their profession and eager to enforce the new school ordinances of the state. Not surprisingly, young men who had been armed with these tools and responsibilities in an institution detached from rural life often experienced their first village assignments as a baptism of fire. They found that, unlike seminar training, the teacher's work was still enmeshed in the local social and cultural fabric. Despite the new ordinances and surveillance of the sections they could not ride roughshod over traditions of their communities or stand aloof from internal feuds.

In the mid-1820s, Wilhelm Wander, a graduate of the Bunzlau seminar in Silesia, dubbed his first assignment "Battle Village" in letters to a former classmate. Over forty years later he still remembered himself as the torchbearer of a new profession, struggling against the forces of darkness. Wander had been sent to Giessmansdorf to assist Schoolteacher Kusche, a Breslau graduate who had been hired despite a local preference for the son of the preceding cantor-schoolmaster. Kusche's efforts to respect local tradition had not spared him petty harassment, but from the start his assistant introduced sweeping changes in the instruction of the younger children. Wander was determined to teach reading as an ongoing skill; rather than have the children simply memorize scriptural passages, he introduced the new phonetic method. Thus parents who were accustomed to supervising their children's scripture reading at home suddenly were prevented from doing so and were cut off from the school. When they discovered that their *Seminarist* had no time for hymns and was relying on "honor" rather than the rod, they threatened to run him out of the village. Wander later claimed that he had gradually won over the village to his enlightened pedagogy; but in any case he transferred to a more lucrative and compatible position in the town of Hirschberg after a two-year stint on the rural front.[51]

By the mid-1840s, Wander was a notorious democrat and anticlerical, and he barely escaped dismissal from office. Aside from its ideological tone, however, his *Die Volksschule als Staatsanstalt* (1842) was an appeal for renewed state intervention and bore eloquent testimony to the professional frustrations of seminar graduates in the countryside.[52] In 1828, Ludwig Kamphausen, a graduate of the Meurs seminar, had anticipated Wander. His appeal to the Düsseldorf section from his first assignment, the village of Velbert, reads like a cry from the wilderness. Kamphausen's appointment to the Lutheran school had occasioned a serious rift between the school committeemen, who had wanted a *Seminarist*, and the village majority, who had petitioned the section on behalf of a native son. To discredit Kamphausen the disgruntled majority had spread the rumor that his parents were Reformed. Unwittingly, though naively, he provided further pretext for slander by seeming to betray the Lutherans in their bitter dispute with the Reformed church over ownership of the village organ.[53]

Kamphausen provoked more venom by undertaking his office with the scrupulousness of a greenhorn. Unlike the schoolmaster who had preceded him, he refused to lead the children's choir in funeral processions. That duty of the sextonship, he reminded the section, had been banned in a recent ordinance and in any case was too undignified and time-consuming for a modern schoolteacher. Parents accustomed to withdrawing their children from school for weeks to work in the fields or in a nearby factory were now faced with a *Seminarist* who insisted on daily, year-round attendance and full payment of the school fee. As the village majority had warned in its petition, the community had ample means to spite an unwanted teacher. To deprive Kamphausen of fees parents sent their children to a nearby school. Meanwhile, the village, ignoring the section's prohibitions, had retained Sunday collections and a biannual "circuit" for a significant portion of the schoolteacher's income; parents now used these arrangements to make Kamphausen, in his own words, "bitterly aware of his dependence on the community." He found counterfeit coins and old buttons in the collection basket, and his circuit yielded far less income and far more abuse than his predecessor's. Aside from depriving him of needed "respect," the circuit involved hour-long treks from farmstead to farmstead that were not exactly "pleasure strolls" (*Spaziergänge*) in bad weather and forced him to close school for nearly two months every year. The section, he concluded from this ordeal, must not only forbid parents to use another school but also extract a salary from the communal treasury or levy a new tax on all Lutheran households. Both requests betrayed a naive optimism about the willingness and capacity of the state administration to intervene at the local level. Though noting that his behavior had been quite proper and that his complaints were legitimate, the section could only advise him to make do with existing arrangements.[54]

Kamphausen described his parents as "very humble [*gering*] and poorly paid," but complained about the "undignified" endowments of his position and the insults he had had to endure from the "crude mob." What emerges from his and other graduates' appeals is the social identity that was integral to a professional ethos. A training that had been very modest by academic standards had nonetheless distinguished them from other local sons who had stayed at home to work in the fields or learn a trade. In 1844 an anonymous graduate was remarkably explicit about the "inner" transformation they had undergone.

> A teacher of the present age must feel an inner disinclination to enter into a more friendly relationship with the peasants if he is in the countryside, or with farmer-townsmen if he is in a provincial town. He cannot do it, it is contrary to him. These people's entire way of thinking and acting contradicts his finer sense, he cannot feel comfortable in their circles. As a seminar pupil he moved only among educated men, and above all stood in a certain friendly relationship with his teachers. The further he progressed in knowledge and thought, the more he raised himself above the circles to which he perhaps belonged by birth. That was not arrogance on his part, but the entirely natural and unsurprising result of his higher education. Thus he felt compelled to approach the circle of officials [*Beamte*] living near him, . . . but very soon he was confronted with the unfortunate contradiction between his achievement and his enforced inferiority.[55]

One might conclude from this witness that the Cassandras had been vindicated: the seminars had uprooted young men from their backgrounds and "overeducated" them for desolate islands in the countryside. But the more accurate conclusion is that an "entirely natural and unsurprising result" had not been avoided by keeping the curriculum nonacademic or by limiting the pupils' exposure to town life. The irony of the seminar experiment is that it had backfired despite these controls.

In 1843 a Silesian graduate echoed Kamphausen in a published letter to one of his teachers in the Breslau seminar. He could not imagine "vegetating" for the rest of his life in his first village assignment; the farm plot attached to his position required more time and energy than his teaching duties, and the peasants refused him help at harvest if he was too strict about summer attendance. Though he missed Breslau, where he had spent some time after graduation, the essential problem was that "the seminar pampers us; it educates us for higher, nobler purposes, and spoils us for an existence [*Wesenheit*] and fate [*Bestimmung*] as peasant and teacher in one person." If he and his classmates had merely done some kind of apprenticeship, he noted, they would not have found such treatment intolerable.[56] The acute sense of deprivation that informed this appeal was typical of seminar graduates' public protests from the mid-1830s onward. Their self-image as educated practitioners of an intellectual profession had not required academic trappings. Inevitably the sons of the lower orders among them came to regard upward mobility not as a privilege that the state could withhold but as a social right. The dilemma that produced the emancipation movement was that state-sponsored reform deprived them of their right.

Part Two

THE EMANCIPATION MOVEMENT IN

PRE-MARCH AND 1848

Four

EMANCIPATION: THE COUNTRYSIDE

In 1848, when the emancipation movement enjoyed a brief respite from official censorship and retaliation, it built on the basic reform program of Pre-March. By the mid-1840s a small but articulate group of spokesmen had developed a kind of advocacy journalism, with a standard, almost ritualized vocabulary and set of arguments. The key words were borrowed and adapted; they had been the common coinage of social description and political discourse in Germany since the eighteenth century and pervaded the intense discussion of the "social question" in Pre-March. To "emancipate" the peasantry meant to relieve them of semifeudal dues and services. By the 1840s the term evoked economic dislocation, overpopulation, and the attendant specter of a mass "proletariat" in town and country. In teachers' appeals they, like the peasants, were victims of anachronistic, oppressive conditions. But they were more analogous to the new proletariat, since their occupation had not inherited, and remained deprived of, a secure station and their dilemma combined poverty with extreme insecurity. Indeed a contributor to the *Preussische Volks-Schul-Zeitung* complained in 1844 that the teacher, though he obviously belonged in the *Stand* of "educated men" (*Gelehrten*), was in fact a *"Proletarius"* if legal status depended "solely on property [*Grundbesitz*] and capital."[1]

In 1849 about 79 percent of Prussian schoolteachers lived and worked in communities officially categorized as "rural," among the peasant and subpeasant masses who still accounted for the bulk of the population.[2] The emancipation movement included town schoolteachers, but focused on the rural majority and spoke above all for its younger generation of seminar graduates. In the countryside emancipation had several interlocking dimensions; it became the code word for a thorough fiscal and institutional overhaul of the rural teacher's relationship to his community and the state administration. The central theme was to replace shameful "dependence"— and here teachers adopted a common distinction between degradation and respectability—with a healthy measure of "independence."

In the national occupational structure the rural teacher, like anyone else, should enjoy a kind and degree of recognition "appropriate to the *Stand*" (*standesgemäss*). That adjective was rich in connotations; it implied that a new social and official status was *both* an occupational necessity and a professional right.

To outsiders, including some of the supporters of the movement, its reform agenda seemed absurdly ambitious. In retrospect the agenda seems modest enough but nonetheless premature. In Pre-March nonacademic credentials and a predominantly rural environment combined to isolate elementary school teaching from the educated professions and branches of public officialdom. To judge by the past record and present course of rural school reform there was little reason for optimism. The countryside was not stagnant, but by the 1840s the effect of most changes—and above all of the rapid population growth—was to make improvement of school and teaching conditions all the more difficult.

Spokesmen for the emancipation movement harbored no illusions about this environment; for the most part, in fact, they stereotyped it as a stubbornly ignorant and backward world. Emancipation nonetheless seemed feasible because it required the motive power of the state, not a catalyst within rural society. "The state," a teacher wrote from Pomerania in 1842, "will finally issue wise and definite laws to constitute a free, independent *Lehrerstand*."[3] He summarized the cluster of expectations that informed the emancipation appeal and made it fundamentally different from a defense of traditional occupational status. In Pre-March and 1848, for example, guild masters appealed to the state, but wanted it to reverse course. They were protesting legislation that threatened the "honor" of their trades by exposing them to socioeconomic change.[4] But the emancipation movement could hardly wax nostalgic about an honorable past; its spokesmen objected to the title *Schulmeister*, and insisted on *Schullehrer*, because they hoped to erase a dishonorable image from public consciousness. Claiming a new status for a state-created profession, they expected the state administration to proceed on course and complete its reform from above.

THE INCOME CALCULUS

"The truth lies in numbers!" A. Breter, a Berlin teacher, reminded his colleagues in 1843. Once confronted with the cash differential between teachers' earnings and what they should earn, the public would gladly come to the rescue.[5] Other teachers' spokesmen had less confidence in public open-mindedness, but shared Breter's faith in numbers. Their articles and petitions were crowded with official statistics of teachers' annual incomes and comparable figures for other occupations, itemized calculations of household budgets, and projections of an appropriate scale of incomes for their profession.

In teachers' arithmetic differences in income level involved far more than degrees of material comfort or deprivation. They rested their case on a social calculus in which elementary school teaching figured as a new kind of expertise, and indeed one with a critical function in the public sector of an increasingly complex society. Although the calculus was designed for a profession that had developed outside the established ranks of an estate society, it echoed and extended traditional assumptions about the relationship between income and status. The point was that social ranking had to adjust to a new division of labor, but also that the new society, like the old, could and should be ordered into an intricate hierarchy of occupational groups. A standard of living "appropriate to the *Stand*" still meant one corresponding to the nature and importance of its work and allowing it to maintain its proper station. Seen in that light the cost of income reform paled before its urgency.[6]

The official statistics of the early 1840s exaggerated the extent to which rural teaching incomes had already risen. Unlike the figures for 1820 they included funds actually being used to support retired schoolmasters and assistants. Moreover, the pastors' cash valuations of teachers' lodgings and land endowments reflected spiraling rents and food prices rather than new earnings. Even if these roseate terms are accepted, the sections' accomplishments over two decades were quite modest. In 1820 the incomes for 66.5 percent of the rural positions in Prussia, including the sextonship, had been estimated at less than 100 thaler and 52.1 percent of these at less than 60 thaler. French legislation had given the Düsseldorf district in the lower Rhineland a clear head start. Thanks to the minimum salary of 65 thaler, combined with the fees from a growing school-age population, its average rural income had risen to nearly 200 thaler by the 1840s. Improvement had been a more awesome task in the eastern provinces, where the agrarian population offered an especially poor base for school support. In 1820 the rural average in the Königsberg district had been only about 63 thaler; two decades later the number of positions with less than 60 thaler, including the towns, had been reduced to 161, but 883 positions fell between 60 and 100 thaler. For the most part the section had managed to turn unviable incomes into meager ones.[7]

More typical were the patterns of improvement in the Trier

district in the Rhine Province and in the Potsdam and Frankfort districts in Brandenburg. In Trier, where rural incomes had approximated the national distribution in 1820, only 6.7 percent of all teaching positions had less than 90 thaler in 1843. From 1819 to 1841 the percentage of rural incomes with less than 100 thaler dropped from a towering 73.5 to 23.4 in Frankfort. By 1827 the sub-100 thaler category included only 39.3 percent of the rural positions in Potsdam, and by 1841 the percentage had declined to 29.9. Although the sections could boast success at the bottom of the income scales, they had achieved a less dramatic shift at the upper end. In 1843, 51.6 percent of the rural incomes in Frankfort were in the 100–200 thaler category, and 31.3 percent fell between 100 and 150 thaler. The corresponding percentages for Potsdam in 1841 were 59.1 and 37.4. In Trier in 1843, 82.1 percent of the positions, including the towns, had between 90 and 200 thaler, and 67.7 percent between 90 and 160 thaler. Rural positions with over 250 thaler still formed a very small minority (11.0 percent) in Frankfort and were a great rarity in Trier and Potsdam.[8]

Inflation was certainly cutting into teachers' cash gains by the 1840s, but regional variations in prices make it futile to generalize about the scale of real incomes behind these figures. Intent on drawing attention to a national scandal, Breter and other spokesmen frequently claimed that the teaching corps had to be rescued from the "cares of subsistence" (Nahrungssorgen) and indeed from the clutches of real "poverty" (Armut). In the Pre-March countryside the growing mass of landless and near-landless families made it increasingly difficult to circumscribe the state of poverty. Though poor by any standard, so many families still managed to subsist, and so many others, though better off, were on the brink of destitution. Teachers' relative position can be gauged by locating their incomes in the categories for the Prussian class tax, which excluded only the population of several larger towns. According to the instruction of 1820, categories seven to nine were intended for "small peasants and townsmen" and the very bottom category (twelve) for "common servants, day laborers, and wage hands" who owed only the personal tax of a half thaler per year.[9]

Even in the most advanced provinces a scattering of rural positions were still at the bottom of the Prussian income pyramid in the 1840s. Like day laborers, married teachers making less than 100 thaler were on the edge of real poverty, and those with large families surely were in its clutches. In 1846 the ministry itself acknowledged this scandal by allocating 45,000 thaler to relieve the many teachers in "dire need." It tried to stretch this emergency relief by ordering

	Number of Taxpayers (nearest thousandth)	
	1821	*1848*
Seven–nine (200–500 thaler)	543,000	458,000
Ten–eleven (100–200 thaler)	709,000	976,000
Twelve (sub-100 thaler)	2,389,000	3,339,000

the sections not to raise any income above 80 or 90 thaler; but in 1847, with the onset of drastic inflation, the ceiling was raised to 100 thaler or more for married men.[10] While population growth had swollen tax category twelve, however, reform had lifted most teachers above its ceiling. In more cautious moments spokesmen claimed that the typical teacher was still worse off than most artisans,[11] but that comparison glossed over a critical distinction in a period of overpopulation and rapid economic change. Though the teacher might fall short of a neighboring artisan in sheer income, he was at least guaranteed the bulk of his livelihood and could be dismissed only for gross incompetence or neglect of office. His position did not allow him to exploit the advantages of a free market, but it also spared him the perils.

The emancipation movement measured deprivation by a higher standard. To exaggerate teachers' proximity to the lowest occupations was to dramatize the injustice of their exclusion from the narrowing pyramid of more affluent incomes and living standards. In a petition to the ministry in 1842 thirty-one Westphalian teachers, hardly conscious of their leap, complained that existing incomes required "the life style of a Diogenes to satisfy even the most essential needs of human life and do honor to the class of educated men, among whom the schoolteachers should be numbered."[12] Though most teachers were not starving on their diet of potatos, bread, and water, Karl Böhm wrote in his "New Year's Wishes" for the same year, they had a right to meat, vegetables, and an occasional glass of beer or wine. And they wanted to dress "respectably" as members of the "middle class"—by which Böhm meant men "whose industry and wit [*Spekulation*] allow them to stand on their own two feet and confront the eternal vicissitudes of life with some placidity."[13] To Böhm and other spokesmen such aspirations were perfectly legitimate; they did not betray the pretensions of the social climber or the crass materialism condemned in the catchword *Luxus*. It was integral to their arguments that, by the nature of their work and function, modern schoolteachers had "needs" not to be found among "lower" manual occupations. Side-jobs increased their incomes but were incompatible with an "intellectual" profession whose work, unlike the artisan's, could not be measured by hours spent in a shop. If the rural teacher gave private lessons he had to rush from school every day, and if he served as communal clerk he had to set aside a part of his week to copy documents for the local council. Such tasks not only prevented him from preparing his lessons properly but also deprived him of leisure and thus sapped the mental energy and enthusiasm that was essential to his work. Unable to relax and "restore his powers," he approached his hours in the schoolroom as another drudgery in a wearing daily routine.[14]

These heartfelt arguments also reminded the state administration of the low returns on its seminar investment. To fulfill his assignment the seminar graduate needed not only leisure but also a margin of income well beyond subsistence. Without extra cash for books he could not deepen his knowledge of elementary subjects and keep abreast of new developments in pedagogy; thus he inevitably succumbed to the intellectual stagnation and rote instruction of schoolmastery. Though not an occupational necessity in the narrow sense, "middle-class" consumption habits were indispensable accoutrements of professional status. On that score, in fact, spokesmen posed as reluctant but hard-nosed materialists, nodding respectfully to the ideal of a better world but planting themselves in the reality of status consciousness and its material base in Prussian society. The sad truth was that intellectual superiority and refined manners did not guarantee the "respect" that the teacher so obviously needed. "The people," a Rhineland teacher complained, "are so accustomed to measuring the invisible value of an activity by its visible reward, the importance of an office . . . by the clinking coins it brings in." The peasants, a West Prussian teacher added, were particularly noted for measuring a man by his outer display, whatever his "inner worth."[15] Though not a propertied resident the rural schoolteacher had to cut a respectable public figure by maintaining a proper household and above all by clothing himself and his family as members of the "middle class." A Brandenburg teacher calculated that, if household expenses were kept to a minimum, a village teacher with a wife and four children nonetheless needed at least 207 thaler a year in cash. In addition to 8 thaler for books his budget included about 23 thaler to maintain a wardrobe of topcoats and jackets.[16]

The emancipation movement called for a sweeping income reform—not just attention to the worst positions. In the early years and again in 1848 most proposals fixed 250 thaler—still a rare fortune in the countryside—as the minimum rural income, intended only for young, unmarried men. Periodic increments would guarantee every rural teacher at least 450 thaler by the end of his career.[17] On the one hand these were very ambitious figures; the extra cash would catapult about twenty thousand communal employees to a modest but secure level of conspicuous consumption, well above the poverty of their immediate predecessors. But the figures were also offered as proof that seminar graduates were willing to accept an "appropriate" rung on the national status ladder. Although Böhm and others sometimes drew a sharp boundary between the "lower" and "middle" class, they were well aware that their profession did not qualify them to cross that boundary according to the prevailing criteria of property (*Besitz*) and education (*Bildung*). Indeed, the careful estimates of "appropriate" rewards for various kinds of work in their income calculus denied that the brutal simplicity of class existed or ought to develop in the middle ranks. What they saw was an expanding, multitiered hierarchy—the modern sector of the *Mittelstände*. In it professions and public offices were, or at least should have been, ranked by a formula combining their educational credentials with the relative importance of their contributions to the public welfare.

By that formula seminar graduates could not compare themselves with academic graduates. Instead they claimed equality with the chancellists, secretaries, and still lower state employees who had attended high school but had not attained an *Abitur*.[18] These "educational equals" began their regular tenure with salaries of 200–300 thaler and in some cases advanced to 600–700 thaler. Since these were mere *Bureaumenschen*, the gap between their salaries and the incomes of teachers seemed all the more shocking. Teaching, after all, could not be equated with "rote" office work: it was more "difficult" because it required "intellectual vitality," and it "provides the state with more blessings than the registry councillors by educating loyal subjects, upright *Bürger* and officials."[19] For five to ten trial years—that is, before tenure with a regular salary—the clerks had to survive on a pittance, and the chancellist positions were open only to regular army officers after twelve years of service. Against this the emancipation movement matched the sacrifices teachers had had to make—many by paying for a part of their seminar training, most by beginning their careers in especially poor-paying rural positions. In any case the movement was preoccupied with the rewards for services rendered, not with the initial sacrifices. From that standpoint the "educational equals" became unequal foils, used to throw the teachers' professional identity and public role into bold relief and to underscore the modesty of their aspirations.

Schoolteachers are obsessed with money, a pastor in the Rhineland complained in 1839, and they ignore the other, less tangible, but more abiding satisfactions of their offices.

> The *Lehrerstand* is and will remain a very honorable and re-warding profession [*Stand*]. If it does not wear its reward on its sleeve, it wears it within. How fortunate is the life of the well-loved, capable village schoolmaster in his rustic sphere! A school that is not overcrowded, children who consider his every word the gospel, a fair-minded pastor over him, a not-too-demanding public around and beside him. And add to this many a wedding and baptismal feast, braced with the sweat of a healthy village youth. Considering all this and much more not stipulated on the collection lists, the teacher very often leads a happy life if only he knows enough to appreciate it.[20]

For all its naiveté the pastor's idyll evokes the nest warmth peculiar to small, familiar rural communities. But in Pre-March the teachers who were likely to share his appreciation were to be found among the older generation. What emerges from the emancipation movement is a markedly negative stereotype of rural life, rooted in seminar graduates' alienation from the terms and conditions of their employment. Men conscious of their professional training and public function found themselves bound in a host of ways to the identity of schoolmastery. They experienced the village nest as a tangle of frustrating, often humiliating dependencies. Only a genuine public office that was based on solid financial support and extricated from the local tangle would end this social and psychological bondage.

The most widespread anachronism, the sextonship, was also the one to which rural communities clung most tenaciously. Its endowments were still indispensable to rural positions, but its duties, teachers protested repeatedly, had become intolerable. The only exceptions were the "higher" duties of church cantor and organist, which allowed the seminar graduate to use his musical training and capitalize on rural tradition. Like teaching, music was an art requiring skill and practice. Unlike teaching, a strong voice or a virtuoso performance at the organ commanded the locals' respect. Adults

who had little notion of their schoolteacher's feats in the classroom
became an appreciative audience at Sunday services. The organist
"has to lead the hymn," Nehm wrote, "and since song is the community's oral prayer, that is an essential part of the service."[21] However,
other time-honored duties, still inseparable from schoolmastery in
the eyes of parishioners, now seemed "alien" and "demeaning" to
the men who had to perform them. The sections had been chastened
by local opposition to their recent meddling and in the 1840s proved
unwilling to ban customs that had long been considered incompatible with teaching. In 1843, for example, younger teachers in the
Potsdam district, with the support of two superintendents, requested release from serving as village criers at local funerals and
weddings. For the weddings the sexton had to wear a striped scarf
and a garland of flowers and play the buffoon, and the peasants, one
teacher complained, "say . . . that's the only reason we have him."
Councillor Meyer replied that "an old duty of the sexton's office,
[though clearly] inappropriate to the teachers' present educational
level," could not simply be wiped out by administrative fiat. Teachers would have to rely on the pastors and civic officials to win their
communities' consent.[22]

What rankled most sexton-teachers were the petty custodial chores
that were still stipulated, often in great detail, in their contracts. A
man trained for intellectual work and expected to command respect
in that capacity might also be required to set the village clock every
morning, ring the church bells, shovel snow from the entryway, or
keep the pews clean. These "alien" tasks were not "dishonorable in
and for themselves" (or were they?); but they interfered with the
demands of a full-time job and, as important, fastened an educated
man to the wrong end of the local hierarchy, below the laboring
classes.[23] Aside from requiring manual labor, the sextonship formed
a particularly exposed, sensitive area in which the countrymen could
deal with a *Seminarist* on their own terms, as a "servant" in the old
sense; they had ample opportunity to impress on him the servant's
dependence or simply to indulge whims at his expense. In 1842 the
Westphalian petitioners summarized the many tales of woe surrounding tower clocks and churches: "Sometimes it is the church,
sometimes the tower which can give the common man occasion to
abuse the teacher, who is dependent on him in so many ways. The
steps or the church pews are not clean enough for him; the tower
clock runs too fast or too slow, or is in need of repair—in short,
when an occasion is sought a hundred petty details can result in the
greatest vexation for the teacher."[24]

The details were particularly vexing when they became weapons in the vendettas to which the teacher, like any other local resident, might fall victim. In a West Prussian village, one story went, the reigning parish elder turned his neighbors against a young teacher who had declined his matchmaking services. To teach him a lesson the village had the old tower clock repaired and resurrected the sexton's obligation to keep it wound and oiled. The bachelor's woes multiplied when the clock ran fast and the hired hands, vexed at being awakened too early, assembled before the schoolhouse one morning to regale him with insulting songs.[25]

Local attachment to the sextonship was matched by indifference, if not hostility, to the needs of the teaching office. The traditional and, from the standpoint of the communities, very convenient "pensioning" system awarded the outgoing schoolmaster with a portion of his successor's income. Unwilling to antagonize the countrymen with another school burden, the sections had merely tried to fix the pensioner's share at one-third and, less often, to provide his successor with a small compensation. Seminar graduates protested the loss of income and decried the fate of men who, having devoted their lives to the "public," were reduced to beggary in retirement. "Every teacher who has to end his years in this way without being guilty himself," Wander wrote, "is an indictment against his people."[26] Hardly less scandalous was the treatment of the teacher's widow, who usually had to vacate the schoolhouse a few months after her husband's death and had no special claim to public support. A West Prussian teacher reported that a widow with young children, not wanting her neighbors to witness her "lowliness," had moved to another village to find day labor. She was driven out when she ran out of money and proved unable to do the work. *Kreis* officials forced her readmission, since the headman in her old village was equally determined to keep her out. But for her support she had to "live with day laborers' widows who were no longer fit to work and go with them from house to house every day for meals."[27] To the reporter and his readers the point was that a teacher's widow should not have to resort to either common labor or poor relief. Unlike the artisan's widow, Silesian petitioners noted in 1848, she could not take over her husband's shop. "Such a woman stands almost helpless," they concluded, since she cannot find work "appropriate to [her] *Stand.*"[28]

One of the standard proposals of the emancipation movement was that a state fund support pensioners as well as teachers' widows and orphans.[29] Security against old age and early death was only one advantage of public office; the others would rescue teachers from daily indignities. Since the early nineteenth century the sections had tried to mend the crazy quilt of rural school support; but their councillors were too far away, and too busy, to tend to all the details and close the remaining loopholes. Typical were the complaints about the land endowments attached to the sextonship or the teaching office itself. Although farming cushioned the teacher against rising food prices, it also "peasantized" him and, in the absence of hard-and-fast communal obligations, made him beholden to the local landholders for extra hands to harvest his crop and for wagons to transport it. Whether the community had to provide a shed for the teacher's cow or keep the shed in repair was sometimes an open question. In some communities the teacher had to heat the school-room from his own pocket; in others school parents, and particularly the landless among them, failed to pay a weekly or monthly wood fee.[30]

These were petty but symbolic details; they embroiled seminar graduates in feuds with their communities and reminded them of the continuing absence of the state administration. By the early 1840s, for example, the village of Dobberzin (Potsdam district) and Eduard Krause, its first *Seminarist*, were at odds about firewood, the cow shed, and a ditch that had been dug across the land endowment. In 1834 the school committee had promised to expand the shed, but with the fateful proviso that "it remains only to hold the community to doing it." Meanwhile the committee protested that Krause was storing fodder, brought from land he had rented in another village, in his lodging. In 1844, Krause insisted that a gang of local farm hands be fined for plundering his apple trees, and the culprits—or someone—retaliated by throwing a rock through his window. Welcoming this opportunity, the committee would not be persuaded that the General Code obligated it to compensate Krause for the repair of the window. Inspector Albrecht finally arrived to mediate and tried to secure compensation by dredging up an ordinance from the sixteenth century, but to no avail.[31]

In the tangle of school support "dependence" meant vulnerability to local evasion and spite. The school fee was a particularly annoying example; it constantly reminded seminar graduates that the state administration had not replaced outmoded endowments with a secure, public salary. By the 1840s, to be sure, the sections had achieved a considerable improvement in school attendance and fee collection. But it remained intolerable that most rural teachers were still compensated for their professional work with a kind of wage from individual parents. If the fee marked local attachment to tradition, it also dramatized teachers' vulnerability to change in the Pre-March countryside. From 1816 to 1846 the school-age population of Prussia increased by 44.7 percent, and thanks to stricter enforcement of attendance the number of pupils in the elementary schools more than doubled—from 1,167,350 to 2,433,333. Despite a marked increase in teaching positions the average number of pupils per teacher jumped from 53.6 to 79.7.[32] By the 1840s many of the rural teachers who were overburdened with pupils were being compensated for their extra work with a higher fee intake. But others had suffered losses or had at least been deprived of potential windfalls. Reluctant to expand their meager school budgets, some rural communities supported a second teacher or an "assistant" by granting him a token salary and supplementing it with a portion of the incumbent's fees. Teachers in several provinces protested that, like the pensioning system, this expedient burdened teachers with the sacrifices their communities should be making.[33]

More important than the sheer increase in population was the accompanying multiplication of landless and near-landless families in virtually all regions of Prussia. In teachers' complaints it made little difference that fee collection had improved despite this rural "proletariat"; here again reform was more than offset by new expectations. Men plagued by "poverty" and aspiring to a "middle-class" life-style regretted the loss of even a few thaler. Their most bitter grievance against the fee was that it put them in an irreconcilable conflict of interest with the local poor. A report from West Prussia claimed that the village teacher "could not proceed with heartless severity against his debtor," since "painful sacrifices" were preferable to "the loss of his good conscience." Yet the teacher who might want to "make a sacrifice for the good of the poor," the Westphalian petitioners explained a few years later, was "usually prevented by his own limited circumstances."[34]

Both creditor and debtor were victims of the failure of the state administration to remove the old conflict between the school fee and poverty. Typically, section policy had stopped halfway; while recognizing that an annual rate of one or two thaler per child was an onerous burden for poor parents, it also acknowledged communal inability or at least unwillingness to compensate for them from public funds. In Westphalia the community had to pay the fee for its "public poor," but only at two-thirds to half of the normal rate.[35] The Potsdam section had hoped to limit nonpaying children to one-tenth of the school-age population. To judge by the surviving school budgets, most communities were barely managing that ratio in the 1840s (with occasional setbacks), and some were far below it. Part of the problem, Councillor Ferdinand Striez had noted in 1839, was that neither the estate lords nor the communities were willing to take responsibility for new settlements (*Vorwerke*) of day laborers.[36]

In the Düsseldorf district teachers complained about fee losses despite their relatively high incomes. The ordinance of 1825 had required compensation only for children on the poor roles and only for days of actual attendance. These qualifications remained significant in the 1840s; in 1843 only 1.7 percent (2,328) of the school-age children in the district were not attending at all, but another 12.9 percent (17,384) were attending "irregularly."[37] In an era of mass poverty the teacher also had to contend with arrears and recriminations from parents on the regular collection lists. If he persisted, the mayor had to proceed to forced collections, and indeed seize property in lieu of cash. As early as 1832, Councillor Grashof had described the ensuing legal morass: "The many costs and coercive measures snuff out the last spark of concern for the school," and in the end "the teacher goes empty-handed."[38] Such procedures did not endear teachers to their mayors and pastors, who fretted about the time spent on fee collection and were most reluctant to harass the local poor. The worst of it, one teacher recalled, was that the creditors bore the brunt of local wrath: "The people, and especially the less understanding among them, fell into the error that [they] had induced all these measures with their cry for pecuniary gain."[39] In 1842 a group of teachers in *Kreis* Lennep petitioned the ministry to require local compensation for arrears. However, the ministry rejected their first petition and referred a second one to the Düsseldorf section. Confronted with a problem that had defied solution, the section rebuked the "complainants" for not cooperating enough with local officials and for failing to live on "good terms" with their neighbors. Teachers "mistake their office and profession," it concluded, "when in pursuit of their own interests they disregard the circumstances of the communities by which and for which they are hired."[40] At a subsequent meeting with teachers and pastors, local officials would not consent to expanding communal fee compensation for either the public poor or uncollectable arrears.[41]

The response by the section confirmed that, in policy as well as practice, the balance of power between state and local school administration had tilted since the Reform Era. By the 1840s the sections had allowed their reform drive to come to a near standstill; unwilling to override the communities, they had no choice but to lay the burden of adaptation on their employees. The local school committees had been established to implement reform from above and eventually to generate it from within; now their authority became an obstacle that teachers could not bypass, and that could be used to veto their requests for improvements and redress of grievances. Not surprisingly the emancipation movement indicted the committees as, at best, symptoms of local neglect. Although some committees actively obstructed reform, the majority were, in Balster's simile, "like bodies of the living dead, moving their stiff limbs only after the most jolting outer stimulus."[42] A more supportive approach could hardly be expected from the uneducated laymen who made up the committees; often they were appointed merely because they were the local bigwigs, and they were also likely to suffer the heaviest loss in the event of new financial sacrifices for the school. In 1842 the Westphalian petitioners complained that the typical committee did little beyond attending the annual school examination and approving attendance lists and described the "unbridgeable chasm" that teachers faced.

> There are so many wants and deficiencies in office, as well as encouraging signs, and how much they stir the teacher, who alone can know them! How much he would like to share the former, for purposes of united improvement, and the latter to prove his industry in the good work. Do not object that the teacher neglects the opportunity to do so with written communication of his wishes and proposals. This tiresome route remains unused because it usually leads to mere formalities and is calculated only to increase the obstacles. And so the typical committee and teacher remain isolated, and agreement in policy is to be expected as little as mutual encouragement and stimulation. "Divide and you create hate!" also applies here. If they had been placed in a closer relationship they would have drawn closer personally. The superiority-dependence relationship may be necessary and purposeful in other spheres, but here it creates a harmful partition.[43]

This petition and several others in the 1840s requested that teachers be admitted to the committees as voting members. What produced mutual isolation and hostility, they argued, was the subordination of trained professionals to uneducated laymen. Once joined by the man who had devoted himself to the school and had "a deeper view into the matter," the laymen would surely be persuaded of the need for reforms. In that one sense the emancipation movement hoped to complement reform from above with communal participation; committee membership would allow the teacher to transform "bodies of the living dead" into levers of emancipation.

ADVANCEMENT

In 1839, a "Doctor Werther" imagined an exchange of views between an old schoolmaster and two young colleagues who were passing through his village. His exercise was intended primarily to advertise the new pedagogy, which the visitors contrasted rather patronizingly with rote schoolmastery. But when the young men looked around their host's cramped, dilapidated lodging and asked why he had not moved on to another village, they received their comeuppance. "Should the school office," he asked indignantly, "really be nothing more than a cow that supplies us with butter" and is exchanged as soon as possible for a better one? His villagers were like his children; he had instructed most of them, had attended their baptisms, their confirmations, their weddings. You will not find satisfaction in a new position, he warned the visitors, because "the specter is in your hearts." And they "weighed the obvious truth in these words."[44]

This image of the teacher as a local patriarch, well loved in his "little circle," had long been contradicted by reality. In the eighteenth century it had been common for rural schoolmasters to move from place to place, and many who had remained in their first or second positions had probably wanted to move. The great range of incomes, even in a small region, meant that a better or at least more lucrative position always loomed around the corner. Moreover, there were too many occasions for feuds between the schoolmaster and his neighbors—too many reasons why he might be willing to try his luck elsewhere. The career of Julius Fetting in Prussian Pomerania was a three-stop quest for less vexatious, more secure employment. To judge by scattered reports from other regions, any half-decent vacancy drew a plethora of applications; what seems to have limited the competition was that it was difficult to learn about vacancies.[45]

In school reform there was an implicit tension between the schoolteacher's local mission, which required that he settle in one community for an extended period, and the need to provide him with professional incentives. One obvious way to attract and hold better men was to transform the existing haphazard job mobility into an orderly system of advancement up the scale—and particularly the income scale—of rural positions.[46] But in the eighteenth century church and state officials could directly assign teachers only to the small minority of schools under royal *Patronat*. Elsewhere they merely reviewed and usually confirmed the choice of the estate lord, the parish elders, or the pastor acting in their name. These authorities could not be expected to weigh professional merit; they were more concerned to provide employment to a native son or to secure a competent organist or a useful artisan. In the middle and lower Rhineland many communities filled vacancies by holding elections; all adult male parishioners voted, and sometimes public examinations of the applicants preceded the voting. The problem with this more democratic procedure was that it gave more scope to local prejudice and favoritism. In the early nineteenth century French officials in the Trier region had simply arrogated the appointment power and had matched teachers and communities without regard for local sensitivities.[47] In the Grand Duchy of Berg, where the state school commission had allowed communities to propose three candidates, Commissioner Johann Anton Küpper proposed to take appointments entirely out of local hands and entrust them to higher state officials, who could select "with strict nonpartisanship and justice." The communities, Küpper argued, had proven unworthy of their appointment right; they used irrelevant criteria, were unable to distinguish between competent instructors and charlatans in the examinations, and exploited the abundance of applicants to avoid raising teaching incomes. It made some sense to allow local nominations for the pastorate, since "to some extent the communities are in a position to judge the most suitable among several pastors." But "with the schoolteachers there is no difference as to their suitability for this or that office."[48]

In Pre-March neither the ministry nor its district sections took this drastic step of canceling the right of the communities to select their children's instructors. The Düsseldorf section merely refined the Berg procedure: notice of a vacancy had to be published in the official gazette (Amtsblatt) and the state inspector had to oversee a local election, limited to the present and former members of the parish executive. In most other districts no new legislation was forthcoming; the sections merely insisted that vacancies be published and reserved final approval of the local choices.[49] The ministry's seminar ordinance of 1826 required that preference be given to graduates, but the sections probably shirked from applying the letter of the law in the face of local resistance. Here again the emancipation movement resurrected the unfinished business of school reform and pursued it with a vengeance. From the late 1830s onward the movement accompanied its proposals for an appropriate income scale with schemes for "advancement." These included periodic increments (every five or ten years) for stationary teachers, but their main purpose was to allow intercommunity promotion on the basis of professional merit. In 1848, in fact, anticipating that competition would be for reformed vacancies, several provincial conferences stipulated that new men begin their careers in the "lowest" rural positions.[50]

Wanderlust had been strongest among recent graduates. Aside from those in particularly low-paying positions, an increasing number of "assistants," particularly in the Rhine Province and Silesia, received room and board and perhaps a portion of the school fee due to

regular teachers.[51] Older men who had advanced a bit still could not
satisfy their needs and in any case might still be on the lookout for
more dignified employment. In the countryside the problem was not
simply that job mobility was limited. Again emancipation meant an
end to the rural teacher's dependence on his community and its
officials. Arbitrary and degrading hiring procedures frustrated win-
ners as well as losers, since success brought no illusions about the
nature of the game. In 1845 a Westphalian teacher complained that
school committees were still addressing applicants as "subjects";
that title insulted the man who would occupy "one of the most important offices in the community" and made him "appear to be . . .
of very inadequate education in the eyes of the educated public."[52]
Often enough the public examination that survived in some communities was a time-consuming farce; the decision had already been
made behind the scenes, and in any case the local audience was not
qualified to choose the most competent teacher. In an 1848 petition
Silesian teachers were willing to maintain the examination only as a
formality and recommended that, to insure "honorable" appointments, applicants be spared any direct contact with the community.[53]

With or without the exam local or even personal considerations
overrode professional merit in too many cases. The relative of an established family in the community, the fiancé of one of its daughters, the retiring schoolmaster's son-in-law or assistant—these were
the chosen few. One teacher reported that a plum position in Upper
Silesia had fallen to the young assistant, although more than twenty
older and more experienced men had applied, and asked, "When will
this abuse end?"[54] Indeed the very pressure to move left teachers at a
grave disadvantage. One poetic teacher in the Potsdam district used
an animal fable to describe the buyers' market that often prevailed.
The local councillors deliberated for hours, waiting to see which of
the many applicants would settle for least. They leaned toward the
dog ("He is satisfied with lousy bones / We can have him make the
rounds for food"), but ended up hiring the stag ("We will have to give
him the least / What he needs he can earn privately").[55] The only
way to end these abuses, a teacher in Magdeburg wrote in 1843, was
to give the sections "a free hand to crown merit."[56]

In 1848 the emancipation movement hoped to accomplish that
purpose, without centralizing appointments to the degree Küpper
had proposed forty years earlier. The most popular scheme allowed
the community to select among a few (usually three) candidates
who had applied directly to the section. That would insure a "just"
and "honorable" promotion system and spare teachers undignified

contact with the locals, though not entirely eliminating the latter's traditional voice. The sections, it was assumed, would limit local freedom of choice to the most deserving applicants.[57] The new hiring procedures were a corollary of emancipation, not a substitute for it. Combined with higher incomes and other rewards of public office, they promised to transform an unrecognized profession into a vehicle of upward mobility with career opportunities in its own ranks. "Advancement" in that sense made it imperative that scattered thousands of communal employees be organized into a corps of public officials. At the same time periodic salary increments were meant to avoid an overly rapid turnover, which would not enhance respect for the teaching office, and to allow settlement in a first or second assignment for personal reasons. The rural teacher who married one of the daughters of the community, for example, or simply grew to like his neighbors was not to be penalized for developing local attachments. But the proposals for intercommunity promotion marked both the alienation of seminar graduates and the broader implications of their new professional identity. As strong as the push—the reaction against the village nest—was the pull of ambition. The graduates envisioned a state-ordered *Berufsstand*—a bureaucratic corps in which they could prove merit and reap the appropriate rewards. In that light rural communities were not places in which to settle for a lifetime; they had to be arranged, in all their variety, as steps in a career ladder.

TEACHERS AND CLERGYMEN

In its original and most frequent usage "emancipation" was a rallying cry against the pastors and diocesan superintendents who served as school inspectors. In the late 1830s and early 1840s teachers in the Rhineland and Westphalia used a popular journal, *Der Sprecher*, to raise the cry and counter the objections of affronted clergymen. Meanwhile teachers in Brandenburg and Silesia were airing the same complaints in their own journals. Their appeals were suppressed in the mid-1840s, but in 1848 emancipation from the clergymen-inspectors became a standard plank in teachers' reform programs. According to most proposals, the local inspectorate was to be eliminated, and the pastor, though he might retain membership on the school committee, was denied a "natural right" to its chairmanship. Likewise the superintendents were denied their virtual monopoly of state inspection. They were to be replaced by full-time, salaried "schoolmen," elected or at least nominated by the teachers themselves.[58]

It was partly to avoid the expense of salaried inspectors that the state administration had continued to rely on the superintendents in the early nineteenth century. But expediency had gone hand in hand with respect for the heritage of popular education. The confessional division of the new seminars had reflected and confirmed the strict separation of Catholic and Protestant schools, even in the same village. Not surprisingly the division also limited interconfessional cooperation in the teaching corps. In Pre-March Catholic teachers, even in provinces where they were numerous, supplied the emancipation movement with far fewer spokesmen than did their Protestant colleagues. Though Catholic seminar graduates surely had professional grievances, particularly in view of their relatively low incomes, they were inhibited by membership in an authoritative church and by obedience to its ecclesiastical hierarchy. In 1848 some Catholic teachers in the Rhineland and Silesia participated in the emancipation movement and joined the Protestants on most issues. On the issue of church and state, however, they tended to part ways. At the conference for *Kreis* Geldern in the Düsseldorf district, for example, the Catholic majority vetoed a proposal for election of the school committee chairman on the grounds that the pastor was the only qualified man. In the light of recent state interference in church affairs they probably saw clerical inspection as the guarantor of Catholics' right to their own, strictly confessional schools.[59]

Protestant seminar graduates had received an orthodox religious instruction, but their churches, Lutheran and Reformed, were less cohesive and more secular. To judge by the emancipation movement in 1848, however, Protestant teachers spanned a broad spectrum of opinion on the proper relationship between state, church, and popular education. Bitter personal experience and political beliefs had reinforced each other in a few cases—Wilhelm Wander in Silesia, for example, and Ferdinand Schnell in Brandenburg. To these anticlericals the confessional churches and their "clerisy" were tools of reaction, holding the faithful in political ignorance and splintering the nation into antagonistic sects. It was the responsibility of the state, they argued, to enlighten and unify its citizenry with a nonconfessional elementary school offering a general, primarily ethical introduction to religion. Most Protestant teachers' representatives were unwilling to carry emancipation to that extreme. Although some remained committed to their confessional heritages and regarded teaching as a kind of lay diaconate, others were pragmatists who accepted the confessional division of the schools as a legacy that could not be overcome.[60]

The crux of the matter is that, in its restricted sense, the emancipation appeal was not aimed at guardians of confessional orthodoxy. The various shades of opinion on religious instruction did not prevent widespread agreement on the need for a strict *administrative* separation of church and state in popular education. In the countryside the pastorate inevitably had become a focus of seminar graduates' resentments; its prestige was a handy foil to their lack of recognition, and its "alien," obstructive authority represented virtually everything wrong with their relationship to community and state. A degree of rivalry was to be expected between the pastor, who was the established mandarin in his community, and the seminar graduate who wanted his place in the sun. But the newcomer found the rivalry frustrating because its unequal terms were plain for the entire village to observe. Reform had not closed a social abyss that extended well beyond incomes and living standards. In the Rhine Province and Westphalia, where the Protestant pastor presided over the local Presbyterium, the sexton-teacher was not even eligible for election to its lay membership. The result, one teacher noted in 1845, was "isolation that only too easily turns to opposition."[61] More humiliating were the sexton-teacher's liturgical and custodial chores, which made him a servant-at-large for the pastor as well as the parishioners. In 1848 the Brandenburg provincial conference included among the "oppressive" sexton duties a long list of menial services owed the pastor—from carrying his coat to collecting parishioners' offerings.[62] In Westphalia a revised sexton ordinance, issued in 1835, had been remarkably faithful to historical detail. It required the sexton to carry messages to the next parish, assist on night calls with a lantern, and—if there was still any doubt that he was at his master's beck and call—report to the rectory every morning for orders. A humane pastor, the Westphalian teachers admitted in 1842, would spare his teacher these humiliations; but to others, jealous of their prestige and authority, they were a handy weapon.[63]

It was this glaring inequality that made seminar graduates so resentful of the pastors' central role in the administration of local schools. In fact it was often impossible to disentangle the lines of authority in parish and school; the two jurisdictions—if they did not coincide—intersected in confusing ways. Louis Balster, an early spokesman for the emancipation movement in Westphalia, had faced that problem as sexton-teacher in Lindenhorst. Balster had been feuding with Pastor Friedrich Frahne since the latter's arrival in 1836. As pastor of the Brechten parish, Frahne was also *Parochus* of the chapel and chairman of the chapel committee in Lindenhorst, but the issue was whether his authority extended to Balster. Hairsplitting legal arguments became their medium for a bitter struggle over matters of face. In 1843, Balster agreed to summon the combined chapel and school committee to meetings only as a "favor." Even as sexton, he protested to the superintendent, he was not subordinate to the Brechten pastor, and in any case there was no connection between sexton duties and school matters. That made it all the more offensive that Frahne had "ordered" and "charged" him in "categorical tones." "I am only a schoolteacher with little income," Balster lamented, "but that is no reason why I should be stepped on by someone more privileged whenever he has a mind to do so." Frahne responded that he had merely issued the kind of order he was accustomed to receiving from his own superiors. Departing from legal niceties, he informed the superintendent that "in our day there is a class of men who immediately cry about injustices, or sharpness, or oppression when they are consigned to the limits of their occupation . . . and who in their conceit make demands on the church, the state and social life which cannot be met in view of their education and achievements." In the end Balster received little comfort from the superintendent, who sympathized with his complaints about the contested obligation but also reprimanded him for accusing a superior of "inhumanity" without just cause.[64]

Liberation from the sextonship would not end subordination to the local school inspector; the pastor occupied that office by virtue of his higher education as well as his religious authority. Although seminar graduates might dismiss the lay members of the school committee as ignorant laymen, their diploma was far less impressive than an *Abitur* and university degree, their training no match for an education in the classics and academic theology. Graduates tried to topple that obstacle, or at least circumvent it, by accentuating their professional identity and insisting on their rightful place in a modern, complex world of *Berufsstände*. What mattered in its division of labor was not the level of "education" (*Bildung*) in the general, humanistic sense, but the requisite kind of expertise. As the Westphalian petitioners argued their case, "Pedagogy has certain subjects which, even without the Roman and Greek authors, suffice to give the teacher a scholarly training for his profession; as the sphere is different, so is the education."[65] Despite their traditional guardianship of popular education the pastors now had to recognize the masters of a new discipline and consign themselves to their own equal but separate, or "alien," field of expertise.

The problem was not simply that most pastors had not been introduced to the new pedagogy. They did not qualify as "schoolmen" and could not appreciate what it meant to be a modern teacher because they lacked practical, workaday experience in the instruction of young children. On that score Wander was willing to compare teachers with "apprentice masons" and asked his readers to imagine the apprentices' reaction to supervision by "a doctor or theologian." The supervisor could "astound them when the opportunity arises," but they would "soon discover that he knows nothing about building and will laugh when he tries to lay down the rules."[66] Balster had learned that lesson in the early phase of his feud with Pastor Frahne. In 1836, Frahne had demanded an explanation for the "shameful" absenteeism in Lindenhorst. Balster answered that by instructing the older children in religion on Wednesday and Friday mornings the pastor made it virtually impossible for them to attend school in the afternoons. Frahne countered that the teacher was "arbitrarily" holding his afternoon classes from twelve to three and had eliminated Saturday sessions so as to have more time for pleasant chores and visits to neighbors. To Balster the charge betrayed a woeful lack of "sympathy" (*Huld*) for the school and teacher. The pastor simply did not understand how exhausting it was to instruct eighty or ninety children of various ages and keep them all occupied for five hours a day. Such work did not require "speculative thought," but it did involve "reflection" and constant formulation of "clear concepts." The issue, Balster insisted, was not whether religious instruction should be eliminated or even curtailed. It belonged in the school and indeed should be the "center" of an "instructional development" aimed at "the entire spirit of the child." Frahne merely had the children recite a few hymn verses or a biblical aphorism, and that was hardly surprising; he could do no more precisely because they could hardly read and write.[67]

Seminar graduates had learned from bitter experience that the typical pastor—who had never actually taught children and who in fact entered the schoolroom only on the rare occasion of an inspection or a public examination—knew nothing about "building." The irony is that members of an "alien" profession often seemed guilty of a betrayal of kin. As an educated official, after all, the pastor knew how difficult it was to maintain the proper respect among the locals. A West Prussian teacher described a typical village baptism, with the pastor seated beside the headman and parish elders at the head of the table and the teacher relegated to the bottom end, and concluded: "How wrong it is for him [the pastor] to neglect this opportunity to impress the peasants with the dignity of the teaching office."[68] The explanation was not always that the pastor wished to keep down a rival; he might also be reluctant to forfeit his parishioners' cooperation, and risk the loss of their contributions to his income, by pressuring or contradicting them. To teachers, however, the pastors' handicaps only confirmed the uselessness of the local inspectorate. A Brandenburg teacher related the tribulations of a colleague who, having made an example of two schoolgirls for their poor hygiene (he had discovered insects in their hair), had been insulted by their parents. When the matter reached the pastor, he warned the teacher, "Don't be so impulsive in the future!"[69] Another village teacher drew this conclusion: "So long as we teachers remain subordinate to the clerical school inspectors any resident of your community will be allowed to submit even the most unfounded complaints to your superior; so long as the latter, whether he likes it or not, has to heed these complaints and intervene as judge—usually with investigations conducted so that the claims of the grown man, the teacher, need public confirmation by the child, the pupil in the school—this abuse will not end."[70]

If the pastors often merely channeled local attacks, they also deprived teachers of direct access to the state administration. Aside from annual tours of their jurisdictions the superintendents—and through them the sections—had to rely on the pastors to appraise teachers' work and general conduct. The annual conduct lists (*Conduitenlisten*) were submitted in secret, and that intensified teachers' fears that they were being judged on the basis of ignorant, sometimes prejudicial witness.[71] Likewise the local inspectorate intruded when teachers appealed to the sections for help. A complaint about a local school policy or a request for an income subsidy from local or state funds had to receive the pastor's approval if it was to carry any weight. The hazards of this procedure were well illustrated in the village of Lintorp (Düsseldorf district) in the summer of 1848. By then Wilhelm Hagen, a graduate of the Soest seminar, had fallen into debt trying to support six children on a 150-thaler income. Pressed by two of his creditors, he petitioned the section for a subsidy. The section referred the petition to Pastor Petersen, who instructed Hagen to submit an affidavit of his "competence in office" from the school committee of Lintorp. In his response Hagen anticipated the complaints of the committee and dismissed them as the *Pedantismus* of "unprincipled" and "incompetent" men. He urged the pastor to rely on his own judgment, since an "educated man" knew how to value a teacher's work "from a higher perspective" without being swayed by "stubborn prejudice" or "the mob's standard" (*Pöbelmasstab*). The affidavit that Petersen nonetheless submitted aired the usual complaints—that Hagen was not devoting enough attention to singing and prayer, for example—and added that he almost never attended church, played cards in the local tavern every day, and seldom visited local residents. "It seems that everything here is too petty and common for him," the committeemen concluded with the venom of men snubbed, "and we can only hope that higher authorities will assign him to a larger sphere as soon as possible." In an accompanying letter Petersen, though regretting Hagen's snobbery, wanted it made clear to him that his pastor had "unequivocally" supported his request. But the affidavit achieved its end; the section refused Hagen with a reminder that "the granting of a subsidy depends not only on the teacher's need, but also on the judgment of his behavior in office."[72]

Elimination of the local inspector would remove an alien filter from the evaluation of the new profession and, as important, allow state officials to intervene more effectively on its behalf. The only way to insure this two-way administrative traffic was to replace the superintendents with full-time, salaried schoolmen. The superintendent lacked expertise in the new pedagogy, and in any case could spend only a few hours in each school on his annual tour. He might make a special trip to a village to settle a dispute, but only if it was brought to his attention and usually after it had escalated into a feud. In the state administration itself liberals like Diesterweg and Landfermann were not the only critics of this part-time inspection. In 1839 the Potsdam section admitted in private that the typical superintendent—aside from his lack of expertise—was too busy with his clerical duties to devote sufficient attention to the many schools in his jurisdiction.[73] Even the more active superintendents could offer only sporadic, often inconsequential help to Rhineland teachers who were protesting school fee arrears, or to a beleaguered teacher like Krause in Dobberzin. Once the inspectorate became a full-time job it could serve as the strong arm of state intervention in the countryside.

The "truth" in which "the teachers' consciousness of today is rooted" and which "can never be eradicated," Rhineland petitioners submitted in 1847, is that "only a teacher can understand, correctly interpret and evaluate another teacher. [He] knows his colleague's position, profession, cares and troubles" and "can advise and lead him and satisfy his innermost needs."[74] In 1848 some conference delegates took that truth literally and wanted to exclude clergymen without exception from the new inspectorate. Most conferences avoided that degree of occupational chauvinism by allowing exceptional clergymen who were also full-time schoolmen.[75] In its efforts to eliminate clergymen, however, the emancipation movement was not simply denying the legitimacy of ecclesiastical supervision. Implicit to its reaction against the teachers' peculiar predicament was the conviction that professions, including those in the state service, had the right to supply their own supervisory officials. In that sense the state administration, like mother church, had to recognize that its child had come of age. The movement wanted state intervention without bureaucratic tutelage.

Five

EMANCIPATION: THE TOWNS

In Prussia school policy respected the administrative and socio-economic barriers that had long divided the towns from the countryside. Reformers in the late eighteenth century had carefully distinguished the two worlds and had planned a more ambitious curriculum for urban lower schools. The national ideal of the Reform Era, with its principle of "general education," erased that distinction only in theory. In practice it was still assumed that skilled artisans, shopkeepers, and other *Bürger* needed a more extensive education, particularly in practical subjects, than the countrymen. The ministry tried to meet that need, without distracting the other seminars from their rural mission, by establishing a special seminar for town schoolteachers in Berlin in 1832.

In 1849 only about 21 percent of the entire teaching corps was classified as urban in official statistics. The Berlin seminar had been kept small, but with urban growth an increasing portion of graduates from the other seminars had ended up in the towns.[1] It is not surprising that they played a disproportionate role in launching the emancipation movement and articulating its goals. Karl Böhm and several other spokesmen in Berlin were in frequent contact with mentors like Diesterweg and Doctor Kobitz, the liberal editor of the *Preussische-Volks-Schul-Zeitung.* In the larger towns teachers who publicized their grievances risked official retaliation, but were not vulnerable to the kinds of local reprisals that rural teachers faced. Some graduates in the towns—like Wander in Hirschberg—had begun their careers in rural schools, and all knew that the countryside was a particularly hostile environment for their profession. The more important reason why town spokesmen transcended the split between *Stadt* and *Land* was that they did not see an essential difference between their grievances and those of the rural majority. They had the same basic perspective on the dilemma of a new profession and called for the emancipation of the teaching corps as a whole.

REFORM AND EXPANSION

Despite the occasional efforts of state and ecclesiastical officials the towns had been as impervious to school reform as the countryside in the late eighteenth century. Stein and his collaborators hoped to create showpieces of national renewal with the Municipal Law of 1808. Once endowed with elected councils and magistrates, the towns would assume responsibility for their public institutions and thus cultivate national citizenship at the local level. One such institution was the elementary school; like poor relief and other branches of municipal administration it was assigned its own committee (*Schuldeputation*), staffed by appointed citizens and members of the city government.

It was characteristic of the Reform Era that the new school officials in Berlin and the district sections accompanied this gift of self-administration with a healthy dosage of centralized reform from above. In fact the sections often began to reorganize town schools without bothering to solicit opinions from the new school committees and in some cases without waiting for their establishment. In the teens the better Latin schools were elevated to classical high schools (*Gymnasien*) with a preuniversity curriculum; most of the others, together with the less ambitious parish and private institutions, were limited to elementary instruction. With the help of municipal officials, the sections and their school inspectors began to ferret out the many unlicensed schoolmasters who had survived in towns of all sizes. They were now required to pass an examination or find other work.[2]

But the limitations of reform from above had long-term effects in the towns as well as in the countryside. State officials tried to solve the fiscal dilemma by squaring the circle. Although they prodded the towns to make room for the elementary schools in their communal budgets, they were unwilling to apply the tax provision of the General Code or impose any other general tax for school support. In 1809, Humboldt had drawn up a tax-based plan for the entire school system in Königsberg; but following his departure the new magistrate and city council, with the approval of the section, left the elementary schools in the hands of the neighborhood parishes and offered token municipal aid.[3] Threatened with a tax in 1811, the council in Breslau pleaded poverty and the issue was dropped.[4] In most other Prussian towns the issue was never raised. Recent war burdens, Humboldt's successor noted in 1814, made a school tax as ill timed for the towns as for the countryside.[5] While waiting for the state-wide law that was never issued, the sections had to make do with improved collection of the school fee and other patchwork measures. Schools that had been reorganized and rid of their most glaring deficiencies entered Pre-March on a shoestring budget.

In the first decade of reform the absence of a tax did not prevent a marked rise in town teachers' incomes. By 1820 the yearly average was about 212 thaler in all of Prussia and exceeded 250 thaler in five districts. However, for 54.8 percent of the 3,745 town schoolteachers incomes were still below 200 thaler.[6] Figures that were high in the countryside were less impressive in the towns, which were expected to attract the best-educated, most competent teachers and had to compensate them for the higher cost of urban living. More important, the new income packages included a host of traditional endowments that allowed municipal administrations to limit their aid. Like their rural colleagues, rectors in small towns were still farming small plots and receiving payments in kind. In many cases the school and teacher were still dependent on their original sponsor, the parish, for the bulk of their support. Even in larger towns many rectors and other well-situated men were earning less as teachers than as parish cantors or sextons.

From the 1820s onward the imperatives of growth put municipal officials and the section councillors who brooded over them to a more severe test. The population of the towns, like that of the countryside, increased by more than 50 percent in the first half of the nineteenth century, and the urban percentage of the Prussian population crept from 25.6 in 1834 to 26.7 in 1849.[7] Since the rapid increase in school-age children coincided with enforcement of attendance, the elementary schools, from the smallest provincial outposts to the capital, were particularly jolted by this demographic leap. Institutions that had barely entered the public sector required breakneck expansion of facilities and multiplication of personnel. An expansion that would have strained municipal resources under any circumstances now exposed the critical weakness in the arrangements for school support. Parish funds were virtually exhausted; for purposes of expansion the elementary school became, for the first time, a full-fledged municipal responsibility that had to be met largely with cash.[8] The problem was not simply that, in the absence of a general tax, propertied residents escaped the main burden of support. An increasing percentage of the fee-paying public belonged to the proletariat who overcrowded traditional livelihoods and swelled the new working class in domestic and factory industries. Faced with a growing number of pauper families, Breslau, Königsberg, and many other towns had to establish free *Armen-*

schule.[9] In others a significant portion of the fees for poor children remained "uncollectable." At the same time the magistrates and councils, as well as older town administrations (where the Municipal Law did not apply), proved most reluctant to grant teaching incomes a high priority in their budgets. In part their thrift reflected indifference toward an institution that had attained public status only because of outside meddling and that now competed with poor relief and other public services that also demanded higher expenditures. But the fate of the schools was also a symptom of the general fiscal dilemma of the towns. State taxes left a very narrow base for municipal taxation, and often enough a portion of the latter was already earmarked for service on the war debts.

This was, in rough form, the social and fiscal straightjacket of urban school expansion in Pre-March. Its most striking result was a bottom layer of new teachers, some paid meager cash salaries, others supported with a variety of more expedient arrangements. The capital itself illustrates both patterns on a grand scale. In 1812, when a school commission was established in Berlin, only about 2,000 children were being instructed at the cost of the municipal poor treasury. In addition to the four *Armenschule* there were about sixty parish schools, scattered through the city without regard to the population distribution. Private institutions often operated without licenses and mixed elementary instruction with an old-fashioned Latin curriculum to attract as many fee-paying customers as possible.[10] In 1821 the ministry and its commissar, Beckedorff, began pressing for a complete reorganization and brought Doctor Reichhelm from Königsberg to serve as the first school superintendent in Berlin. A year later the city council hoped to limit costs by assigning pauper children to the parish schools. In 1826, Reichhelm proposed a more ambitious plan for a capital which, like other large cities, harbored "the most bitter poverty . . . side by side with considerable prosperity." The poor administration had estimated that the parents of 4,500 school-age children could not afford a fee, but only 900 of those children were attending the *Armenschule*. Reichhelm's plan called for fourteen *Armenschule*, each divided into boys' and girls' sections, to provide all 4,500 children with completely free instruction. Despite recent schemes for a national system of education these would offer only minimum preparation for the "common trades" and would lack any "organic unity" with the new high schools.[11]

Anyone familiar with similar projects in middle-sized towns, Beckedorff wrote in praise of the plan, could appreciate the "geometrically increasing difficulties" involved in this "colossal work."[12] The city council quickly approved the scheme because the extra burden on the municipal treasury was estimated at only 8,100 thaler per year. Reichhelm had kept the bill low by trimming teaching salaries to a bare minimum. The "principal" of each school was salaried at 300 thaler, which was below the income of many small-town rectors, and his "class teacher" had to get by with 100–120 thaler. If the latter figure was modest by any standard, it was markedly low in view of the notoriously high rents and food prices in the capital. By 1847 there were fifteen *Armenschule*, each with two principals, and the number of classes—and class teachers—had mushroomed to 114. Thanks to a series of raises, the minimum salary for a class teacher ranged from 180 to 300 thaler from 1846 onward (depending on the number of teaching hours), and he was guaranteed a 50-thaler increment every five years. But the raises came late, and even with them the council had to approve emergency aid for married teachers during the inflation of 1847–48.[13]

A more striking result of low-budget reform was the survival and growth of private schools. In 1826, Reichhelm had hoped to drive them out of business, but he had not anticipated the accelerating population growth of the next two decades. In 1816, Berlin had been an oversized *Residenzstadt* with a civilian population of about 182,000. By 1846 in-migration had turned it into a sprawling European capital with over 389,000 civilians, and enforcement of attendance had more than tripled the number of elementary school pupils. Most of the immigrants were countrymen and provincial townsmen from Brandenburg and provinces farther east who found cheap lodgings within and outside the old city walls. Perhaps the most fortunate were those employed in the new factories or as domestics in prosperous homes. Most had to survive on meager, precarious earnings in the traditional trades, already severely overcrowded by the 1830s, or compete for unskilled wage labor.[14]

In 1835, when the net expenditure by the city on the elementary schools was 70,062 thaler, its net expenditure on poor relief was already 435,325 thaler. Ten years later the corresponding figures were 269,421 thaler and 767,979 thaler. In the 1840s one-seventh to one-fifth of the families in the city were exempt from the rent tax used to meet the mounting expenses for poor relief and other public services. This financial squeeze explains why state and municipal officials avoided building and staffing a sufficient number of *Armenschule*; instead they shunted the surplus of pupils classified, for school purposes, as "poor" to the private schools and paid their fees. In the distribution of poor children, in fact, the *Armenschule* had barely taken the lead by 1847, and only by limiting nearly 1,500 pupils to part-time instruction:

| | ARMENSCHULE | | PRIVATE |
	Day School	Part-time	SCHOOLS
1837	4,013	1,198	6,360
1847	8,266	1,414	8,418

The irony is that the fee subsidy for private schools amounted to nearly 57,000 thaler in 1846—nearly twice as much as the city was spending on teachers' salaries in the *Armenschule*.[15] The school commission had attached strings to its generosity: the private school "manager" (*Vorsteher*) had to pass a regular teaching examination and service one of the school districts. Aside from the subsidy, however, the managers were still private entrepreneurs who rented their own facilities, supplied their own equipment, and competed for fee-paying customers. In 1844, Superintendent Otto Schulz calculated that a manager entirely dependent on the fees for 225 poor children could earn—after paying rent and other overhead costs—no more than 220 thaler per year.[16] He was not likely to be strict about the attendance of poor children; their absence made room for others at a higher fee rate. He catered to the "whims of the public," that is, fee-paying parents, by continually adjusting the curriculum to its tastes. Though one manager regretted these business practices, he reminded critics that "with the loss of parents' favor his [the manager's] precious bread vanished."[17]

As semiprivate entrepreneurs the managers were an embarrassing anomaly in the new era of public education. What had changed was the scale of their enterprises. To handle the flood of poor children the managers had hired a large number of "assistants." These had to pass an examination and submit progress reports to the school commission, but otherwise were mere wage-hands paid by the week or month and dismissible on short notice. Although some had qualified only for the private schools, others were former seminar pupils who had been expelled or teachers who, dismissed from positions elsewhere and barred from teaching, had gravitated to the capital in search of work.[18] The illegitimate employees survived as the underworld of the Berlin teaching corps. In the late 1840s, after the school commission had required the managers to raise their wages, the assistants were earning 180–240 thaler per year.[19]

The sheer size of the capital made it unique among Prussian towns, but in many others population growth and accompanying poverty had a similar impact on school expansion. In the former Kurmark Brandenburg, for example, the population of the eighty-one *Städte* (excluding Berlin) increased by 83.4 percent from 1815 to

1846.[20] Since the 1820s special commissars dispatched by the Potsdam section had combined legal muscle with moral exhortation to extract salaries for new teachers. Every town, the section announced in 1838, finally had "a fully organized school system corresponding to its needs—which of course awaits completion everywhere and will have to be expanded because of the increase in school-age children." In a private report, Councillor Striez noted that the growing poverty kept everything in flux and prevented reform from taking root.[21] Greiffenberg, a town with only 965 residents in 1816, illustrates the flux in miniature. It was one of the many agrotowns, mixing farming and trades, that became overcrowded with landless laborers and struggling artisans. While its larger neighbors established magistrates and councils, Greiffenberg remained under the *Patronat* of the local estate lord and *Landrat*, Wedell-Parlow; the "mayor" was his appointee and in turn appointed four "section men" (*Viertelsmänner*). In 1815, when the cantor-schoolmaster died, his position was worth 223 thaler, most of it in sexton fees and payments in kind. It did not bode well that Wedell-Parlow and local officials rejected a proposal by one wary candidate that the school fee be replaced by a fixed salary of 100 thaler.

By 1846, Greiffenberg had 1,375 souls and was hosting a modest *Stadtschule* with a four-man teaching staff. However, foot dragging and penny pinching had accompanied every step. In 1822 local officials reluctantly scraped together 166 thaler for a second teacher (most of it in surplus school fees), but two years later there were 150 children in his class. The section men, hoping to avoid further expense, recommended that a local tailor instruct the younger children. This time the parish church came to the rescue, and by combining school funds with a hodgepodge of pastoral incomes, Greiffenberg managed to hire a clergyman-rector at 450 thaler. Meanwhile, Wedell-Parlow resorted to forced collections and indeed imprisoned the school treasurer for embezzlement. In November 1829, after charging the mayor with fee collection and appointing a new school committee, he reported to the section that the "school system" was "beginning to gain more solidity."[22]

By 1832 there were about 300 school-age children and 175 of them were crowded into the third teacher's class. Superintendent Albrecht saw no alternative to a communal tax, but when local officials pleaded the incapacity of the town, he retreated, noting that "the poverty of the small towns is ever increasing." In response to admonishments by the section the school committee reported that most of the 83 thaler in fee arrears for 1834 could not be salvaged. Four years later, after much wrangling, local officials agreed to sacrifice 30 thaler from the communal treasury and a fourth teacher was salaried at the very modest sum of 110 thaler. In 1848, when the section had to relax its grip, Greiffenberg slipped back into old habits. In June the school committee attributed parents' failure to pay a school fee for the past three months not to "bad will," but to "the general poverty which unfortunately prevails here as elsewhere in the Ackermark." Despite the orders of the section forced collections were impossible, since "no citizen is willing to accompany the court clerk and he dare not enter the houses alone." Meanwhile a new local regime, the product of a "general citizens' protest," had struck the fourth teacher's salary from the communal budget. In the winter of 1848–49, when fee payment again stopped for three months, the pastor admitted bad will. Parents had misinterpreted the school provisions for a new constitution, and lacking strict orders from on high, local officials had been content to let everything run amok. In June the section, exasperated by this latest recalcitrance, finally ordered Greiffenberg to introduce a limited school tax.[23]

Although school expansion was less traumatic in the larger towns in the Potsdam district, their new magistrates and councils also faced mounting poverty and were reluctant to dip into public revenues in the absence of parish funds. The population of Schwedt grew from 4,221 in 1815 to 7,024 in 1846. By 1828 the town was salarying a nine-man teaching staff from the communal treasury. When the section insisted that it urgently needed three new teachers, the magistrate pleaded incapacity—noting that, if pressed, the council might restore a school fee. Schwedt managed with one new position for a few years because the local tobacco industry limited the overcrowding. In 1834, Commissar Striez agreed to the establishment of a "small school," limited to twelve hours per week, for about eighty children who were employed in the tobacco "factories" and shifted summer vacation to accommodate the sharecroppers who needed their children's labor from mid-June through the fall. By 1847 the treasury was salarying three more teachers at 160 thaler.[24] Though local conditions varied, this pattern of expansion was repeated throughout the district. From 1827 to 1841 the number of town teachers grew by 35.9 percent; the percentage with 100–200 thaler increased from 26.8 (1827) to 42.3 (1841), and the percentage with 100–150 thaler from 10.2 to 16.3.[25]

By the early nineteenth century many of the towns in the Düsseldorf district in the lower Rhineland were burgeoning textile centers. Under French administration the mayoralties had had to accept new obligations for elementary education. But without a tax neither recent French tutelage nor new industry made an effective difference in the economy of school expansion. The fee-paying public simply shifted from the traditional lower orders to a new working class that earned its wages in domestic and factory industry. In the ordinance of 1825 the section required minimum cash salaries and compensation for poor children, but these impositions made municipal officials all the more determined to limit new burdens. Most of the towns in the district accommodated their growing school-age populations with "assistants" lodged and fed by the regular teachers and perhaps given a token cash allowance. Though that solution inconvenienced married men and deprived their younger colleagues of independence, it was a cheap alternative to regular salaries. By 1849 more than one-third of the urban teaching corps in the district were assistants. Barmen, a major textile center, had twenty-eight of them (out of forty-six teachers), and Düsseldorf, the administrative center of the district, had twenty-one (out of thirty-four teachers).[26]

In most Prussian towns the school fee was kept very low and hard-pressed parents were exempted from paying it. The lesson of Elberfeld, another textile center, was that a more ambitious strategy was politically risky. In 1828 the Elberfeld school committee responded to encouragement from the section and launched a project to reorganize the six parish and eleven municipal schools into a unified, publicly supported system. New contracts awarded the fifteen incumbent schoolteachers with salaries of 300–800 thaler from a central school treasury. To fill the treasury the committee doubled the fee rate and announced that henceforth the municipal tax collector, not the teachers, would make the rounds. Though suspecting that the proposed budget was unrealistic, the city council agreed to subsidize it with an annual grant of 3,560 thaler and cover any deficit for the first year. But since the interest on the school capital of the parishes was not transferred to the new treasury (as the council had expected), the reorganization depended entirely on a higher fee rate. That made its timing all the more unfortunate. In the late 1820s Elberfeld entered one of its periodic trade depressions; confronted with unemployment and reduced wages, the textile workers, like parents in Greiffenberg two decades later, simply refused to pay. The city council reacted by returning the fee to its previous rate, requiring the teachers to collect it themselves, and scrapping their fixed salaries for 1831. Alarmed by recent popular disturbances in nearby Crefeld and Aachen, the mayor and *Landrat* urged the section to approve this retreat. Parents found the higher rate "hateful" and above all objected to the new collection procedure, which made the fee seem like another tax and deprived them of personal contact with their children's instructors. The mayor saw no reason to provoke discontent among the "middle and lower classes" at a time of inflation and unemployment. Complaints about the fee, the *Landrat* reported, had been heard in "recent disturbances" and had found their way into "anonymous threatening letters."[27]

In December 1830 the section approved the council's decision. The teachers understandably felt cheated; their new contracts had been violated, and they did not relish a renewal of personal contacts with parents. Summoned before the council, they announced that they would make the collection rounds again only if their salaries, along with subsidies for assistants, were guaranteed "forever." They relented when the mayor threatened to withhold their salary payments, but the lowered fee rate had not placated parents or at least had not loosened their pocketbooks. In October 1831, when the year's deficit promised to exceed 7,000 thaler, the council voted to dismantle the entire reorganization. At that point the section dispatched a special commission; with its guidance the council voted 7,000 thaler per year and to raise the money approved a new tax on the 600 residents in the upper thirteen tax classes. In the spring of 1832 the school committee worked out a new arrangement with the teachers—one that ignored their contracts and required them to collect the fee, but at least provided 100–200 thaler salaries for instructing an assigned number of poor children.[28] That settled a "school plight" (*Schuljammer*) that had cost at least one town official, School Inspector Johann Friedrich Wilberg, his good reputation. Wilberg had been the protegé of school reformers in the Rhineland and was the only schoolteacher there (and perhaps in Prussia) to be honored with an inspectorate. But he had been caught in the crossfire. Whereas school parents saw him as the chief culprit behind the reorganization and other residents blamed him for the new tax, the teachers concluded that he had not done enough to defend their interests.[29]

Elberfeld emerged from its school crisis a step ahead of most Prussian towns. It was typical of urban school economy, however, that the city fathers had burdened the more prosperous residents with a new tax only as a last resort—to buttress a precarious school fee. More important, Elberfeld kept entirely in step with its neighbors by continuing to meet the imperatives of growth with assistants. From 1833 to 1846, when the school-age population more than doubled (from 2,583 to 5,537), the number of regular teachers remained at fifteen but the number of assistants jumped from fifteen to twenty-one.[30]

VIEWS FROM THE BOTTOM

It was the legacy of school reform that created a united front in the emancipation movement. Despite the differences in their occupational conditions town teachers supported and echoed their rural colleagues because they also lacked an "appropriate" financial reward and social status. Likewise they saw emancipation as the necessary conclusion of state-sponsored reform. Its levers, money and career opportunities, would benefit both branches of the teaching corps.

As victims of urban school economy, town schoolteachers, like those in the countryside, found themselves caught between the neglect of their communities and the limited, often ineffective intervention of the state administration. In many of the smaller towns, where the sextonship and its endowments had survived, the teacher was still dependent on his neighbors' contributions and the yield from "peasantizing" farm work. But emancipation spokesmen saw no reason to congratulate the larger towns for their record on school support, despite their more impersonal terms of employment and relatively high salary scales by the 1840s. "The honor of a city," Karl Böhm judged in 1842, "consists in guaranteeing an existence to its residents corresponding to their service and education, and to date neither Berlin nor any other town has merited that honor."[31] Ultimately the responsibility lay with state officials who had allowed the towns to scrape together inadequate budgets and expand their school systems at the expense of new generations of teachers. In fact Eduard Mücke, a young teacher in Rathenow (Potsdam district), publicly charged that the section commissar, not the city fathers, had trimmed his salary to 160 thaler in 1827.[32] The charge proved false, but what mattered was that the state administration had failed to honor its debt to a new profession in the public service. As early as 1837, Ferdinand Schnell, a teacher in Prenzlau, had used this clumsy but revealing metaphor: "The school and its men are stepchildren of the mother or, perhaps better, the father—since he is the master over salary and wealth. . . . Of course it might appear unnecessary to touch on politics when it comes to the elementary school system. But the appearance is false; the school can evaluate its circumstances correctly only when it tries to understand its relationship to the state, and that relationship is as close as that of the child to the father. To guarantee its own survival the state must guarantee the school its right of family inheritance by word and deed."[33]

The private school assistants in Berlin were the most glaring examples of neglect. Since the 1820s they had been required to meet the standards established by public officials, and had spared the city the expense of more public schools. Superintendent Schulz was impatient with cries of poverty among municipal teachers, but in 1845 he admitted that the assistants, and particularly the married men among them, were in unique financial "distress."[34] Perhaps more scandalous than their income level were the terms of their employment. Unlike the lowest paid municipal teacher, or even the assistant in a Rhineland town, they had not been drawn into the relative security of the public sector. Some managers, an assistant complained in 1836, liked to underscore their employees' wage-earning status by paying them in class, right in front of the children, and one had the children deliver the money.[35] In the same year another reporter described many of his fellow assistants as "nomads," constantly changing schools in a vain search for more humane conditions of employment. Twenty years ago, an older man reminisced, both the managers and their employees had enjoyed "decent incomes" and "respect"; but the employees' incomes had declined sharply, and they could not escape because the *Armenschule* preferred younger men. We are "the sacrifices in the reorganization of the Berlin school system," he lamented, and so "it is doubly painful for us to have to stand below younger men who have been trained in the pleasant atmosphere of the seminars, partly at their own expense, but partly with the support of the state."[36]

It was a measure of the assistants' vulnerability that they fell silent in the late 1830s and early 1840s. In 1848 they organized and voiced their grievances in two petitions to the magistrate. City officials, they charged, had tolerated the managers' "extreme selfishness" and "false conception of freedom and private rights," and thus had left their employees to "languish in an entirely unworthy relationship." It was a blatant contradiction to demand "the same education and work . . . without securing them the same rights and pay as its other teachers." The petitions requested equality with municipal teachers in salaries and opportunities for promotion. One of them, in fact, proposed that every teaching candidate in Berlin "prove himself" in a private school as a prerequisite to municipal employment.[37] If full adoption by the city was overdue, it was only an interim solution. Six assistants helped revise the original draft of the Tivoli petition, approved by about three hundred teachers assembled in Berlin in April 1848. They were probably responsible for the new provision that the private schools, like all other elementary schools, be made "state institutions."[38]

In Berlin and other towns municipal teachers at least had public status. The seminar graduates among them entered a world already overcrowded with educated young men, and their sense of deprivation was far from unique. To judge by credentials, in fact, they had less reason to complain than the university-educated trainees who survived on a pittance, or on their own resources, while waiting for tenured positions in the higher administrative and judicial ranks.[39] However, seminar graduates were the lowest of the low; they found themselves on the bottom rungs of a profession which, far from approaching the income and status of the academic elite, had yet to achieve parity with its "educational equals" in the subaltern ranks of the state bureaucracy.

In 1842 a fictional character named Rothe, speaking for his creator, described a typical day in his life as a young schoolteacher in a provincial town. Awakening before dawn in a small, barely furnished room, Rothe regrets that there is no "dear wife" at his side. A man with a salary of 135 thaler has no choice but to put off marriage. It was only a dream, he recalls, that a colleague suddenly died; but he cannot help coveting the 190-thaler salary he would have inherited. The reality of his day is that the curriculum has been expanded and he will have to work harder. At lunchtime and again before supper he hurries off to give private lessons to the son of a "higher official" and has to bear with the father's unsolicited advice on pedagogy and the virtues of frugality. On his evening stroll Rothe spies another young teacher who is known to be an "idiot" but has been cunning enough to secure one of the most lucrative positions in the local high school. Later he passes one of the most imposing residences in the town; gossip has it that its owner curried favor with those on high and was even willing to sacrifice his wife to an influential friend for his sinecure. Returning to his room, Rothe pours his frustration into an article on the importance of the teaching corps and its urgent need for "means." But a messenger arrives with a rejection notice from the journal to which he has already sent a similar piece. Though his complaints are all justified, he reads, they have been published too many times already. He leaves off in disgust, goes out again, and ends up gazing at the window of the blond-haired, blue-eyed maiden for whom he has long pined. Overhearing voices next door, he is shattered to learn that she will wed on the morrow.[40]

Melodrama, but it made palpable the bitterness among Rothe's real-life counterparts. Under more favorable circumstances they might have prided themselves on being genuine municipal employees (*Angestellten*), distinguished from the great majority of rural teachers by their regular salaries paid entirely or almost entirely in cash. Yet the modernity of their employment could not compensate for lack of money. In 1827, Commissar Striez had deemed 180 thaler the bare minimum for a single man;[41] over a decade later, in the inflationary 1840s, the salaries of many new positions had not yet reached that sum or were only slightly above it. If the occupants of those positions had more cash than younger teachers in the countryside, they also had to buy all their food at inflated prices and pay higher rents. In that light, in fact, cash salaries seemed a disadvantage; town teachers looked with envy on the land endowments and payments in kind attached to rural positions.[42]

In the towns material deprivation was intensified by the lack of opportunities to escape it. While few better-endowed positions had been established since the 1820s, the 100–200 thaler variety had multiplied severalfold in most towns. The result—the inevitable by-product of extreme economy in school expansion—was a bottleneck. In the 1840s, when natural attrition allowed some new men to move up the ranks, the sheer arithmetic left recent arrivals wondering whether they would ever escape their shoestring positions. Those who were prudent enough to put off marriage were understandably impatient; men who had completed their training and begun their careers saw no reason why the hardships of initiation should continue in their mid-to-late twenties. Those who did marry found that they could not make ends meet and had to crowd their off-hours with private lessons. In 1842, Schnell bore witness to the despair among his colleagues in Prenzlau. "The simple truth," he wrote, "is that young men with the richest potential, the highest examination grades and the best intentions sink down together and mutter with heavy sighs: 'If only I could—if I did not have a wife and children—I would learn a trade now.'" It might be different if they were "teachers of the old stamp," Schnell noted, but seminar graduates had a new "consciousness" and new needs.[43]

Despite salaries of 120–132 thaler, a correspondent reported from Stettin in 1844, younger men in the *Armenschule* would "face the future with hope and contentment" if they had "the prospect of advancement or transfer to more lucrative positions."[44] He cited Magdeburg as a more generous town, but one of its angry young men, Eduard Hesse, would not have agreed. Hesse had transferred to Magdeburg in 1836 after a brief stint in the countryside. Though he had moved from an outlying district to the inner city by 1848, he was still earning only 200 thaler. Not surprisingly his *Appeal to Prussia's Schoolteachers* proposed that, aside from enjoying a higher salary scale, teachers receive a promotion at least every five years.[45] In Berlin, where the salaries for class teachers in the municipal schools were relatively high by the mid-1840s, the overcrowding and long wait tended to cancel out that advantage. Most older men with families, Schoolteacher Schneider had complained in 1842, have spent their lives waiting for a better lot: "Our good positions loom before us like a 'Fata Morgana,' an optical illusion, and unfortunately we have come to realize it."[46] Two years later Superintendent Schulz hailed the recent hike in class teachers' minimum salary scale, but had to admit that the ratio of class teachers to principals was now more than three to one. Even when salaries were as low as 100 thaler, Schneider responded, "earlier teachers were sustained in life by the hope of a principal's position soon."[47]

The bottleneck probably caused more friction among the ranks than teachers were willing to admit publicly. But Böhm, Schnell, and other better-situated spokesmen for the emancipation movement made common cause with their younger, or at least lesser paid, colleagues because they counted themselves different only in degree. Though at the pinnacle of the income hierarchy they tended to minimize their apparent advantage over rural teachers, insisting that inflated prices in the towns, and particularly in the larger ones, made it difficult to support families. At the same time they looked in the other direction, and not just to their "educational equals" in the subaltern ranks of the state bureaucracy. The clerks were their standard of reference, but their envy extended to the "middle-class" comforts and opportunities of university graduates in the higher state offices and academic schools. In 1842, Breter calculated that a Berlin teacher with a wife and three school-age children needed at least 646 thaler in cash to maintain "an extremely modest and thrifty household." He figured rent at 85 thaler, which was relatively low for Berlin, but included 24 thaler for a maid, 44 thaler for the husband's wardrobe, and 54 thaler for school fees, with one son attending a gymnasium and one daughter attending "one of the better middle-level girls' schools." Likewise, in a petition to the magistrate in 1848, teachers in Breslau requested free instruction for their children in the high schools of the city as well as higher salaries.[48]

Teachers who had reached the middle and upper ranks faced another, more imposing bottleneck. In the towns the presence of classical high schools and universities reminded seminar graduates that they had been relegated to the "lower," self-enclosed end of the Prussian school system. In addition to being excluded from academe, they were being deprived of nonacademic positions for which they possessed professional qualifications and experience. Rectors and principals could have no further prospects so long as the state inspectorate was monopolized by clergymen. To make matters worse, theology candidates were encroaching on plum teaching positions in the seminars and the few nonclassical high schools (*Bürgerschule*) and, in some provinces, received appointments as rectors of elementary schools. Faced with a surplus of graduates from the theology faculties, the state administration was relying on these positions to support some of them until they could secure pastorates or academic positions.

To town schoolteachers this preference for academic degrees in their own preserve was one more proof of their unique dilemma. Whereas the member of every other profession (*Stande*) can advance to the highest rank, Eduard Mücke wrote, "the teacher remains what he is even if he was an angel or could become one."[49] Professional consciousness made it virtually irrelevant that the seminar was a nonacademic institution and indeed that elementary instruction was radically different from academic teaching. In 1841, a Berlin teacher who was struggling to support a wife and five children asked why the elementary teacher earned half as much as the gymnasium teacher and "a young man one year out of the university, that seat of scholarship and brawling, is appointed rector although many deserving and experienced men have long placed their hope in that office. . . ." His answer to these rhetorical questions was "That's just the way it is!"[50] In April 1848 the Tivoli petition condemned a system in which "the university graduate was entitled to advance to higher positions not because of 'greater practical capacity' but merely because of 'deeper scholarly training,'" and continued:

> There would be no objection to that, of course, since the practice of teaching is just as noble in a lower position as in a higher one; but with the lower position he [the elementary teacher] also had to manage forever with a proportionally lower salary. In fact it did the elementary teacher no good to equip himself with all the scholarly disciplines and attempt the higher examination—that was denied him, since he had not studied at the university!—Was it not inevitable that university graduates would have contempt for elementary teachers, and that the latter, conscious of their practical capacities, would harden in resignation?[51]

The Tivoli petition was drafted in the immediate aftermath of the "March Days"; confronted with new horizons, its authors did not limit their goals to higher positions in the elementary school system. They wanted to guarantee future generations of elementary teachers "an equal birthright with the theologian, the doctor and the jurist," and to that end proposed that the seminars be eliminated and teacher training be incorporated into the universities.[52] This radical route to emancipation was not taken by the other spring assemblies and the later official conferences. What they produced was a reform agenda combining the aspirations of urban and rural teachers. In several provinces the conference delegates established a minimum salary of 200 or 250 thaler for all teaching positions. Others, in Brandenburg, Silesia, and Saxony, scaled the minimum as high as 400 thaler for the larger towns. More important were the "advancement" schemes to circumvent the bottleneck in town school systems as well as the arbitrary hiring practices of the countryside. If many town teachers could not escape the bottom ranks, they could at least look forward to salary increments every five or ten years. Merit-based promotion would not allow ascent into the academic ranks, but combined with the use of "schoolmen" in the inspectorate, it offered career opportunities in a professional corps.[53]

𝕾𝖎𝖝

THE STATE AND ITS WARDS

In Pre-March the emancipation movement pressed its claims on a resistant state administration, and it proved impossible to settle accounts. The conflict marked the growing tension between bureaucratic rule and social change. On one level the seminars and their graduates became touchstones in an ideological arena. From 1840 onward the Ministry of Culture occupied an ambiguous middle ground in that arena, but nonetheless regarded emancipation as both illegitimate and dangerous. Pressed to extend reform from above, the ministry began a crackdown on the seminars so as to preclude dissatisfaction among future generations of schoolteachers. The choice of means seemed as alarming as the goals. Veteran officials were still committed to reform, but on their own terms. They were accustomed to dealing with individual subordinates rather than group spokesmen and collective petitions and would extend help only through the communal links of an administrative hierarchy. Now they were faced with subordinates who, aside from their ingratitude, sought recognition of the teaching corps as a *Stand* and tried to strengthen its claims with a liberal form of corporate self-help. Suppressed in the mid-1840s, this new corporatism revived in the more convivial atmosphere of 1848.

CRACKDOWN

Baron Karl von Altenstein, the minister of culture from 1817 to 1840, was a bureaucratic weathervane who adapted to changes in the political winds without committing his ministry to any one of them. He was succeeded by Friedrich Eichhorn, a bureaucrat more eager to chart a fixed course. Soon after taking office, Eichhorn compensated for his lack of expertise in public education and brought his staff more in line with his own views by appointing several new councillors. Among them was Gerd Eilers, the former school councillor in Koblenz (and, ironically enough, Landfermann's predecessor there), who was to become his most influential adviser. On Eiler's recommendation Ferdinand Stiehl, the director of the Neuwied seminar, was called to Berlin in 1844 to conduct a general review of elementary school policy.[1]

In 1846, Heinrich Deinhardt, a liberal partisan, surveyed the "overhaul plans" of the ministry. Though he dubbed them a "simple reaction," he also noted that the ministry "vainly fancies that it can hold fast to the good which it recognizes in the present educational system while binding its richest veins."[2] Deinhardt's judgment suggests the difficulty of locating ministerial policy in the emerging ideological spectrum. If there was a "simple reaction" on the issue of popular education in Pre-March, its advocates were the estate lords and academics who were formulating a conservative ideology. To them the new "rationalistic" school was a particularly unfortunate example of the state activism with which enlightened bureaucrats and national reformers had plagued Prussia. The "pedagogical ultras" of the Reform Era, Eduard Glanzow charged as early as 1824, had created "schoolmaster universities" whose graduates' "philosophizing, catechizing and dogmatizing ... struck at the very roots of earlier generations' 'prejudices.' "[3]

It was in the countryside that conservatives found the social deference and political subservience that seemed essential to the survival of an estate society. The school had a place there, but only as an agent for preserving and transmitting (or renewing) the masses' time-honored beliefs and values. Its central mission was to translate an orthodox, neo-Pietistic Protestantism into an emotionally based, unquestioning belief in dogmatic tradition, a belief pitted against the theology of the Enlightenment and calculated to insulate the rural lower orders from its corrosive rationalism. A rural schoolmaster with an artisanlike training and dependent status sufficed for that purpose. Indeed he figured in idylls of the old, unspoiled peasant community precisely because he was not in a position to uproot prejudices. To uplift rural teachers with the props of public office was to create bureaucratic levelers at the very base of the social hierarchy. For the conservatives improvement of teachers' "objective situation," if it were needed at all, would be limited to providing them with more farm land; thus they could improve agriculture with their good example while remaining bound to their neighbors' occupational and intellectual sphere.[4]

In the 1840s the ministry leaned toward this conservatism without abandoning its own traditions. Eichhorn and his councillors were veteran officials trying to preserve yet bind a reform legacy, not outsiders opposed to that legacy in principle. Still committed to a

Volksschule offering some kind of "general education," they rejected proposals to include direct preparation for agriculture in the rural curriculum. In 1841, in response to complaints from the *Landtag* of Province Prussia, the ministry insisted that rural school reform must progress to completion—with stricter enforcement of attendance laws, more effective inspection, and above all improvement of the most poorly endowed teaching positions.[5] To accomplish the latter it continued work on a new set of provincial school laws. While rejecting the conservatives' alternatives, however, the ministry was engaged in a more precarious balancing act than eighteenth-century reformers had attempted. Committed to a more liberal dosage of popular education, it nonetheless was determined to counteract the symptoms of social and political unrest that were multiplying in the "hungry forties." The rural curriculum might remain "general" in content but was to be trimmed to the essential subjects, and these were to help preserve the traditional moral-social fabric, not just develop "rationality." In that sense rural education should be, in Eichhorn's words, both "useful" and "homogeneous." The primary purpose of religious-ethical instruction was not "development of the understanding" but "nurturing of sentiment and reliable character, suitable to the conditions of popular life."[6]

In 1843 this rather cryptic phrasing was elaborated by a school official who, if not a member of the ministry, at least shared its perspective.[7] The author paid his respects to the principle of "basic general education" as "the declaration of the people's majority, the highest respect for their rights, the surest trust in their moral capacity." As for the pedagogy that had become entrenched in the seminars, however, it had neither arisen from nor adapted to "existing popular circumstances." Instead it had developed in a vacuum, from a merely formal principle into a systematic discipline (*Wissenschaft*). The tragic result was hardly surprising: the seminars were producing scholar-professionals who were alienated from and spurned by the population they had to serve. State policy now had to repudiate a misguided reform from above and return to a "truly popular education," geared to the "existing, unique educational needs of the people as well as their indisputable intellectual, moral and physical characteristics."[8] In a sense, then, the state was to assume a populist role, defending the rural masses' genuine culture against an alien professionalism. But the author's list of "regrettable developments," inevitably accompanying a one-sided "development of the understanding," covered the entire litany of conservative alarmism: ". . . a raging, chronic passion for reading, particularly in the lower orders; a grasping for appearances without regard for the consequences, which results in *Luxus* in social life and violation of its estate conditions as well as in a greater demand on life and the state and less consciousness of duty; further an effete egotism in family and community, a hollow liberalism in political attitudes, . . . and whatever similar developments may accompany a formally edu- cated but heartless and sometimes conscience-less contemporary trend."[9]

This specter would become reality, the author concluded, if schoolteachers continued to present religion as a rational theologi- cal system—as the seminars were training them to do. Instead they had to concentrate on biblical history so that the children could ac- quire "in a living view . . . the individual's personal circumstances as well as popular and state conditions." Likewise the German lan- guage had to be taught as "the expression of the German people in its spiritual life," with minimal attention to the logical rules of grammar.[10]

Respecting the legacy of the Reform Era in name more than in spirit, the Eichhorn ministry posed this version of "general educa- tion" against the contemporary trend. In the logic of its tortuous policy the rural teacher, though he could not provide instruction in agriculture, should nonetheless be equipped with agricultural skills in the seminar.[11] The point was not simply to improve his income or to turn his land endowment into a shining example of new agri- cultural methods. Though unwilling to reincarnate schoolmastery, the ministry envisioned a man rooted to the rural masses by his "cir- cumstances" as well as his beliefs. That vision reinforced the usual reluctance to impose new burdens on the countrymen and brought school reform to a near standstill in the early 1840s. The law pro- mulgated for Province Prussia in 1845, and the only one to be pro- mulgated, had originally been drafted by the province's president, Theodor von Schön, a key figure in the Reform Era who had survived the subsequent reaction. Schön had combined the traditional school communities into larger, more viable units and had included a tax on all landed property to finance teaching salaries. But the Eichhorn ministry took a second, considerably modified draft in hand and ended by merely tinkering with the province's *Regulative* of 1746. The minimum cash income for a village schoolteacher (in addition to free lodging, use of a plot of land, and specific deliveries in kind) was raised from fifteen to fifty thaler—a very modest sum indeed for the 1840s and one that the communities could continue to raise with a school fee.[12]

The emancipation movement collided head-on with the assump- tions behind this official reform agenda. To the ministry emancipation was not a social right but a particularly alarming symptom of a political malaise. The new aspirations among seminar graduates betrayed their miseducation and were thoroughly incompatible with their assignment in an educational policy oriented toward preservation. The proof lay in the intellectual affinities and direct contacts between the emancipation movement and the liberal opposition. Diesterweg was the most active and outspoken mediator, but not the most prominent one. In 1842, Friedrich Harkort, a Westphalian industrialist, presented the ministry with a petition from teachers in his province. In a public critique of the elementary school system, Harkort supported teachers' pleas for radical improvement of their incomes and status and advised them to unite under effective leadership.[13] Related to the liberals but within the jurisdiction of the ministry were Protestant clergymen who styled themselves, provocatively enough, "Friends of Light" and preached against the authoritarian government and neo-Pietistic obscurantism of the established churches. Schoolteachers in Berlin itself had signed their petitions, and others were reported to be attending their meetings in Saxony and Silesia.[14]

It was little comfort that the emancipation movement was limited to a tiny minority of the Prussian teaching corps or that a few threatening circulars had sufficed to silence them by the mid-1840s. What the ministry saw was a political chain, and it led directly back to the seminars. Eichhorn had suspected "excesses" and "false directions" in seminar training when he took office.[15] The final link between an overly "rational" or "scholarly" curriculum and the liberal malaise was, appropriately enough, the towns. In the 1840s distrust of the moral environment of the towns, which had marked seminar policy for several decades, received a distinctly political impetus. The opposition, after all, was primarily an urban phenomenon. The ministry had only to look to the capital itself, where Diesterweg and several other liberals were encouraging the emancipation movement. In the western provinces the most prominent liberal spokesmen, including Harkort, were town merchants and industrialists. The "Friends of Light" were holding their open meetings in Breslau, Magdeburg, Merseburg, and other urban centers.

In the fall of 1845 a curious incident in the Protestant seminar of Breslau rattled all the links in this political chain and dramatized the excesses of the seminars. Breslau was the wrong place at the wrong time: a center of liberal opposition in politics and church affairs and capital of the province that had produced the Weavers' Revolt and Wilhelm Wander, the most notorious "radical" among seminar graduates. The disturbance in the seminar began harmlessly enough; faced with an uncooperative class, an instructor in the Polish language singled out one of the pupils for disciplinary action. When the class protested en masse, Director Gerlach tried to punish the ringleaders with confinement. They refused to comply, and the class then petitioned the provincial school college to rescind the punishment or release them from the seminar. Not content just to release the twenty-three pupils who stood by the petition, the school college barred them permanently from teaching.[16]

A classroom squabble had escalated into an open revolt, an unprecedented act of insubordination. Its result was that twenty-three young men found the door shut on their chosen livelihood. Behind the pupils' action lay a variety of motives whose relative importance is difficult to assess. To some extent the ripples of dissatisfaction among Silesian teachers, together with the broader currents of opposition in the province and its capital, had spilled over into the seminar. Some of the pupils may have become disillusioned with their future occupation while apprenticing with older, embittered men. Despite later denials, Christian Scholz, a seminar teacher who had launched a reform journal in the province, may have been proselytizing among them. In any case the language teacher's problems were hardly surprising; the reward for high marks in Polish was assignment to one of the least desirable positions in Upper Silesia. Before the open revolt, in other words, the class had been engaged in a passive protest.

The religious opinions of Director Gerlach may have antagonized pupils who had been influenced by the liberal church movement in their regions or exposed to it in Breslau. In 1842, Gerlach had been promoted from a remote pastorship to the directorship of the seminar largely as a reward for his stolid orthodoxy. Eichhorn had foisted the appointment on the Breslau school college, despite its objection that Gerlach was disqualified by his lack of experience in elementary education as well as his "willful" and "impatient" personality.[17] The irony of the story—if we can believe the only available witness who was a pupil under Gerlach—is that these shortcomings exasperated the pupils without making them either respectful or fearful. From the start, it seems, Gerlach was unable to win the pupils' confidence as a professional model; his classroom procedure was distinctly unorthodox, and when he tried to demonstrate his pedagogical mastery in the adjoining elementary school, he seemed ineffective and, worse, laughable. More important, Gerlach was no patriarch; insecure in the cramped, adolescent environment of the *Internat,* he oscillated between threats of severe punishment, left unexecuted, and professions of friendliness, contradicted by his distant behavior. In 1844, his attempt to salvage his authority with a draconian house rule failed. In this atmosphere a disciplinary action could easily backfire; in fact the pupils may have seized on an opportunity to discredit their unpopular and mercurial director.[18]

In the aftermath of the Breslau incident the ministry in effect admitted its mistake by not recommending Gerlach for another directorship.[19] Nonetheless the incident stood as proof that the "opposition"—in what was now the multidimensional, politically charged meaning of that word—had entered the seminar itself. According to that version the villain of the piece was the city of Breslau, not Gerlach. Sent to investigate on the scene, Ferdinand Stiehl failed to uncover any evidence that the citizens of Breslau had exercised a direct influence, political or otherwise, on the "oppositional step by the *Seminaristen* as a corporation" (Eichhorn's words). But there were telltale signs. The "public," Stiehl reported, had supported the pupils' requests to attend the theater and had even taken up a collection for the expelled pupils. Notebooks filled with quotations against "tyranny" and "clerisy" from *Don Carlos* and other objectionable readings testified to the intellectual contamination of the town.[20] Following Stiehl's recommendation, Eichhorn reported to the king that Breslau was unsuitable for future rural schoolteachers—a conclusion, he noted, that found confirmation "not only in the outer appearance of the pupils . . . but also in the frequent complaints of sensible school patrons about the presumptions and pretensions of the teachers educated in the Breslau seminar."[21]

By October 1848, when the Breslau incident occurred, Stiehl had already drafted a cabinet order empowering the ministry to conduct a general crackdown on the elementary school system. On December 25, just one week after Eichhorn submitted his report to the king, the order was issued with a wording still harsher than Stiehl's.[22] It marked the hardening of long-standing misgivings into an official policy of restraint, an attempt to fasten the seminars to a clearly circumscribed definition of the proper role of the rural school and its teacher's corresponding station. The teachers' recent participation in "disorderly partisan efforts," the order began, had revealed attitudes "as little compatible with the duties of their office as with their outer situation." Henceforth the seminars were to emphasize "moral education" over "development of the understanding" and were to follow this no-nonsense dictum: "Particularly in regard to rural teachers, the entire emphasis is to be on insuring that the instructional sphere and life-style remain appropriate to their later lives—Nothing has a more pernicious effect on the formation of a man's character, and is more likely to provoke dissatisfaction with his profession, than habituation to forms of life, needs and intellectual habits for which the profession provides neither room nor means."[23]

The ministry set about drafting the statewide regulations that the seminars had thus far lacked. At the same time, Eichhorn, jolted by the fresh example of Breslau, revived a more radical cure: locating the seminars in rural or at least semirural settings. Despite the *Internat* the seminars had failed to protect a generation of rural teachers from the corrupting "forms of life, needs and intellectual habits" of the towns. The difficulty of finding replacements for existing town facilities paled before the need to keep future candidates in rustic incubation. In 1846 the Breslau seminar, which had been shut down as a result of Stiehl's investigation, was reopened in the small town of Löwen in Upper Silesia. Most of the inhabitants, Eichhorn informed the king, lived "in limited circumstances" and were "renowned for their sobriety and frugality." Unlike most Silesian towns, Löwen had been spared "the agitations and disorders of recent times."[24] Eichhorn planned to remove a few more seminars to quiet new homes, but the "March Days" of 1848 swept him and most of his councillors from office. The relocations had to wait upon the postrevolutionary, unabashedly conservative ministry of the early 1850s.

A NEW CORPORATISM

In 1839 the Münster section anticipated ministerial policy by bluntly reminding a group of teachers that they had chosen "a lifelong fate [*Lebenslos*] far removed from all circumstances requiring greater expenditure or making greater demands."[25] While the ministry was formulating new guidelines, however, the sections were still involved in the laborious task of implementing recent school laws. Their reaction to teachers' aspirations combined a practical fatalism about the pace of reform with a strong note of injured paternalism. Seasoned veterans, men who had entered the state administration in the teens and twenties and who had gotten its reform drive underway despite the obstacles, found themselves reproached for not doing enough. Occasionally, in fact, they were told that they had accomplished virtually nothing. In their responses to petitions the sections were not content to censure "inappropriate" demands. They lectured on the past and present realities of school reform—with markedly positive interpretations of their own income statistics and with denials of charges that local officials were violating the law. Petitioners were informed that their complaints ignored the priorities of the state budget as well as the limits of communal capacity, and in fact, by angering the communities, made the work of the state administration all the more difficult. Though improvement was necessary, it would come only if teachers trusted in higher officials' good intentions and unflagging commitment to reform.[26]

Petitions were not the only proof of teachers' ingratitude. Literary efforts in their own journals and in the general press were still more offensive to officials who were unaccustomed to the glare of publicity. One particularly goading example was an article on the "poverty" of the teaching corps published in the *Vossische Zeitung*, a major political journal, in 1842. Its author was Eduard Mücke, a young schoolteacher in Rathenow (Potsdam district), but he had managed to persuade a retired *Landrat* to affix his signature. Thus, a claim that teaching incomes had barely risen in the last three decades seemed to have official sanction. In 1827, Mücke charged on the basis of his conversations with local officials, the state commissar had trimmed the salaries for new elementary teachers in Rathenow to 160 thaler, though the magistrate had wanted to approve 200 thaler.[27] The commissar was Seminar Director and Section Councillor Ferdinand Striez, and Rathenow was one of many towns whose school reform and expansion had been his responsibility. Not content with publishing a refutation, Striez pressed for a disciplinary proceeding against Mücke that might result in his removal from office. The ministry advised him to be content with a formal warning, as it was beneath the dignity of a section councillor to attribute so much importance to an elementary teacher's complaints. Striez dredged up the protocol of his negotiations with Rathenow, which proved that he, not the city fathers, had been at the generous end of a 40-thaler difference, and had the school inspector read it to Mücke in the town hall. Having absorbed this history lesson, the young man had to admit his carelessness and promise to refrain from further public comment.[28]

Injured paternalism was typical of Prussian higher officialdom in Pre-March. In popular education, as in so many other spheres, officials in Berlin and the provincial centers had stimulated and sustained the national renewal after Jena. They constituted the *Staatsstand*, distinguished from civilian society by their expertise in public affairs and unique in their ability to balance particular interests in the service of the national welfare. Now they faced social unrest and "partisan" opposition, and, above all, grumblings on the bottom edge of the bureaucratic hierarchy. Long accustomed to guiding and indeed monopolizing reform from above, they would accept neither criticism nor participation from below and could not understand why bureaucratic tutelage seemed increasingly oppressive and less and less legitimate.[29] In 1843, Karl Mager acknowledged the "true triumph" of the state administration in popular education over the past thirty years but continued:

> The one-time guardian cannot believe that a child whom he has nurtured so carefully has become a grown young man so quickly, and indeed is already sporting a beard. It would sadden him if their existing relationship were changed even in the slightest. Also, he is a little piqued at the boy's saucy notions, since the young gentleman deigns to criticize his guardian's relations, finds something to expose here and there and above all finds fault with the meager fare with which he has to suffice. The ward is unwilling to be treated always as a child, partly because that injures his young pride (since others among his peers are their own quasi-masters), partly because he is convinced that he could improve much if his guardian would only let him.[30]

From its outset the emancipation movement was bent on a radical overhaul of the guardian-ward relationship. What happened, in the long view, was that the movement informed the term *Lehrerstand* with a dimension it had previously lacked. In teachers' appeals *Stand* assumed a mediating role as a unified corporation able to speak and act for its members. A state-created profession developed outside the estate society, elementary school teaching had not inherited the internal cohesion or the outer defenses of the artisan trades and other long-established corporations. In official usage the term *Lehrerstand* distinguished trained teachers from schoolmastery without endowing them with a corporate unity, much less a corporate will. It was simply an occupational category which, for purposes of administration, broke down into thousands of individual subordinates, each accountable to his district section, and ultimately to the ministry, through his school inspector. Since the early nineteenth century the state administration had gradually extended its supervision over these scattered subordinates with new school laws, circulars defining their responsibilities in great detail, and regular school inspections. In 1819 the ministry had introduced secret "conduct lists" for schoolteachers as well as pastors. Three years later it had assumed the right to remove them from office with an internal disciplinary proceeding (without appeal to the civil courts).[31]

In these ways the teachers had become "state servants" (*Staats-*

diener) and received the same treatment as subaltern clerks and trainees in the lower ranks of the state administration. What set them apart was both their lowly status and their extreme insecurity. The problem was not simply that they lacked state salaries; communal office of the kind stipulated in the General Code and foreseen in the Reform Era was still far from realization. From the late 1830s onward, Wander and other spokesmen protested that the teacher's dual subordination was increasingly tension ridden and increasingly intolerable at each end.[32] The "higher supervision" of the state seemed so illegitimate, and so hypocritical, because the teacher remained subject to the mediate authority of his community. Though the district section held him accountable for his work, it left him vulnerable to an indifferent, often hostile population, particularly in the countryside, and dependent on that population for his rewards. That contradiction was made all the worse by superintendents who were clergymen and devoted only part of their time to school inspection. Besides lacking pedagogical training and classroom experience, the superintendents were too distant and too occupied with ecclesiastical matters to offer effective support against the locals. In 1848, Schoolteacher Gollnisch illustrated the teachers' singular insecurity by running the entire gamut of his superiors. "Was he [the schoolteacher] a state official [*Staatsbeamter*]? That is not to be found in any law. Was he a communal official? That too has never been declared. And who are his superiors? The provincial school college, the district section, the school councillor, the superintendent and the school inspector, the pastor as local inspector, the local school committee, the headman, the mayor, the patron, the *Landrat*. All demand obedience, often contradicting each other. What a position!"[33]

One way to circumvent this morass was to pose the *Lehrerstand* as a corporate entity and demand that it be recognized as such. The dispersion of teachers over thousands of communities made that route difficult. By the 1840s, however, seminar training had created a fundament of professional consciousness and solidarity, and indeed in some regions the sections had helped sustain this *Standesbewusstsein* by sponsoring teachers' conferences. Though quick to proclaim the existence of solidarity, spokesmen realized that it had to assume organizational forms if the new profession was to overcome the contradictions of its origins. An organized *Berufsstand*, a professional corporation, would allow its members direct access to the state administration without local interference, while mediating their subordination to its higher officials. Both goals informed proposals to replace clergymen with "schoolmen," elected or at least nominated by the teachers themselves, in a new *Kreis* inspectorate.

To penetrate the state administration with this kind of corporate representation was to professionalize its supervision and, as important, to maximize its impact at the local level. In 1848, some assemblies and conferences took that penetration a step further by requesting that the higher levels of school administration, from the sections to the ministry itself, likewise be staffed by schoolmen.[34]

Since the late 1830s the emancipation movement had hoped to supplement this administrative self-regulation with both independent and official forms of corporate self-help. These evolved from the very role that its early spokesmen assumed. Hoping to excuse his public attack on higher officials in 1842, Mücke claimed that he had acted "out of love for his *Stand.*"[35] His declared hero, Wilhelm Wander, and other colleagues were the first *Standespolitiker* of a new profession. They were pioneering a role that would become acceptable in a later age of interest-group politics, but was still novel and threatening to the bureaucratic guardians of Pre-March. Though self-appointed, they dared to speak publicly for their provincial colleagues and ultimately for all schoolteachers in Prussia. Their ritualized arguments were designed to justify the emancipation of their *Stand* as a whole—with a professional inspectorate, with membership on the local school committees, and, above all, with an "appropriate" salary scale and promotion system. As Karl Böhm, perhaps the most precocious *Standespolitiker*, had written in 1837: "The state must recognize the *Lehrerstand* as a *Stand*, not as a surrogate" and must "constitute it."[36] The appeals by Wilhelm Nehm and others, Riepe wrote from Barmen two years later, represented the struggle "not of individuals but of an entire *Stand*" and "therein lies a phenomenon singular to our times."[37]

It was a small-scale phenomenon; but the collective petitions of the next few years in the Rhine Province, Westphalia, Brandenburg, and Silesia did initiate corporate self-help and assert a common will. The petitioners turned to the provincial *Landtagen* for new school legislation only after submitting their grievances directly to the district sections or the ministry. The state administration, one critic objected, had no choice but to ignore "opposition from officials pursuing personal or professional grievances." To Böhm this was "the language of the most blatant servility," implying that Prussia was a "despotism." The great discovery of the era was that strength lay in numbers: "If a hundred thousand teachers submit a petition . . . it would perhaps be deemed inadvisable to allow men who have already brought so much benefit to the state to go hungry any longer."[38] Faced with more modest petitions, the sections recognized that they were violations of normal bureaucratic procedure and summarily refused to countenance them. They responded to each signator through his school inspector and rebuked him not only for expecting too much of his community but also for bypassing it with a "corporate initiative." Any teacher who had complaints about the fees for poor children, the Düsseldorf section wrote, "must present [them] individually, and with modesty, to his school committee" (though that route had already proven a dead end). Only then, after the communal employee had turned to his "immediate superiors," might state officials intervene on his behalf.[39]

These rebuffs did not prevent the emancipation movement from advancing to a new stage of corporate self-help with voluntary associations, which were designed to enhance "consciousness" and render group pressure more effective. As early as 1829, at an officially sponsored teachers' conference in the Düsseldorf district, Diesterweg induced several participants to launch an "independent" *Verein*. The only other unoffical gatherings of teachers were the annual music festivals in some provinces. These were primarily a holiday entertainment, attended largely by older men whose common bond lay more in church music than in professional skills and concerns. Diesterweg envisioned a genuine professional association for the district, with an elected executive, local chapters, and an annual assembly. The Düsseldorf *Verein* was stillborn, but the experiment revived in the late 1830s, when the music festivals seemed to be declining for lack of interest.[40] By then there were many more seminar graduates in the field—men in the Rhineland and other regions who had already acquired the rudiments of a corporate spirit before scattering to their individual assignments.

Diesterweg and the teachers who answered his call extolled corporate self-help primarily as an "inner" road to reform. Teachers could compensate for the shortcomings of seminar training with lectures and work sessions on pedagogy and other subjects. And they need not struggle for recognition in isolation; the individual could find sustenance and develop self-confidence in the group, among his colleagues. Through association, in other words, a new profession might emancipate itself despite the continuing inadequacy of state intervention.[41] But this inner, uplifting kind of self-help was inseparable from, and often provided public camouflage for, use of the associations to formulate demands and press them upon the state administration. In June 1842, Böhm justified the establishment of a Brandenburg association by insisting that "we teachers must do something ourselves, we cannot let everything be done to us." What was needed, he reminded his audience, was "an effort to improve the outer situation of the *Stand*" as well as "intellectual emancipation."[42] A few weeks later an assembly in Berlin, attended by about 250 teachers, elected an association executive, with Diesterweg as chairman and Böhm as one of the secretaries, and scheduled an inaugural assembly for late September. Meanwhile Dyckerhoff, a Rhineland teacher, had ended his appeal for higher salaries by proposing that the teachers in the province elect five deputies, one from each district, to draft a collective petition to the king.[43]

Even the music festivals had required a paternal nod. Suspecting that the festivals might be too frivolous and expensive for the participants, the Altenstein ministry requested reports from the sections in 1835. It had been sufficiently reassured to tolerate the festivals, but only if they limited their repertoire to "ecclesiastical" and "serious" music and were held under the supervision of a seminar staff or school inspector.[44] Not surprisingly the sections were quick to forbid professional associations a few years later. When Diesterweg nonetheless sought official permission for the Brandenburg assembly on the grounds that its purpose was merely to discuss innovations in pedagogy, the ministry and the Brandenburg school college demurred. Such a large, noisy gathering, their response noted with unwitting irony, would "distract [the individual teacher] from the small communal circle in which he is called to calm, quiet, but therefore all the more useful work." Despite Diesterweg's reassurances a few participants might stray beyond pedagogy and raise the "unsuitable" or "ill-considered."[45] In January 1843 an official reporter put the matter less delicately: the "great efforts" that the state administration had launched during the Reform Era and was still carrying forward required neither assemblies nor associations.[46] Diesterweg was warned to stop meddling, and in February 1844 the Potsdam section finally moved to throttle, though not ban, the most outspoken organ of the emancipation movement, the *Preussische Volks-Schul-Zeitung*.[47]

These measures squelched the organizational efforts of the movement and kept its *Standespolitiker* relatively quiet for the next few years. But by the mid-1840s the movement had found approval in another quarter. To the liberal opposition, "association" offered an alternative to the *Bureaukratie* that was stifling the entire society. In the constitutional *Rechtstaat*, free *Vereine* would allow professional colleagues or neighbors to promote their private interests while enhancing their contribution to the general welfare. Their elected executives and open discussions would complement and provide training for citizenship under a parliamentary government. As Diesterweg put it in 1839, "The abstract, French kind of freedom, by itself, amounts to nothing," and elimination of all traditional associations (*Genossenschaften*) "brings us no benefit." He conceived of "state life" as "a living constitution, membered with occupational types and corporations."[48] In 1842, Friedrich Harkort, perhaps the most enthusiastic advocate of association in the liberal camp, forwarded a teachers' petition to the ministry; when it was rejected he drew the lesson that "emancipation" of the school could not wait upon reform "from above" and urged the teachers to achieve "unity" by electing an executive committee.[49] Karl Mager pointed to the recent veto of the Brandenburg assembly and asked why industrialists could represent themselves in associations but teachers could not. As state servants, in fact, teachers would acquire a broader perspective from the experience; rather than blame everything on their guardians, they would soon realize that neither "the other branches of the state administration" nor "communal poverty and indifference" could be ignored.[50]

While defending voluntary associations in the private sphere, Mager and other Pre-March liberals also encouraged teachers to incorporate self-help in an official form. The teaching corps, like the clergy, might elect synods to deliberate on its affairs and participate in the formulation of school policy. Here the Reformed Church of the lower Rhineland had long offered a model. After abandoning statewide plans for ecclesiastical self-administration, the Altenstein ministry had extended the synodal system to the Lutheran Churches in the Rhineland and Westphalia in 1835. By the mid-1840s, the "Friends of Light," reacting against increasingly orthodox and bureaucratic rule, were calling for synods as the keystone of a "constitutional" reform of the established churches.[51] Heinrich Deinhardt, like Diesterweg and Mager, saw no reason why teachers should not enjoy a similar kind of representation. Only synods, he argued, would replace "mechanicalness" with a "living organism" and thus end the "head-on opposition between the state administration and its subordinates."[52]

In 1848 self-help and association finally achieved legitimacy in a constitutional monarchy. Veteran and new *Standespolitiker* responded to the March Revolution by holding assemblies in Berlin, Düsseldorf, Breslau, Erfurt, and several other provincial centers. Their hope was that teachers' petitions to the upcoming national assembly would prevail over other, often hostile interests in the framing of constitutional provisions and a state law for the elementary schools. On May 31, probably at Diesterweg's suggestion, a liberal ministry provided for a corporate expression of opinion in *Kreis* elections and provincial conferences of delegates. At the *Kreis* level the *Landrat* presided and the state inspectors attended, and the provincial conferences included district and provincial school officials as well as seminar directors. This official presence may have inhibited discussion, but did not prevent teachers' delegates from submitting detailed and far-reaching reform programs.[53] Like the spring assemblies, they called for officially sponsored "school synods" at the *Kreis* and provincial levels, perhaps capped by annual or biannual assemblies. These were modeled on the church synods, with seats for "laymen" as well as "schoolmen"; but their primary purpose was to guarantee the schoolmen professional representation and perhaps even legislative power.[54] In Silesia, Westphalia, and several other provinces elected committees had already begun to organize voluntary associations so as to buttress the synods in that role and to draw as many teachers as possible into the corporate movement.[55] Even in the new era, the organizing committee in the Rhine Province explained in early 1849, a provincial association was indispensable: it would prepare "a secure basis for the effectiveness of the teachers' deputies" (i.e., to the synods).[56]

In March 1849, Diesterweg, acting as chairman of the new "General Teachers' Association of Berlin," proposed that provincial representatives convene in the capital to inaugurate a national association for Prussia or perhaps all of Germany.[57] By then the Prussian revolution had collapsed, and the emancipation movement did not survive the subsequent reaction. But the movement set a precedent for later generations of schoolteachers who did succeed in establishing associations. What mattered in Pre-March was that schoolteachers, though better off than schoolmasters, had not escaped a peculiarly dependent kind of communal employment. At the same time, as products of reform from above, they were increasingly subject to arbitrary bureaucratic supervision. Their official demi-world combined extreme vulnerability to both local society and the state. In reaction the emancipation movement did not try to reincarnate the forms of group solidarity and self-protection that had characterized an estate society. It had not inherited those forms, and in any case its very goals required a different social and political structure. Whereas traditional corporatism had fixed the legal ranks that were, as a rule, inherited, association assumed a framework of legal equality. The latter was more appropriate for a movement that represented a new occupation, outside the estate ranks, and wanted to make it a vehicle of upward mobility.

Likewise the movement could hardly replace one kind of hierarchical coercion with another, internal kind. Membership in the new *Vereine* was voluntary, and both the *Vereine* and the synods were intended to exemplify democratic representation and procedures. As the authors of the Tivoli petition explained, a national parliament would not suffice; the principle of "representation" must prevail in every *Stand*, since "any *Stand* which does not incorporate the constitutional element will harden into monarchic dictatorship despite the general state constitution."[58] In these senses, Diesterweg and his disciples were pioneering a new corporatism that promised the advantages of the old but would realize a distinctly liberal ideal.

Seven

1848: STATUS AND IDEOLOGY

To the liberals of Pre-March and 1848, associations promised to perpetuate the benefits of corporate life while transcending its historic disadvantages. As intermediate units they would buffer the individual against both social chaos and the political despotism that might accompany it, and thus, in Adolph Diesterweg's phrase, avoid an "abstract, French kind of freedom." But associations were also an alternative to castelike selfishness. In a newly constituted society they would reconcile private self-interest with the public welfare, and indeed in a way that would insure the promotion of the latter.[1]

To judge by its rhetoric, the emancipation movement exemplified this ideal. What was at stake, its spokesmen argued, was not simply or even primarily the rights of a new profession. Teachers wanted to escape "poverty" and "dependence" so that they could fulfill their unique and vital public mission. In 1848 the emphasis remained, but the argument shifted to an ideological level. In speeches, journal articles, and petitions to the ministry and national assembly the movement profiled an emancipated teaching corps as the guarantor of political democracy and national unity.

But the emancipation movement differed from traditional corporatism more in perspective than in priorities. While other groups defended historic rights by appealing to a vanishing past, the movement tried to justify new ones in a postrevolutionary future. Its spokesmen in 1848 formulated an ideological rationale for status aspirations. As it had been in Pre-March, the central objective was to reposition the teacher, and particularly the rural teacher, at the intersection of community and state. If the movement assumed a radical posture, it was also flexible and selective in appropriating liberal ideals. Its *Standespolitik* underscores the need to trace the tensions in German liberalism back to the interests of constituent groups.[2]

COMMUNITY, STATE, AND NATION

What was the proper relationship between the local community and its children's instructor? Should the teacher be accountable to parents and local officials, and if so in what form and to what degree? These questions had been central to school reform from its outset— whether the issue was elimination of the school fee and other traditional endowments, the procedure for appointing teachers, or the role of the pastor and school committee. Particularly in the small, familiar communities of the countryside the typical arrangements for school support had kept the schoolmasters bound to local priorities and cultural norms. Since the late eighteenth century reformers had decried this kind of accountability; but attempts to establish a tax-based salary, the most solid foundation for an independent teaching office, had succumbed to political and fiscal caution. By the 1840s the practical obstacles had not disappeared; indeed, they seemed more imposing in view of rapid population growth, the spread of poverty, and the resulting drain on communal finances.

In Pre-March, conservatives and likeminded school officials who hoped to enlist popular education for their own purposes turned the unavoidable necessity of the teacher's dependence into a virtue. It was the liberals who sponsored the unfinished business of the early nineteenth century. To call for a new reform drive, however, was not necessarily to approve a drastic, jolting reversal of teacher-community relations. Heinrich Deinhardt, the same liberal who defended teachers' right to representation in associations and synods, objected to their appeals for advancement through state appointment. The elementary schools, he argued, were not comparable to the high schools, which were "in the state service" and were "the conscious continuation of the *Stände* with a self-conscious unity transcending the local boundary of communal life." More than any other communal official, in fact, the schoolteacher "needs trust in his moral character and must enter a friendly relationship with his community if his work is not to be hampered." Since the community had to approve an "entire personality," appointment could not be reduced to a simple reward for professional achievement.[3] School reform had always acknowledged Deinhardt's objection, at least implicitly. Ultimately, enlightenment was a matter of popular conversion; the teacher might only provoke resistance if he faced his community as a man completely apart, as an outside agent rather than as a neighbor. Thus a new profession had to accept a degree of social ambiguity, outside the ranks of true *Staatsstände*; in Deinhardt's words, its work would become "independent, free and satisfying" only if it occupied an "intermediate position between community and state authority."[4]

Deinhardt ignored the more pressing reason why most liberals continued to regard the elementary school primarily as a communal institution. The Reform Era had combined a new centralization with an attempt to promote local initiative and responsibility. With the Municipal Law of 1808 the towns had received a limited but nonetheless significant measure of control over their internal affairs. The new school committees in both town and country were intended to make the lower school one of the most important communal institutions. In Pre-March there was little enthusiasm for this gift of "self-administration," if only because it brought new financial burdens without producing new revenues. But by the 1840s liberal merchants, industrialists, and professional men—many of them frustrated by their participation in municipal government—were blaming the "official caste" for the economic and political stagnation of Prussia. *Bureaukratie*, with its arbitrary and stifling tutelage, had to accede to constitutional government, and a national parliament, by itself, did not guarantee the transition. The new *Rechtstaat* required a pyramid of intermediate organs, staffed by elected representatives rather than salaried officials, from the communal to the provincial level.[5]

In a review of Wilhelm Wander's *Die Volksschule als Staatsanstalt*, Karl Mager, a moderate liberal, explained the role of popular education in this scenario. Mager was unwilling to blame the bureaucracies for all the "inconveniences" and "conflicts" of the transition to representative monarchies. If the bureaucracies were allowed to exercise "absolute tutelage," that reflected a "fault in the popular character." The problem was that "the people" preferred that their state serve as "the master of a thousand arts, the witch doctor who can and should do everything," and would only resent the responsibilities and problems attendant upon true freedom. As for Wander, he glorified officialdom as the "source of intellectual life," the "distilled essence" of a dumb "pile of potatoes," because he was infatuated with the "Hegelian misconception" of the state as a "moral universal." In that conception the elementary school system was reduced to a "philanstère" or "intelligence factory," its managers directing production from the capital and provincial centers and its teacher-foremen delivering "no wares but those conforming to the sample sent down from above." Though Mager did not approve of democracy, his point was that self-administration, essential to the exercise of freedom, must extend to the school and its teacher, even if that handicapped or at least postponed concrete improvements that were long overdue. Decrees can be "implemented in a few weeks," but "the people's own effort has something lasting" and "provides a school for moral and political education that is completely lacking to a people ruled by ordinances."[6]

In 1848 political principle was reinforced by fiscal realism; both required that elementary school policy be tailored to a new communal law instituting self-administration. On June 23, Count von Schwerin, the new minister of culture, summarized ministerial plans before the national assembly. His message was that education must be "linked primarily" to the community and "only when the powers of the community no longer suffice may the state enter with its central power." Aside from the principle at stake, he noted, the state simply could not afford the nearly one million thaler needed to salary about thirty thousand teachers at a sufficient level.[7] The full assembly never debated school provisions for a new constitution, but in the fall of 1848 its central committee completed a draft that elaborated Schwerin's formula. The draft eliminated the school fee and included a state guarantee of a "definite, sufficient salary"; but school support was to be a communal responsibility, with state aid promised only in cases of proven incapacity. Likewise, the communities were assigned the management of "external affairs" and the selection of teachers.[8]

The liberal commitment to self-administration coexisted, often in considerable tension, with continued reliance on the state bureaucracy to impose reforms.[9] Indeed to Adolph Diesterweg, the mentor of the emancipation movement, the urgent need for reform from above precluded even a minimum of local autonomy in popular education. Unlike Mager, Diesterweg was a working schoolman who often styled himself a *Volksschullehrer*. His formula for a liberal school policy derived from his experience in seminar training and his empathy for graduates in the field. Since the late 1820s, Diesterweg had indicted Prussian communities for their neglect of the schools and their stubborn refusal to abandon the stereotype of schoolmastery. Echoing the complaints of his graduates, he portrayed the trained teacher as a helpless victim under the existing conditions of communal employment. The problem was that state-sponsored reform had stopped halfway; it must now proceed to the creation of a thoroughly centralized school system.[10]

In late July 1848, Diesterweg and twenty-one assembly deputies published a draft of school provisions. The wording was moderate, though flexible enough to allow a marked advance in state centralization.[11] In the spring the major teachers' assemblies had approved less compromising reform programs, and in the summer the provincial conferences confirmed their most important details. Included were reforms of local school administration, designed to remove obstacles and provide leverage *within* the community. As a voting member of the school committee the teacher would escape subordination to uneducated laymen and have a forum to explain the "needs" of his school. Elimination of the local inspectorate spelled an end to the pastors' degrading tutelage and obstructive authority in school administration. With rare exceptions, however, the assemblies and conferences demanded "elevation" of the *Volksschule* to a "state institution" in the strict sense. The state administration, not the communities, was to provide every teacher with an "appropriate" salary, without the school fee and the sextonship, and guarantee him an increment every five or ten years. Pensioners and teachers' widows deserved support from state funds. The communities could fill vacancies only with candidates already selected by the sections; their traditional power of appointment was incompatible with a merit-based system of advancement.[12] Though these proposals sometimes were prefaced with assurances of communal "participation" in the new era,[13] their implications were clear enough. By virtue of salary and appointment every teacher, from the smallest village to the capital, would be a full-fledged state official (*Staatsbeamter*) in a branch of the national bureaucracy.

The very raison d'etre of the emancipation movement explains its lack of substantial concessions to communal self-administration. What mattered was the record of local neglect and its accompanying social injuries. Even in the capital and other larger towns the extreme economy of school support had deprived seminar graduates of a "middle-class" life-style and frustrated their career ambitions. In the countryside communal employment had meant the sextonship, the school fee and its entanglements in local poverty, inadequate arrangements for firewood and other details, and pastors and school committeemen who had, at best, failed to shield teachers from these indignities. Because state-sponsored reform had lagged so far behind teachers' expectations, the emancipation movement preferred to abandon its middle road and to leap over the communal office that had long been planned and was now promised in a new constitution. Particularly in rural communities, the conference in *Kreis* Henneberg (Rhine Province) explained, many teachers had been reduced to "fawning subservience" (*Kriecherei*) as communal employees. They had "felt only too deeply the immeasurably harmful effect of local authorities on the work and character of the teacher, and the teacher's unworthy relationship to those authorities in view of their usually lower educational level."[14] The same experience led a group of Silesian teachers to petition the ministry for state salaries in late November 1849, a year after the revolution had collapsed. Their fear was that their communities, which still regarded the school as an unwanted "burden," would now harden in old habits. If the *Volksschule* were placed in the "strong hands of the state," however, "our dependence on the communities, and the many unpleasantries to which we are subject, would cease, and our work would be much more successful. . . . Facing our present situation and the hopeless future if our dependence on the communities remains, we are filled with despair. Even if Your Excellency has the most powerful will to improve our situation, he will fail in view of the force of circumstances, and when the community is forced to provide a raise in salary the poor teacher will be the object of hatred and persecution."[15]

If state office would bring obvious benefits to the teachers, it was justified above all as the necessary platform for their public mission. In Pre-March *Standespolitiker* had simply extended the logic of school reform since the late eighteenth century. In 1844, Richard Baron, a Silesian teacher, began his essay on "making the *Volksschule* a popular affair" with the admission that the school was still a burden to the people, aiming far higher than they could understand. He drew the standard conclusion: the state—if it was finally to "raise" the people to the proper level—had to guarantee its teachers "as much independence as possible."[16] Baron did not specify the route to "independence," but others had already argued that any kind of dependence on the local population, even in the form of a fixed communal salary, would handicap the teacher in his efforts to lift an ignorant, resistant population to his own enlightened level. In view of the vital contribution of the teaching corps to public morality and welfare, Böhm had written, it was "the most necessary of all *Stände*," and was particularly deserving of state office. "Imagine a school," he had concluded, "whose teachers are emancipated, with incomes appropriate to their work and not dependent on the community; how much could be accomplished in it!"[17]

The "March Days" allowed the emancipation movement to shift from reform logic to revolutionary ideology without fear of official retaliation. The mission of the teaching corps was no longer to enlighten the natives in the traditional sense but to realize and secure the democratic, unitary nation-state that a reluctant king had just promised and the national assembly was in the process of legislating. Nearly four decades earlier Emmanuel Kriegskotte had anticipated the new theme by arguing that the modern schoolteacher needed state office to escape his predecessors' "slave mentality" and to educate his community to freedom.[18] In the spring of 1848 Kriegs-kotte was echoed by Theodor Hegener, another precocious West-phalian teacher, in an article on "the educational issue from a demo-cratic and national standpoint." To Hegener the decisive point was not the teachers' right to a new "independence" and "dignity," but the state's obligation to enable its citizens to exercise their newly-won political rights. As a state-salaried official the teacher would be a local agent of the new regime, protecting his community from the seductions of both "anarchy" and "reaction or partisan efforts," and above all preventing education from raising "one segment of the population . . . to aristocratic arrogance, the other to the slavish feel-ing of subordination."[19] Likewise, Schoolteacher Gollnisch, the key-note speaker at the Silesian provincial conference, saw no need to dwell on professional self-interest. The crux of the matter was that the teachers' "completely insecure" and "unworthy" position would be a disadvantage to the people in a constitutional state. "I ask: can the free state's demand for a national education of its citizens—for their development into a people worthy of, and able to preserve, free-dom—be realized without a unified, independent *Volksschule*? Can un-free teachers, dependent and hamstrung in so many ways, edu-cate a free people?"[20]

To Gollnisch and other spokesmen political democracy and na-tional unity were inseparable. To emphasize the latter, in fact, the Silesian teachers' assembly of April 1848 and the later provincial conference defined the *Volksschule* as a "national" rather than as a "state" institution. One of its requirements was a uniform cur-riculum, transmitting the national heritage. The other was a state corps of schoolteachers, free to integrate popular culture into a new whole—into a German or at least Prussian cultural and political unity—despite the stubborn particularism of local life. To be sure, Gollnisch argued, teachers did not aspire to become a "school gen-darmerie"; but if the teaching corps was to serve the "communities of the free state," its place belonged between "the nation and its youth," not "under the tutelage and arbitrary power of communal officials."[21] The conference in *Kreis* Henneberg had claimed the same intermediate—or, better, transcendent—role in its petition to the ministry. The *Volksschule* must become a "state institution in every aspect of its administration" (including teaching salaries and appointments) so that it could cultivate "German nationality" rather than "the most petty kind of particularism."

> The unity of Germany remains a dream if the children are
> not raised for it and inflamed with it. For that reason the

teacher must stand over, not under, his community. Do not misunderstand us—particularly in rural communities he must be the band which ties the constituent parts to the great whole, and in every way keeps them in living communion. Therein we see the great and sublime mission of the *Volks-schule*, and therefore we demand that the teacher be a state servant—i.e., nothing other than the band between the individual and the whole.[22]

Thus *Standespolitik* bypassed communal self-administration with appeals to liberalism's most far-reaching goals. Although the mission of the teaching corps had changed, it was still to play a strategic role in a state-centralized reform from above. On the one hand, the emancipation movement was reminding the Prussian public, and above all the legislators, that political democracy and national unity were experiments in grave danger. But its ultimate defense was that the March Revolution had already made the dream a reality. The teaching corps could enter the state bureaucracy without becoming a "school gendarmerie," Gollnisch reasoned, because the state *was* the nation. Since a national, democratic parliament had superseded the bureaucratic despotism of the old regime, there could no longer be any fear that the *Volksschule* would "keep the people dumb and enslaved."[23] As a later speaker put it, the administration was "no more than the mandator of the people"; its duty was simply to "execute the popular will."[24] Hegener had given this logic its most elaborate and idealistic expression.

So long as the state consisted of a caste of officials, and the population were only state subjects, popular instruction was a tool against popular freedom, like everything else—and indeed all the more so as the state took it in hand and managed it according to its principles. Thus the wish at that time could only be that the school system be exclusively a communal matter . . . and it was quite right to warn the teachers against being accepted into the ranks of the army of state officialdom. But today everything is quite different. The officials are no longer the people's wardens, but rather its servants; laws and governmental policy will flow from the popular will; in short, the state is the people itself. Where then is the danger if the state manages popular education? One may object: the situation could change, we still are not protected against a reaction, and if it comes the centralized school system will be a tool in the hands of despotism. But this weakhearted and faithless objection, if it were to be accepted, would make doubtful, and hinder, many other splendid innovations and establishments which justify [*bezwecken*] the power of the state. Believe in freedom and trust in its survival![25]

Depending on the context, democracy was a precarious experiment, an accomplished fact, or an article of faith that could withstand any test. The rhetoric juggled the present and future of a political ideal. In the process it ignored the reality of a bureaucratic state that had not been toppled and was scheduled to retain a central role in postrevolutionary Prussia. Moreover, reaction was not the only potential problem. Would the teacher-cum-*Staatsbeamter*—even if he believed in "popular sovereignty" or the "national will"—avoid resentment as an outside agent, as one more arbitrary official? Would his work seem any less foreign or draconian to the community, particularly if he threatened to violate its traditional values?

The point is not that *Standespolitik* involved a conscious use of ideology as a camouflage. The ideology was a naive (and unoriginal) but sincere adaptation; it was based on the conviction that political progress and professional emancipation were overdue and henceforth must reinforce each other. Yet the lesson that informed virtually every plea for independence was that professional status was a function of power over the public. Representing men who had been deprived of power, the emancipation movement sought as much of it as the state, with its salaries and immediate, overriding authority, could offer. To award the teacher with that kind of professional status was to exempt him from accountability to his community, even in a modern, liberal form. The underlying paradox of *Standespolitik* was that the teacher could educate his community to "freedom" only if he was free of its control.

The failure of the revolution meant that emancipation, in this radical sense, was impossible. But it had become apparent in 1848 that a reactionary bureaucracy was not the only obstacle. In the liberal movement sympathy for the teachers' aspirations was offset by objections to state centralization, and there remained the awesome problem of financing sufficient incomes for nearly thirty thousand men. To judge by its plans the liberal regime might not have offered teachers any more than they received from its successors. The school provisions of the "decreed" constitution that followed the dissolution of the national assembly in December 1848 were not reactionary. Although confirming communal responsibility for school support, in fact, they also maintained the state guarantee of a "definite, sufficient" teaching salary and added that teachers had "the rights of state servants." The constitution of January 31, 1850, specified "duties" as well as "rights" and changed the salary promise to a "secure income measured to local conditions."[26] If the latter formula invited abuse, it also acknowledged the practical limits to communal support and state subsidies that the revolution had not overcome.

THE TEACHERS AND THE PEOPLE

The "entirely natural and unsurprising result" of "higher education" in a seminar, a graduate had explained in 1844, was that the modern teacher rose above "the circles to which he perhaps belonged by birth." His dilemma was that he could not "feel comfortable" among peasants and farmer-townsmen but lacked the credentials to enter the "middle-class" ranks.[27] In appeals for emancipation upward mobility became a right the state owed its wards, not a privilege it could limit, or indeed postpone, as it pleased. It was precisely because *Standespolitiker* were so convinced of that right that they discussed their own and their colleagues' deprivations with such blatant snobbishness. In 1846, for example, a Silesian contributor complained that the teachers' "personal" legal status kept them on a par with the lower classes and forced them to endure insults from apprentices' wives in court. His conclusion was that they should be made "equal to other educated men" by joining the *Eximierten*— that is, those exempt from local and regional jurisdiction. Factory owners and artists, he admitted, did not enjoy that privilege; but they were already assured a higher regard before the law as members of the "higher" *Bürgerstand*.[28] In 1848 the emancipation movement clearly repudiated this kind of elitism by committing itself to legal and political equality. More common had been blunt remarks about the private wounds of status deprivation, and particularly about teachers' "mismarriages." In the countryside, a Silesian graduate had complained in 1844, the teachers' marriage prospects were limited to "farm servants" who were willing to "clear the dung out of the barn" and "plough the field." To marry an "educated girl" was to court disaster.[29] "Do you know what it is like," Dyckerhoff asked the educated public, "to have a wife whose eyes light up only when the talk comes round to the most banal subjects, who remains dead when heartfelt matters should be stirring within her?"[30]

Teachers who missed intellectual stimulation at home were probably glad to entrust domestic management to sober, practical housewives. If they appreciated their wives, however, they could not reconcile themselves to a "public" that regarded the modern school as a useless burden and refused to acknowledge their professional credentials. Their resentment was sometimes tempered by understanding of the economic plight of the lower orders. However, they stereotyped their neighbors, and particularly the countrymen, as a woefully ignorant, materialistic, and even malicious lot. That stereotype informed pleas for state office in 1848 and assumed more or less explicit form in teachers' complaints about parental disregard for their authority, the countrymen's tenacious use of the sextonship and other indignities, the uselessness or downright vindictiveness of school committees. To emancipate the profession meant to impose social distance and erect protective barriers between the teachers and the people they had to serve.

In the logic of *Standespolitik* negative images coexisted with an abstract ideal of "the people" (*das Volk*). The same population that was blocking professional emancipation was also its indispensable justification and had to serve as its lever. In that sense, Richard Baron, having admitted popular indifference to the school's "higher aims," did not hesitate to remind the rich and educated that "the people in the mass is and remains the basis of all intellectual, social and political life in the state, and with the basis stands or falls the whole."[31] The lower orders, though ignorant and selfish in their present state, were still innately capable of enlightenment. Despite its indictment of an unappreciative public, in fact, the emancipation movement sometimes claimed to represent pressure from below. The modern teacher needed a higher education, a Rhineland petition argued in 1847, because "our people strive after a more complete education and must strive after it."[32]

In 1848 the masses' potential for enlightenment became their capacity to exercise the rights and responsibilities of political democracy. An ideological leap, an abstraction still more distant from the concrete stereotype, offered a creative solution to the teachers' status dilemma. Professional and popular emancipation were to enter into a radical alliance in postrevolutionary Prussia. Though the alliance conveniently ignored past performance, it also justified teachers' more extreme status claims by committing them and their schools unreservedly to the cause of popular freedom. As Gollnisch argued at the Silesian conference, the schoolteachers—aside from their professional right to independence—needed that independence to develop "a people worthy of and able to preserve freedom." A few months earlier, C. Felde, a teacher in Province Saxony, had offered this near utopian vision of a democratic state to justify emancipation: "A new *Volksschule*, constructed in the spirit of our era, will be a cornerstone for a *Reich* in which no more mob [*Pöbel*] is to be found. True popular education is the foundation on which our German state structure must be established. Without it true peace is no longer possible in the world. . . . No God can bless conditions in which only a very small part of the nation can raise itself to human consciousness, while the great crowd is raised like cows, and lives and dies like cows."[33]

In the wake of the "March Days" Berlin teachers had blueprinted a more radical alliance between the teaching corps and the people, offering higher returns to both parties. Their Tivoli petition had been drafted by Eduard Hintze, a Potsdam graduate who taught in the Berlin seminar and, like its director, considered himself a *Volksschullehrer*. In a lecture before colleagues in 1844, Hintze had omitted the usual complaints about teachers' poverty and other sufferings, and had demonstrated a theoretical range not evident among most *Standespolitiker*. It was no accident, he began, that the educational system had evolved into a "state institution"; that reflected the "innermost essence" of a "free state," within which each of the three estates—production, defense, and teaching—included "practical" as well as "theoretical" professions. Hintze numbered elementary school teachers among the "practical," though noting that their seminars differed from the academic schools in function rather than rank. Though the system remained to be perfected, there was no reason for impatience or discouragement. The "world spirit" (*Weltgeist*) took its own course and its "coming to consciousness" could not be hurried; but a "rational development toward freedom" was inexorable.[34]

This young Hegelian was too enamored of dialectical theory, or at least too fearful of the official reaction, to bother with the institutional and social realities still blocking a "rational development toward freedom." In 1848, Hintze abandoned his faith in the world spirit for radical activism. "The revolution is at an end," he announced in the preamble to his draft petition, but "the reformation must begin," and "now or never the teaching corps must prove that it is entitled to be the bearer of popular intelligence."[35] Hintze envisioned a thorough overhaul of the social structure as well as the political system in Prussia. His tool was, appropriately enough, a reorganization of the school system, designed to establish at last an "organic" unity between elementary and academic education. That goal justified and indeed necessitated Hintze's most radical proposal: elimination of the seminars in favor of a university education for *all* teachers. Abandoning a functional division, he now wrote that a "higher education that could perpetuate itself only in the estates in actual possession of money or other exterior privileges" had been "a disastrous sin against the popular spirit." Only by creating an "equally trained *Stand* of teachers" would the state guarantee "an equal level of intelligence . . . to the younger generation in all its branches" and thus allow every citizen "to achieve a position adequate to his talents."[36]

Hintze's draft was revised by a twelve-man committee, including both municipal and private school teachers in Berlin. The committee not only accepted his scheme for an "organically" united system with an "equally trained" teaching corps but also completed his assault on academe by denying that "the classical languages could be . . . the foundation [*Hauptfundament*] of a German education." More important, it proposed to guarantee a "uniform instruction" to all by transferring the entire cost of education, including teachers' salaries, from local to state hands. "The school will become a matter of the state in the most far-reaching sense. Therefore all religious, confessional, patronal and communal privileges must fall. . . . But the costs of [school] support also belong to the state, since instruction must be the same for all. Talent, not the accident of property, must determine the future life course [*Lebensrichtung*]; and poverty can be eradicated only through intelligence and morality, which no one in the state can be denied the possibility of achieving a priori."[37]

With this rationale for state centralization the Tivoli petition advanced from political democracy to equality of opportunity. A school system that had helped perpetuate the rigidities of the Prussian social hierarchy would now institutionalize widespread social mobility. That kind of radicalism was rare in the liberal camp; even left-wing democrats tended to assume that a political revolution would suffice to eliminate, or at least lessen, social injustice. But the emancipation movement claimed to represent men who had been, by social origin as well as professional function, in a unique position to understand how the schools had separated the ranks of *Bildung* and *Besitz* from the vast majority. Seminar graduates recruited among the lower orders had had to return to "lower" or "popular" schools which, despite the principle of "general education" that survived the Reform Era, had neither institutional nor curricular links with the *Gymnasien* and universities. They had found painful confirmation of that reality in their own careers; their diplomas relegated them to a status far below academic teachers and forced them to accept the tutelage of pastors in their professional domain. In that sense, Hintze and the Berlin committee had distilled their radicalism from the experience of their profession: they were generalizing from the status dilemma of the teacher as well as from the fate of his pupils. Even if the teaching corps were emancipated, they had concluded, its recruits did not wish to enjoy upward mobility as a state-sponsored exception. In postrevolutionary Prussia a state-salaried, university-educated corps would make equality of opportunity the rule and thereby extend its own hard-won right to all talented sons of the lower orders.

Approximately three hundred teachers attended the Tivoli assembly and approved the petition. However, many of them may not have realized its more extreme implications. In any case the Tivoli petition, though often hailed in later months, did not become the rule of *Standespolitik*. Other spring assemblies and later conferences dubbed the *Volksschule* a "state" or "national" institution and insisted on free instruction; but they limited their reforms to elementary instruction, without daring to institutionalize an organic unity between their own preserve and academe. As for teacher training, it would achieve a modest academic status if candidates completed a regular high school course and the seminar itself was reformed. Elimination of the *Internat*, perhaps combined with the transfer of all seminars to larger towns, would suffice to provide candidates with the "freedom" to cultivate attributes of an "educated man." More important, the seminar curriculum was to be broader and more "scholarly"—though most programs also reflected teachers' retrospective appreciation for the practical side of seminar training.[38] At the Brandenburg conference several delegates who supported Hintze's proposal regarded a university education as a status credential that guaranteed the teacher an "equal birthright" with clergymen and other educated men rather than as a tool of popular emancipation. Several others objected that academic learning was superfluous: the schoolroom required practical skills rather than scholarship. Indeed, echoing the founders of the seminars, one delegate warned that the university-educated schoolteacher would become a perpetual malcontent in the countryside. Hintze came up with a compromise formula that won majority approval but hardly did justice to his original ideal. The "educational institutions" for *Volksschullehrer* would insure both "a complete, free, and scholarly education" and "practical competence" and would accept only graduates of higher *Bürgerschule* and *Gymnasien*. But they were to be "modeled on" (*angelehnt an*), not incorporated into, the universities.[39]

According to the instructions from the ministry, the provincial conferences had to limit proposals to their own branch of the school system. Nonetheless, the draft committee at the Silesian conference requested that the *Volksschule*, as a "national" institution, be "organically united to all the educational institutions of the nation." Co-Rector Ewig was not satisfied with appeals to national unity and popular freedom and protested that the committee had implicitly kept the elementary schools separate from the *Gymnasien*. To him "scholarship" was a "property of the people" and therefore should be "more accessible to the people." Lacking concrete proposals, Ewig could only state his preference for an "organically structured whole from the lowest to the highest educational institutions." The committee, Gollnisch responded, had considered but rejected a broader phrasing; its conviction was that "we should remain within the sphere of activity in which we have belonged and grown until now." Although Ewig's language was "excellent in the abstract," he continued, his ideal was "beyond our capacity" and "we must put aside such thoughts if we do not wish to expose ourselves to the charge of immoderation."[40]

In 1848 the emancipation movement proved radical in that it appropriated left-wing, democratic liberalism. But the Berlin teachers had wanted it to draw the social implications of a political revolution. Gollnisch's point was that that kind of idealism, unlike his own, might endanger the very purpose of *Standespolitik* by branding the teaching corps an extremist element in its own camp.[41] Thanks to one naive listener, he had had to spell out the tactical reservation that most *Standespolitiker* left unsaid. An alliance with "the people" made strategic sense, but had to remain a means to an end. In this case the fusion of professional self-interest and liberal ideology was both radical and limited.

CONCLUSION

In 1854 the Prussian Ministry of Culture issued three *Regulative* for the Protestant elementary schools and their seminars. Their author was Ferdinand Stiehl, the former seminar director who had drafted the cabinet order of 1845. Stiehl had survived the change of regime in 1848 and now, in the post-1848 reaction, completed the crackdown of the Eichhorn ministry with a vengeance. The *Regulative* translated conservative ideology into a new formula for popular education, which replaced "general education" with a heavy dosage of orthodox piety and conditioning for manual labor. Seminar training shrank accordingly; it was not only explicitly denuded of any academic ornamentation but also confined to the needs of a one-class rural school.[1]

In later decades the *Regulative* were condemned as a particularly unfortunate example of the reaction that gripped Prussia after 1848. Yet the irony in the long view is that they did not resolve the basic tension in reform from above: the state had neither abandoned the seminars nor forced the pace of local reform. In the 1860s and 1870s, the climate of national unification and the example of other professions encouraged a new generation of seminar graduates to revive the emancipation appeal. They also returned to corporative self-help; by 1900, Prussian teachers were represented by well-organized provincial associations, complete with elected executives and official newspapers, and formed the largest contingent in an *Allgemeiner Deutscher Lehrerverein*.

A society and political system that had still been markedly traditional in 1848 was distinctly modern by 1900. In the second half of the nineteenth century elementary school teaching, reflecting the general demographic shift, became a predominantly urban occupation. The towns advanced well ahead of the countryside in school reform, but also added complications to the issue of emancipation. Teachers now had to find an appropriate niche in the social hierarchies of large cities and achieve professional independence in their vast, increasingly bureaucratized school systems. At the same time the teaching corps became another interest group in a new arena of party politics. Although the industrial working class may have been less hostile than the countrymen, its Social Democratic party posed the challenge of mass politics on the left. Teachers' associations had to adapt to this context; even if they did not abandon the ideological goals of the activists in 1848, they had more reason to fear revolution and appreciate the advantages of the status quo. A recent study concludes that the "revolutionary pathos" of the earlier emancipation struggle was reduced to "the memory of a heroic phase" from the 1870s onward. Though *Standesideologie* retained a "socially progressive aspect," it was "clearly conservative" in its emphasis on "political reliability" and "national loyalty" and defined teachers as "natural enemies of Socialism and Social Democracy."[2]

For the century encompassed by this study, distinctions between "traditional" and "modern" are unavoidable but ultimately too neat. In the mid-eighteenth century social reality already defied the legal anatomy of Prussia. An elaborate bureaucratic state, superimposed on the corporate hierarchy, was becoming aware of its structural tensions and weaknesses. The estate society gradually succumbed to social and political change in the nineteenth century; but in 1848 the development of an industrial-urban society and a mass political system had hardly begun. By then a reform of popular education had been central to state policy for over a half century. Conceived as a tool of popular enlightenment, it acquired a new urgency as a key to national renewal. In this project, as in so many others, the Prussian state administration pursued limited objectives with inadequate means. The Reform Era marked a brief, tentative departure from a policy whose tortuous via media was to modernize society and state without undermining their basic structures. Though the principle of "general education" survived the era, in fact, state policy came full circle with the prescription of the Eichhorn ministry for rural education and seminar training in the 1840s.

The underlying continuity lay in the failure of the state administration to impose the financial burdens and social-institutional reforms that a modern elementary school and teaching office required. In Pre-March the failure was particularly evident in the countryside, but it extended to the towns, where its consequences were exacerbated by the rapid, makeshift expansion of teaching staffs. By the 1840s the seminar experiment had backfired, or at least had proven ill timed, because two kinds of state intervention were out of joint. In both town and country the expectations of trained teachers, recruited and dispatched by the state, far outstripped the pace of local reform. But although painfully slow, this reform represented an obvious commitment, and it advanced far enough to sustain seminar graduates' expectations and give them a clear direction. In that regard France provides an instructive variant. In the mid-nineteenth century the French government followed the Prussian lead by establishing normal schools, but was far less willing to draw the schools into its jurisdiction. As a result rural *instituteurs* could not hope to win recognition simply as professional teachers; they had to improve their status indirectly, particularly as communal clerks buffering their villages against outside forces of change.[3] Long after the emancipation movement got underway, Prussian seminar graduates likewise had to adapt to communal stubbornness and make do with some kind of semiprofessional status. What remains striking is that the movement, from its outset, pursued a kind and degree of emancipation that allowed for little compromise. A reform agenda that may have been unrealistic, particularly in financial terms, nonetheless seemed the logical culmination of state intervention.

Conservative critics who gave this story an ideological twist at least laid the responsibility where it belonged. A few years after the March Revolution, Wilhelm Heinrich Riehl condemned the "leveling police state" for its assault on the corporate life and "particularist" values of the peasant estate. Its most devastating weapon was the modern schoolteacher, who often became "the evil demon, the Mephistopheles of the fallen peasant."[4] Riehl exaggerated both the helplessness of the victim and the power of the demon; to judge by local reception of school reform and teachers' sense of helplessness, the countrymen were remarkably successful in resisting an intrusion on their resources and sociocultural priorities. Aside from lamenting their impact, however, Riehl singled out the schoolteachers as the embodiment of a new type and mentality. In his social topography the "proletariat of intellectual labor," like the proletariat of manual labor, marked the disintegration of an estate society into a chaotic mass. What made its members particularly dangerous was their "overeducation," which produced pretensions that neither could nor should be satisfied. Most numerous and unfortunate was the "official" branch; the German states had created a horde of petty officials and had unleashed them on society without taking responsibility for their fate. The schoolteacher was a prime exhibit, and the problem was not simply that "he eagerly revealed to the peasant for the first time what a truly modern man, disoriented and embittered toward the world, actually is" and "embodied the demand for restructuring [*Umbau*] in his very person." The peculiar tragedy of the "official proletariat" was to equate "a feud with the imperious stepmother, the existing state authority, with a feud against society" and thus "under existing state conditions have no choice but to disintegrate the entire society into the fourth estate."[5]

Like the mass of urban and rural poor, Prussian schoolteachers lacked the *Eigentum*—whether it be physical wealth or an established profession—that had underpinned "independence" and legitimated rank in an estate society. At the same time they did not meet the new requirements for academic education (*Bildung*), with its access to truly public offices. "Proletariat," in its fundamental sense, signifies the dependence integral to this dilemma, and connotes the acute sense of deprivation that informed teachers' efforts to escape it. Beyond that, however, Riehl's demonology places the teachers in the wrong company and distorts their significance. The emancipation movement spoke for a profession-in-the-making, not an official wing of the proletariat, and pressed a claim to upward mobility via professional and official status. Far from betraying a tendency to revolutionary nihilism, the goal and the route were markedly faithful to the evolution of Prussia. Not surprisingly, teachers borrowed their status criteria from the academic and official elite who had presided over the creation of their occupation. The significance of their emancipation appeal lay in the attempt to stretch those criteria to a nonacademic occupation, most of its members scattered across the countryside and still isolated in rural communities. Seminar training, the movement insisted, was a kind of "higher," specialized education and as such merited recognition as a form of property (*Eigentum*). Indeed a minimum of *Bildung*, even without standard academic trappings, would suffice to separate the new property holders from uneducated peasants and artisans as well as from the growing mass of proletarians or *Eigentumslose*. Emancipation, then, did not involve a leveling process, but an adjustment of the boundary between the lower and middle layers of an increasingly complex society.

Of primary interest here is not the Prussian social hierarchy that can be reconstructed from incomes, educational credentials, and other objective indices. The emancipation movement offers a glimpse of the hierarchy as a subjective reality—as it existed and evolved in the eyes of its members. The movement had a complex perspective, reflecting its constituents' ambiguous, tension-ridden position between the masses and the elite. Ideology aside, its overriding impulse was to prop the teaching corps on a new pedestal, not to identify it with the mass and to voice aspirations from below. That impulse, combined with tactical considerations, explains why the movement as a whole did not pursue the broader implications of the teachers' own case. To the authors of the Tivoli petition the revolution allowed an assault on the privileges of birth and wealth and promised to install the principle of equal opportunity. But their plan to restructure Prussian society through the school system advanced far beyond other reform programs. More revealing was the movement's perspective on its own cause. Whereas it tended to lump the uneducated into a homogeneous mass, it necessarily was more careful to differentiate occupations and tiers when it looked upward. The "middle class" to which teachers sought entry was really the educated and official sector of the *Mittelstände*, and its upper echelons had already achieved legal and social preeminence in the Prussian General Code. To recognize the teaching corps meant to lower the entry requirements and thus to broaden the base of the pyramid. But the movement's conception of a legitimate rank, "appropriate to the *Stand*," and its very standards of measurement, educational achievement and public function, implied that the *Mittelstände* would expand as an intricate, multigraded hierarchy of occupational groups.[6] Using that calculus, the movement kept its sights limited even in the open-ended world of 1848. Seminar graduates' "educational equals," the clerks on the lowest rungs of state service, remained the standard of reference for teaching incomes, and the same criteria that legitimated a path of upward mobility stopped halfway across the academic barrier. Only the Tivoli petitioners hoped to guarantee future generations of teachers "an equal birthright with the theologian, the doctor, and the jurist" by incorporating their training into the universities. Most assemblies and conferences simply wanted them to attend regular high schools and more "scholarly" seminars, perhaps modeled on the university.

If teachers' aspirations were modest in a national context, they were more ambitious in their local settings. Particularly in the countryside, emancipation seemed to require a radical route. Men whose immediate predecessors had been "without station," at the bottom of local society, were to constitute a national corps of state-salaried and state-appointed officials. With that ideal of independence the emancipation movement—aside from its commitment to the democratic and national cause—betrayed a hard realism about the future of Prussia. Its constituents had peculiar reason to understand that state office, even at the bottom of the bureaucratic ranks, offered a lever and shield in Prussian society. Ironically enough the movement, by the nature of its ideological commitment, had to eschew the legal privileges that the *Staatsbürgertum* had long enjoyed. But in a more fundamental sense it envisioned a new *Staatsstand* in an age of legal equality and political democracy.

The conclusion is not that the emancipation movement opted to sacrifice a truly professional status for the security of a bureaucratic niche. In its reform programs profession and office were not mutually exclusive alternatives but the two sides of one coin. Its appeals were permeated with the conviction that elementary school teaching was a genuine *Berufsstand* with its own standards of performance and merit. The instruction of children was a demanding kind of intellectual work, not to be confused with mere pen pushing in a bureaucratic office. By academic criteria the seminar graduate stood below the pastor; but he nonetheless deserved emancipation from pastoral authority because the school was a new field of expertise and he was its trained expert. In 1848 the emancipation movement hoped to institutionalize a new professional ethos with an inspectorate of "schoolmen," with official representation in school synods, and with free associations. In its efforts to escape an official demiworld it ended up projecting an entirely new relationship between the higher and lower ranks of the state bureaucracy. A branch of state officialdom, largely free of local control, would also constitute a self-regulating corporation and represent itself beside and indeed within the ranks. Though this new corporatism was liberal in spirit and form, Riehl, had he noticed it, might not have been so pessimistic about the disintegration of an estate society. All in all an emancipated profession meant one positioned between society and state and enjoying the best of both worlds.

The reasons why the emancipation movement failed, and why its goals remained unattainable long after 1848, are more or less obvious. At mid-century physical isolation was still an important factor; the great majority of teachers lived and worked in a world that was very different from the urban centers of academic education. The traditions and limited resources of the countryside only magnified handicaps that were, in any event, formidable. Although urbanization brought some advantages in the second half of the nineteenth century, it did not lift the teaching corps out of its occupational and institutional isolation. The educational structure that had been taking shape since the Reform Era hardened into a rigidly bifurcated system. Above the great divide stood the university-trained philologists who dominated the *Gymnasien* and formed an official corps of professionals. They instructed a small elite, recruited largely from families with education and property, and controlled the path to university study and official careers. A nonacademic training, a mass public, and a more or less cautious, occasionally backstepping state policy explain why elementary school teaching continued to be relegated to a quasi-professional and quasi-official status.

The emancipation movement of Pre-March and 1848 was not a typical expression of professional aspirations. It represented men in a unique interstice between popular, largely rural culture and academic culture, between resistant communities and a meddling state bureaucracy. Yet the movement protested the dilemma of the excluded and articulated their consciousness, and for that very reason it may be a particularly sensitive guide to dominant social norms and expectations. To return to Riehl's caricature, in some ways the new Prussian schoolteacher "embodied the demand for restructuring in his very person"; but his spokesmen simply tried to modernize long-standing criteria for elite status in Prussia, and in the process confirmed their longevity. It has long been obvious that the Prussian state administration made itself the target of social protest in Pre-March. In this case, and perhaps in many others, the administration nonetheless retained a commanding presence as a model for social aspirations. Perhaps most striking, independence—and indeed freedom—meant both official power vis-à-vis the public and a degree of corporate autonomy in the official ranks. The combination was perhaps paradoxical, but the pursuit of both goals may have been integral to the professional ethos in nineteenth-century Germany.[7] In the transition from a *Ständestaat* to a modern social and political structure, this study suggests, one vital link was *Berufsstand*. Historians are only beginning to understand the social dimensions and political implications of that peculiarly German category.

ABBREVIATIONS

ARCHIVAL RECORDS

HD Hauptstaatsarchiv Düsseldorf, Abteilung Kalkum: Regierung Düsseldorf, Schulwesen.

GS Geheimes Staatsarchiv, Berlin-Dahlem: Pr. Br. Rep. 2, Regierung Potsdam, II. Abteilung, Kirchen- und Schulwesen.

SM Staatsarchiv Münster: Provinzialschulkollegium and II. B, Regierung Arnsberg, Volksschulen.

PERIODICALS

BJ *Berliner Jahrbücher für Erziehung und Unterricht.*

CB *Centralblatt für die gesammte Unterrichts-Verwaltung in Preussen.*

DS *Der deutsche Schulfreund. Ein nützliches Hand- und Lesebuch für Lehrer in Bürger- und Landschulen.*

PJ *Pädagogischer Jahresbericht für Deutschlands Volksschullehrer.*

PR *Pädagogische Revue. Centralorgan für Wissenschaft, Geschichte und Kunst der Erziehung.*

PV *Preussische Volks-Schul-Zeitung.*

RB *Rheinische Blätter für Erziehung und Unterricht mit besonderer Berücksichtigung des Volksschulwesens.*

SC *Schul-Chronik.*

SPB *Schulblatt für die Provinz Brandenburg.*

SS *Schlesische Schullehrerzeitung.*

NOTES

INTRODUCTION

1. For a thorough, insightful analysis of the German educational systems that originated in the early nineteenth century and for comparisons with the French, English, and American systems see Fritz K. Ringer, *Education and Society in Modern Europe*. The most important contribution to the history of Prussian schoolteachers is Folkert Meyer, *Schule der Untertanen*. Meyer concentrates on the late nineteenth century. Our two studies indicate considerable continuity from Pre-March to the end of the century, particularly with respect to the teachers' social origins and status, the tensions of their official position as both communal employees and subordinates of the state bureaucracy, and the role of their associations. For brief introductions see Eugene N. Anderson, "The Prussian *Volksschule* in the Nineteenth Century"; Wolfram Fischer, "Der Volkschullehrer"; Heinrich Busshoff, "Die preussische Volksschule als soziales Gebilde und politischer Bildungsfaktor in der ersten Hälfte des 19. Jahrhunderts." For an insightful analysis of rural *instituteurs* see Peter V. Meyers, "Professionalization and Societal Change." Meyers uses the term "professionalization," but also illustrates how his case "departed significantly from classic examples of professional development." See also Barnett Singer, "The Teacher as a Notable in Brittany, 1880–1914."

2. For a general survey of the literature see Hansjürgen Daheim, *Der Beruf in der modernen Gesellschaft*. For my purposes the most useful contribution is Hans Albrecht Hesse, *Berufe im Wandel*. Proceeding from a historical analysis of German artisans and industrial workers, Hesse proposes a distinction between the "Anglo-Saxon" concept of "professionalization" and *Ver-Beruflichung* in the German context. In "professionalization" the occupational group itself organizes and tries to influence public opinion, primarily to improve its social status. In *Ver-Beruflichung* the emphasis is on raising individual qualifications, in a narrow economic sense, and an outside agent—the state—is primarily responsible for initiating and directing the process. The early history of Prussian schoolteachers does not fit either concept, but includes elements of both.

3. *Deutsches Wörterbuch*, pp. 709–20, and esp. pp. 709, 716. See also Oswald v. Nell-Breuning, "Standischer Gesellschaftsaufbau," pp. 6–11. On *Beruf* and *Profession* see esp. Hesse, *Berufe im Wandel*, pp. 79–84; Werner Conze, "Beruf."

4. Lenore O'Boyle, "The Middle Class in Western Europe, 1815–48," pp. 832–36.

5. The records are in Geheimes Staatsarchiv, Berlin-Dahlem; Hauptstaatsarchiv Düsseldorf, Abteilung Kalkum; Staatsarchiv Münster.

6. Thomas Nipperdey, "Volksschule und Revolution im Vormärz," pp. 137–42.

7. Gottfried Uhlig, *Bourgeoisie und Volksschule im Vormärz*, esp. pp. 125–27.

CHAPTER I

1. Ferdinand Vollmer, *Friedrich Wilhelm I und die Volksschule*; Hartwig Notbohm, *Das evangelische Kirchen- und Schulwesen in Ostpreussen während der Regierung Friedrich dem Grossen*; Alois M. Kosler, *Die preussische Volksschulpolitik in Oberschlesien, 1742–1848*; Gustav Braun, *Geschichte des organisch vereinigten Kirchen- und Schulamtes in Schlesien*; Willi Schwarz, "Die bergische Schule und ihre Wurzeln in der Vikarie- und Küsterschule."

2. The complete text of the *Reglement* is in Theo Dietrich and Job-Günter Klink, eds., *Volksschulordnungen 16. bis 18. Jahrhundert*. For background see Ferdinand Vollmer, *Die preussische Volksschulpolitik unter Friedrich dem Grossen*. In 1765 a slightly revised *Reglement* was issued for the Catholic schools in Silesia; the text is in *Johann Ignaz von Felbiger*.

3. The internal memoranda of the Lutheran High Consistory (*Oberkonsistorium*), in preparation for its report to the king in 1768, are in GS 3822. The other provincial reports are summarized in Vollmer, *Die preussische Volksschulpolitik*, pp. 106–31. For later reports see, e.g., Erwin Schaaf, *Die niedere Schule im Raum Trier-Saarbrücken von der späten Aufklärung bis zu Restauration, 1780–1825*, esp. pp. 88–90; Paul Schwartz, *Die neumärkischen Schulen am Ausgang des 18. und am Anfang des 19. Jahrhunderts*, pp. 179–83; Heinrich Willemsen, "Das bergische Schulwesen unter der französischen Herrschaft (1806–1813)," p. 85; Wilhelm Zimmermann, *Die Anfänge und der Aufbau des Lehrerbildungs- und Volksschulwesens am Rhein um die Wende des 18. Jahrhunderts, 1770–1826*, 1:passim.

4. On Westphalia see esp. Walter Werres, "Die sozialgeschichtliche Begründung der modernen Landschule in Deutschland," pp. 170–221. See also Notbohm, *Das evangelische Kirchen- und Schulwesen*, pp. 167–73; Schaaf, *Die niedere Schule*, pp. 59–60.

5. The *Reglement* had recommended that villages hire cow herders or rotate the children as herders where farmsteads were too scattered. See par. 4, in Dietrich and Klink, *Volksschulordnungen*, p. 133. But Prussian officials continued to cite this problem in succeeding decades.

6. Max van de Kamp, "Das niedere Schulwesen in Stadt und Stift Essen bis 1815," p. 157. On the rural poor see esp. Reinhart Koselleck, *Preussen zwischen Reform und Revolution*, pp. 132–42; Werner Conze, "Vom 'Pöbel' zum 'Proletariat.'"

7. There is still a paucity of historical research on German rural culture, and most of the literature on the lower schools and their reform offers little help. A notable exception is Manfred Heinemann and Wilhelm Rüter, *Landschulreform als Gesellschaftsinitiative.* This monograph focuses on Philip von der Reck, a Westphalian estate lord, and his unsuccessful efforts to reform the parish school in Overdyck. See esp. the assessment of the peasants' reaction, pp. 166–70.

8. Vollmer, *Friedrich Wilhelm I,* pp. 137–41. On sextons, artisans, and other kinds of schoolmasters see Notbohm, *Das evangelische Kirchen- und Schulwesen,* pp. 144–66; Schaaf, *Die niedere Schule,* pp. 76–88; Paul Schwartz, "Die Schulen der Provinz Westpreussen unter dem Oberschulkollegium, 1787–1806"; Wilhelm Meiners, "Landschulwesen und Landschullehrer im Herzogtum Cleve vor hundert Jahren."

9. Vollmer, *Friedrich Wilhelm I,* pp. 126–27, 140–41; Meiners, "Landschulwesen," p. 354; Schaaf, *Die niedere Schule,* p. 77; Notbohm, *Das evangelische Kirchen- und Schulwesen,* pp. 146–47.

10. See par. 13 of the *Reglement* in Dietrich and Klink, *Volksschulordnungen,* p. 137.

11. From a report by Councillor Meierotto in 1793; see Paul Schwartz, "Die Schulen der Provinz Ostpreussen unter dem Oberschulkollegium, 1787–1806," p. 284.

12. Quoted in Alfons Schagen, *Josef Görres und Die Anfänge der preussischen Volksschule,* p. 15.

13. See esp. Koselleck, *Preussen,* pp. 51–77; Conze, "Vom 'Pöbel' zum 'Proletariat.'" Conze refers to the *Standlos* as the *Pöbelstand* (another contemporary term) and the *unterständische Schicht.*

14. See esp. Zimmermann, *Die Anfänge und der Aufbau des Lehrerbildungs- und Volksschulwesens,* 1:passim; Gunnar Thiele, *Allgemeine Voraussetzungen zur Geschichte der preussischen Lehrerseminare,* pp. 1–36.

15. These figures were taken from a pastor's very careful report; see Meiners, "Landschulwesen," p. 354.

16. Friedrich Wienecke, "Statistik des Schulwesens der Kurmark im Jahre 1806." See other official estimates of schoolmasters' incomes in Schaaf, *Die niedere Schule,* pp. 88, 179; Vollmer, *Friedrich Wilhelm I,* pp. 129–30; Carl von Schmieden, *Das Elementar- und Bürgerschulwesen in der Provinz Brandenburg in seiner Entwicklung und seinen Fortschritten,* pp. 13, 16.

17. Joh. Gottf. Dobermann, "Aus einen Schreiben aus Schlesien," DS 9(1794): 92–93. See also Vollmer, *Friedrich Wilhelm I,* pp. 140–41; Schaaf, *Die niedere Schule,* p. 77; Willemsen, "Das bergische Schulwesen," p. 92; Schagen, *Josef Görres,* pp. 16–17.

18. Examples of sexton-schoolmasters' contracts and sources of income can be found in Notbohm, *Das evangelische Kirchen- und Schulwesen,* pp. 160–63; Schaaf, *Die niedere Schule,* pp. 78–82; Braun, *Geschichte des organisch vereinigten Kirchen- und Schulamtes,* pp. 29–32; Schwarz, "Die bergische Schule," pp. 14–16, 46–47. For a survey of Germany see Robert Hillmann, "Lehrer- und Küstereinkommen vom 16. bis 18. Jahrhundert," pp. 513–25, 569–79.

19. Schwarz, "Die bergische Schule," pp. 12–16.

20. Schaaf, *Die niedere Schule*, p. 81; Schwartz, *Die neumärkischen Schulen*, pp. 49–59; Schwartz, "Die Schulen der Provinz Ostpreussen," p. 281.

21. Daniel Schürmann, "Beschreibung des Volksschulwesens und des Lehrerstandes, besonders im Bergischen, während meiner durchlebten Tage," RB, n.s. 6(1832): 44. For other examples of the circuit see "Das abgeschaffte Neujahrs- und Gregoriussingen zu Gaben, in der Niederlausitz," DS 7(1794): 146–52; Schwarz, "Die bergische Schule," p. 84; Walter Schäfer, "Die ideengeschichtlichen Grundlagen der Reform des Volksschulwesens im Grossherzogtum Berg und in der Stadt Düsseldorf von 1799–1816," p. 60.

22. Willemsen, "Das bergische Schulwesen," p. 92. Another mayor reported that schoolmasters were "usually the first beggars of the village" (ibid.).

23. Quoted from a school inspection in Schwartz, "Die Schulen der Provinz Westpreussen," pp. 107–8.

24. See par. 10 in Dietrich and Klink, *Volksschulordnungen*, p. 135.

25. The petition is in GS 3822. In a forwarding letter (Oct. 3, 1801) Inspector Bauer sympathized with the schoolmasters' "hard-pressed situation," but noted that his support of their petition would be "superfluous" and "improper" (*ungebührlich*) in view of his superiors' reform plans.

26. Kriegskotte's petition has been published in Karl-Ernst Jeismann, "Die Eingabe eines Schwelmer Lehrers an das preussische Innenministerium, Sektion für Kultus u. Unterricht, aus dem Jahre 1814." The quotation is on p. 131. For another schoolmaster's complaints about the school fee see G. W., "Warum geht es mit der Verbesserung und Vervollkommung vieler deutschen Stadt- und Landschulen nicht besser und schneller von statten?" DS 21 (1799): 84–85.

27. Quoted in Schaaf, *Die niedere Schule*, p. 81.

28. Councillor Teller used that phrase in 1768; see his comments in GS 3822.

29. "Auszug eines Berichts an die Königliche Regierung zu Lingen, die Beschaffenheit des Landschulwesens in der Inspection Lienen (in der Grafschaft Tecklenburg) betreffend," pp. 290–91. See also Werres, "Die sozialgeschichtliche Begründung," p. 178.

30. This narrative is taken from Bruno Sauer, *Aus dem Leben eines märkisch-pommerschen Dorfschullehrers um 1800*, esp. pp. 43–51. Sauer has used archival records to reconstruct Fetting's biography and occupational conditions in great detail; his book is the best introduction to the rural schoolmaster and his relationship to his community.

31. Ibid., pp. 62–75.

32. See, e.g., Richard Boschan, *Das Bildungswesen in der Stadt Potsdam bis zur Wiederaufrichtung des preussischen Staates*; Albrecht Brinkmann, *Geschichte der Dortmunden Volksschulen*; F. A. Block, *Geschichte des städtischen Schulwesens zu Merseburg*; Schwartz, "Die Schulen der Provinz Westpreussen," p. 121; Schwartz, *Die neumärkischen Schulen*, pp. 10–15; Hillmann, "Lehrer- und Küstereinkommen," pp. 519–20.

33. For background see Karl-Ernst Jeismann, *Das preussische Gymnasium in Staat und Gesellschaft*, pp. 1–148; Friedrich Paulsen, *Der gelehrte Unter-*

richt im Zeichen des Neuhumanismus, 1740–1892, esp. 148–88. For detailed descriptions of lower schools see, e.g., Dietrich Rittershausen, "Beiträge zur Geschichte des Berliner Elementarschulwesens von der Reformation bis 1836"; Emil Hollack and Friedrich Tromnau, *Geschichte des Schulwesens der königlichen Haupt- und Residenzstadt Königsberg i/Pr. mit besonderer Berücksichtigung der niederen Schulen.*

34. Rittershausen, "Beiträge zur Geschichte des Berliner Elementarschulwesens," p. 270. See also pp. 240–42, 266–67.

35. Brinkmann, *Geschichte der Dortmunden Volksschulen,* pp. 21–22, 68–69. On *Winkelschulmeister* see also Boschan, *Das Bildungswesen in der Stadt Potsdam,* pp. 37–48; Schwartz, *Die neumärkischen Schulen,* p. 11; Schagen, *Josef Görres,* pp. 4–9; Hollack and Tromnau, *Geschichte des Schulwesens,* pp. 189–201.

CHAPTER 2

1. Manfred Heinemann, *Schule im Vorfeld der Verwaltung,* is a thorough analysis of the vast literature on school reform in the second half of the eighteenth century and traces the growing importance of the lower schools in Prussian state policy. Outdated but still useful are Walter Götze, *Die Begründung der Volksbildung in der Aufklärungsbewegung;* Kerrin Höber, *Die merkantilistische Nationalerziehung;* Olga von Hippel, *Die pädagogische Dorfutopie der Aufklärung.* Helmut König forces his material into a rigid Marxist framework, but stresses the sociopolitical implications of reform thought and includes the more radical contributors. See his *Zur Geschichte der Nationalerziehung in Deutschland im letzten Drittel des 18. Jahrhunderts.*

2. See esp. von Hippel, *Die pädagogische Dorfutopie,* pp. 19–53; Götze, *Die Begründung der Volksbildung,* pp. 24–27, 57–90. John G. Gagliardo discusses "Pedagogical Reformism"; but the "moral image" on which he focuses emphasized the peasants' "natural," markedly antirational attributes, in reaction against Enlightenment thought. See his *From Pariah to Patriot.*

3. On Rochow see Heinemann, *Schule im Vorfeld,* pp. 111–21; König, *Zur Geschichte der Nationalerziehung,* pp. 170–71, 203–8. On Basedow see esp. Höber, *Die merkantilistische Nationalerziehung,* pp. 18–22. To the anonymous author of *Grundsätze der Kultur* (1785) the peasant not only was incapable of the "active patriotism" of the small elite but also lacked the *Bürgertum's* ability to think in terms of the entire state. However, he could be expected to love his native community and accept the burdens the fatherland required. See ibid., pp. 44–49.

4. Quoted in König, *Zur Geschichte der Nationalerziehung,* p. 62.

5. There is an insightful discussion of "progressive" and "conservative" reform plans in Detlef K. Müller, *Sozialstruktur und Schulsystem,* esp. pp. 92–128. On the advocates of free competition see König, *Zur Geschichte der Nationalerziehung,* pp. 178–81, 336–40; Karl-Ernst Jeismann, *Das preussische Gymnasium in Staat und Gesellschaft,* pp. 132–48; Andreas Flitner, *Die politische Erziehung in Deutschland,* pp. 49–50. On the role of the

churches see Heinemann, *Schule im Vorfeld*, pp. 175–85; Enno Fooken, *Die geistliche Schulaufsicht und ihre Kritiker im 18. Jahrhundert.*

6. The names are from R. Z. Becker, *Noth- und Hülfsbuchlein* (1788) and Christian Salzmann, *Sebastian Kluge, ein Volksbuch* (1789), both summarized in von Hippel, *Die pädagogische Dorfutopie*, pp. 55–86.

7. On the pastors' new role as "popular educators" see esp. von Hippel, *Die pädagogische Dorfutopie*, pp. 46–48, 66–68, 86–101; Götze, *Die Begründung der Volksbildung*, pp. 42–48.

8. Gotthilf Samuel Steinbart, *Vorschläge zu einer allgemeinen Schulverbesserung, insofern sie nicht Sache der Kirche sondern des Staates ist*, pp. 27, 73–94.

9. See esp. Baron von Zedlitz, "Vorschläge zur Verbesserung des Schulwesens in den Königlichen Länden," pp. 103–5. Other examples of the proposed curricula are to be found in König, *Zur Geschichte der Nationalerziehung*, pp. 64–67, 167–70.

10. *Bernhard Overbergs Anweisung zum zweckmässigen Schulunterricht*, p. 21.

11. Quoted in Günther Dohmen, *Die Entstehung des pädagogischen Bildungsbegriffs und seines Bezugs zum Schulunterricht*, p. 71.

12. This section is intended only to illustrate the practical implications of the new pedagogy and ignores the more or less important philosophical and methodological issues that developed. It is culled from *Overbergs Anweisung*; Johann Ignaz von Felbiger's *Methodenbuch* in *Johann Ignaz von Felbiger*; *Christian Gotthilf Salzmanns Pädagogische Schriften*. For a dry but useful analysis of the "concept of pedagogical education" in the Enlightenment, with particular attention to the "artificial" (*künstlichere*) education of the "natural" child in the work of Rochow and Salzmann, see Dohmen, *Die Entstehung des pädagogischen Bildungsbegriffs*, esp. pp. 58–97. There is a brief but refreshingly concrete description of the major pedagogical innovations in Erwin Schaaf, *Die niedere Schule im Raum Trier-Saarbrücken von der späten Aufklärung bis zu Restauration, 1780–1825*, pp. 91–104.

13. For concrete examples of the new discipline see Johann Georg Krünitz, *Landschule*, pp. 757–82. This is a useful compendium on school reform, including advice culled from several of the new teaching handbooks.

14. "Etwas über den ehrwürdigen Schulmeistertitel," DS 7(1794): 156–57; Oberprediger Meyer, "Von dem Verdienst, welches sich ein Schullehrer erwerben kann," DS 20 (1799): 8. A decade later Ludwig Natorp, another pastor, insisted that "artisan-like mechanicalness, deadly to heart and spirit" had to be rooted out if the first generation of Prussian schoolteachers were to be truly "educated" (*gebildete*) men. See Gunnar Thiele, *Die Organisation des Volksschul- und Seminarwesens in Preussen, 1809–1819*, pp. 89–90.

15. Krünitz, *Landschule*, p. 738.

16. Josef Schram, *Die Verbesserung der Schulen in moralisch-politischer-pädagogischer und polizeilicher Hinsicht*, p. 307. This is another useful potpourri on school reform. For other samples from the literature see Margaret Rosenbaum, "Untersuchungen zur Veränderung der Lage und des Selbstverständnisses des Lehrers während der Aufklärung in Deutschland."

17. See esp. Reinhart Koselleck, *Preussen zwischen Reform und Revolution*, pp. 78–115.

18. From 1773 onward Zedlitz had used a small royal grant to establish *Landgnadenschulen*, with teaching salaries of 120 thaler, in the Kurmark. By 1796 there were fifty-five of them, twenty funded entirely by the crown—but in a province with more than fifteen hundred schoolmasters. See esp. Friedrich Wienecke, "Die Landgnadenschulen der Kurmark." In an effort to dampen false hopes Steinbart calculated that the crown would have to spend more than 200,000 thaler to provide all the Kurmark villages with 150 thaler teaching salaries. His estimated bill for the entire monarchy—but just for the rural schools—surpassed one million thaler (Steinbart, *Vorschläge*, pp. 6–9).

19. See, e.g., Meyer, "Von dem Verdienst," esp. pp. 14–15; *Overbergs Anweisung*, pp. 14–16; Heinrich Stephani's essay on "a true improvement of the school and education in the countryside" (1792), in *Heinrich Stephani, 1761–1850*, pp. 137–44.

20. Schram, *Die Verbesserung der Schulen*, p. 30. The need to attract "better men" had been obvious to the High Consistory in 1768; see GS 3822. See also Joh. Christ. Kaeselitz, "Nachricht vom Zustande des Landschulwesens im Preussischen Vorpommern," DS 16 (1797): 124.

21. Johann Friedrich Prenninger, ed., *Landschulbibliothek*, vol. 2, pp. 1–2. Another author proposed that theology candidates be assigned to the lower schools until they found pastorates, and explained, "He [the schoolmaster] speaks, works and lives like the peasant in his village, goes drinking with him and smokes a pipe with him; how can he expect to be honored by him?" (*Einige patriotische Vorschläge zur Verbesserung des Schulwesens auf dem Lande*, pp. 31–32).

22. Krünitz, *Landschulen*, p. 806; *Johann Ignaz von Felbiger*, pp. 40–43; *Overbergs Anweisung*, pp. 18–20; T., "Wie ein Schullehrer auch bey geringe Gehalt sein gutes Auskommen haben kann. Von einem alten Schulmeister," in Prenninger, *Landschulbibliothek*, vol. 3, pp. 130–34. "It is a great achievement," this author wrote, "when one is pious and learns to be content with what is there" (Ibid., p. 130).

23. Wienecke, "Die Landgnadenschulen," p. 315; Ferdinand Vollmer, *Die preussische Volksschulpolitik unter Friedrich dem Grossen*, pp. 145–48.

24. These reform measures were included in several school laws in the late eighteenth century. See, e.g., Schaaf, *Die niedere Schule*, p. 25; Max van de Kamp, "Das niedere Schulwesen in Stadt und Stift Essen bis 1815," pp. 216–18; Wilhelm Zimmermann, *Die Anfänge und der Aufbau des Lehrerbildungs- und Volksschulwesens am Rhein um die Wende des 18. Jahrhunderts*, 1:145.

25. Schram, *Die Verbesserung der Schulen*, pp. 333–34. See also *Heinrich Stephani*, pp. 140–41.

26. See, e.g., the school law for Stift Essen (1786) in van de Kamp, "Das niedere Schulwesen," pp. 216–18; the *Verordnung* of the Magdeburg Consistory (July 20, 1797) can be found in DS 19 (1798): 171.

27. With the rates stipulated in the Prussian *Reglement* the schoolmaster

needed well over 100 pupils to earn 100 thaler per year in school fees. For examples of the great range of local school-age populations see Heinrich Willemsen, "Das bergische Schulwesen unter der französischen Herrschaft (1806–1813)," p. 93; Walter Werres, "Die sozialgeschichtliche Begründung der modernen Landschule in Deutschland," pp. 221ff.

28. See esp. Heinemann, *Schule im Vorfeld*, pp. 212–32.

29. Paul Schwartz, "Die Schulen der Provinz Ostpreussen unter dem Oberschulkollegium, 1787–1806," p. 57. Even with "free schools," Councillor Spalding had noted in 1768, the children of "slight countrymen" might not be able to attend school regularly; they had to work with their parents or enter "foreign service" from age nine or ten, and could not be clothed properly for the walk to school in winter. See Spalding to Büsching (Nov. 21), GS 3822.

30. See par. 8 of the *Reglement*, in Theo Dietrich and Job-Günter Klink, eds., *Volksschulordnungen 16. bis 18. Jahrhundert*, p. 134. The Silesian *Reglement* had stipulated that fee exemptions be limited to "public paupers" and that the pastors should raise compensation money by appealing to their parishioners' "charity" in biannual "school sermons." See *Johann Ignaz von Felbiger*, p. 17 and the two 1771 ordinances in GS 3822.

31. Vollmer, *Die preussische Volksschulpolitik*, pp. 118–19, 252; Alois M. Kosler, *Die preussische Volksschulpolitik in Oberschlesien, 1742–1848*, pp. 32–33.

32. Teller to Spalding (Dec. 20), GS 3822.

33. See Part 2, Title 12, and esp. pars. 1, 26, 29–33, and 65, in *Allgemeines Landrecht für die Preussischen Staaten von 1794*, pp. 584–89. The code provisions for the lower schools are also in Dietrich and Klink, *Volksschulordnungen*, pp. 152–57. The code, it should be noted, specifically eliminated a school fee for those who contributed to the new tax. For a careful assessment of the provisions see Heinemann, *Schule im Vorfeld*, pp. 320–37.

34. Quoted in Jeismann, *Das preussische Gymnasium*, pp. 282–83.

35. K. H. Neumann, *Über die jetzt eingeleitete Verbesserung des Elementarschulwesens*, pp. 35–37.

36. Clemens Menze, *Die Bildungsreform Wilhelm von Humboldts*, is the best analysis of Humboldt's role in the Reform Era and includes a wealth of material on its educational ideals and policies. Still useful are Eduard Spranger, *Wilhelm von Humboldt und die Reform des Bildungswesens*; Thiele, *Die Organisation des Volksschul- und Seminarwesens*; Helmut König, *Zur Geschichte der bürgerlichen Nationalerziehung in Deutschland zwischen 1807 und 1815*.

37. On the consistories see esp. Heinemann, *Schule im Vorfeld*, pp. 169–75. Baron von Zedlitz had created an *Oberschulkollegium*, but it had merely been perched atop the existing chaos and staffed almost entirely by members of the consistories. See Spranger, *Wilhelm von Humboldt*, pp. 74–75. On the reorganization see ibid., pp. 78–87, 130–31.

38. Neumann, *Über die jetzt eingeleitete Verbesserung*, pp. 58–61; Natorp to the Landes-Direktor, Prignitz (July 1, 1811), GS 4803. In 1768 several members of the High Consistory had alluded to the estate lords' lack of co-

operation, but the president had decided to ignore them. See GS 3822. For later complaints see, e.g., Kosler, *Die preussische Volksschulpolitik*, pp. 32, 141; Paul Schwartz, *Die neumärkischen Schulen am Ausgang des 18. und am Anfang des 19. Jahrunderts*, pp. 40–41.

39. Natorp to Baron von Vincke (Dec. 4, 1810), in Ernst Lichtenstein, "Aus dem Krisenjahr der Pestalozzi-Schulreform in Preussen," p. 100. On the superintendents' inadequacies see also Krünitz, *Landschule*, pp. 783–84; Johann Anton Küpper, *Versuch, eine zweckmässige Verfassung für den protestantischen Prediger- und Schullehrerstand zu entwerfen*, 2:180–96. On their new assignments see, e.g., the *Anordnung* and *Dienstvorschrift* for the lower Rhineland (1814) in Friedrich Wilhelm Niedergesäs, *Das Elementarschulwesen in den königlichen preussischen Staaten*, pp. 543–48; Potsdam district section to the superintendents (Nov. 12, 1809), GS 3822.

40. In 1809 the Potsdam section instructed the pastors to submit lengthy reports on school conditions in their villages and supplied thirty-five detailed questions (GS 3822). In 1814 the governor general of the Rhineland declared the pastor "the natural executive and superintendent of the rural schools" (Schaaf, *Die niedere Schule*, p. 272). On the pastors' shortcomings as school inspectors see Küpper, *Versuch*, pp. 180–96; Neumann, *Über die jetzt eingeleitete Verbesserung*, p. 33; Schwartz, *Die neumärkischen Schulen*, pp. 49–56.

41. Alfred Heubaum, "Die Geschichte des ersten preussischen Schulgesetzentwurfs (1798–1807)," pp. 307–8. On Massow's views see also König, *Zur Geschichte der Nationalerziehung*, pp. 305–11.

42. See esp. Humboldt's "Bericht der Section des Cultus und Unterrichts" (Dec. 1, 1809) in Gerhardt Giese, ed., *Quellen zur deutschen Schulgeschichte seit 1800*, pp. 75–83. For background see Menze, *Die Bildungsreform Wilhelm von Humboldts*, esp. pp. 121–30, 190–96; Jeismann, *Das preussische Gymnasium*. On the moral and political importance attributed to the peasantry see esp. Gagliardo, *From Pariah to Patriot*, pp. 174–210.

43. Harnisch quoted in König, *Zur Geschichte der bürgerlichen Nationalerziehung*, 2:124, 137. Jachmann's essays in the *Archiv deutscher Nationalbildung* (1812) have been reprinted in Helmut König, ed., *Deutsche Nationalerziehungspläne aus der Zeit des Befreiungskrieges*, pp. 49–148. See also Jeismann, *Das preussische Gymnasium*, pp. 253–58.

44. Karl-Ernst Jeismann, "Die Eingabe eines Schwelmer Lehrers an das preussische Innenministerium, Sektion für Kultus u. Unterricht, aus dem Jahre 1814," pp. 130–31.

45. Ibid., pp. 122–23; Spranger, *Wilhelm von Humboldt*, pp. 106–7.

46. Quoted in Menze, *Die Bildungsreform Wilhelm von Humboldts*, p. 135.

47. For background see Spranger, *Wilhelm von Humboldt*, pp. 99–106. The *Rescript* establishing *Schulvorstände* and the accompanying instruction (Oct. 28, 1812) are in Ludwig von Rönne, ed., *Allgemeiner Theil. Privat-Unterricht. Volksschulwesen*, pp. 321–25. On their projected role see, e.g., the *Dienstvorschrift* for the lower Rhineland in Niedergesäs, *Das Elementar-*

schulwesen, pp. 549–52; the *Allgemeine Ansichten über die Schulpflege* for the Grand Duchy of Berg (July 15, 1814) in Walter Schäfer, "Die ideenge-schichtlichen Grundlagen der Reform des Volksschulwesens in Grossher-zogtum Berg und in der Stadt Düsseldorf von 1799–1816," *Beilage* 7.

48. Jeismann, "Die Eingabe eines Schwelmer Lehrers," pp. 119–20. See also Jeismann's other excellent article, "Tendenzen zur Verbesserung des Schulwesens in der Grafschaft Mark, 1798–1848," esp. pp. 86–89.

49. Spranger, *Wilhelm von Humboldt,* pp. 106–7. See also Jeismann, *Das preussische Gymnasium,* pp. 331–34.

50. Spranger, *Wilhelm von Humboldt,* pp. 193–94.

51. König, *Zur Geschichte der bürgerlichen Nationalerziehung,* 1:345.

52. Wilhelm Meiners, "Das Volksschulwesen in Mark und Cleve unter Steins Verwaltung (1787–1804)," pp. 128–30. The chamber in Cleve had ar-gued that a school tax was unfeasible in view of "the great poverty of the rural population." Both chambers based their reports on the opinions of tax collectors, school inspectors, and local officials. During the Reform Era, it should be noted, a tax reform was in preparation, but its purpose was to re-store solvency in the traditional areas of state expenditure.

53. The complete text of the draft is in Lothar Schweim, ed., *Schulreform in Preussen, 1809–1819.* See esp. pars. 45, 48, 51, 52. See also the commis-sion's "Nähere Erklärung" (June 27, 1819) in *Die Gesetzgebung auf dem Gebiete des Unterrichtswesens in Preussen, vom Jahre 1817 bis 1868,* pp. 74–81; the opinions of the provincial presidents in ibid., pp. 90–93.

54. Beckedorff's memorandum in Schweim, *Schulreform,* pp. 222–44.

55. Zimmermann, *Die Anfänge und der Aufbau des Lehrerbildungs- und Volksschulwesens,* 3:177–78.

56. The sections' statistics were published in Victor Cousin, *Report on the State of Public Instruction in Prussia,* pp. 136–39, 266–68.

57. Lichtenstein, "Aus dem Krisenjahr," pp. 105–6.

58. Natorp to the Landes-Direktor, Prignitz (July 1, 1811), GS 4803.

59. Neumann, *Über die jetzt eingeleitete Verbesserung,* p. 33.

60. Natorp to Landes-Direktor, GS 4803; Lichtenstein, "Aus dem Krisen-jahr," p. 100.

61. This account is based on the documents in GS 374. See esp. Mielisch to section, April, 1810; Felgentreber to section, Aug. 25, 1819, and Jan. 21, 1820.

62. Felgentreber to section, Jan. 21, 1820, in ibid.

63. See esp. Felgentreber to section, Feb. 5, 1830, and April 14, 1834, in ibid.

64. GS 701. See esp. Nernst to section, 1810.

65. See esp. Hoffmann's report on the meeting in Briest, Sept. 17, 1810; Hoffmann to section, Feb. 11, 1811; Natorp to *Kreis-Direktorium,* Feb. 21, 1811; Hoffmann to section, June, 1815; Schoolteacher Knoth to section, Nov. 30, 1831, in ibid.

66. GS 26. See esp. Voigt to section, April 28, 1810; Natorp to Superinten-dent Hoppe, Sept., 1810; Hoppe to section, April 21, 1811; Felgentreber to Hoppe, May 23, 1811; report of *Amt* Mühlenbeck, July 29–30, 1811; magis-

trate (*Gericht*) and school committee to section, Aug. 30, 1811.

67. Ibid. See esp. Felgentreber to section, Feb. 16, 1813; Felber to section, July 16, 1817; Hoppe to section, Sept. 16, 1817, and June 15, 1818; section to Hoppe, Feb. 10, 1818.

68. GS 586 (Angermünde) and 629 (Zehdenick).

69. The Berg Instruction (Dec. 21, 1812) is in Schäfer, "Die ideengeschichtlichen Grundlagen," pp. 82–84. For an excellent account of French school policy in the middle and upper Rhineland see Schaaf, *Die niedere Schule*, pp. 165–70, 201–33.

70. Alfons Schagen, *Josef Görres und die Anfänge der preussischen Volksschule*, p. 14; Schaaf, *Die niedere Schule*, pp. 212, 275–76, 336; Willemsen, "Das bergische Schulwesen," pp. 90–91, 190.

71. The ordinance and its "Erläuterungen" are in Niedergesäs, *Das Elementarschulwesen*, pp. 216–19, 490–94. For the ministry's attendance decree see ibid., p. 216.

72. See the summary of the sections' reports (1824–25) in K. Schneider and A. Petersilie, eds., *Die Volks- und die Mittelschulen sowie die sonstigen niederen Schulen im preussischen Staate im Jahre 1891*, pp. 38–39; G. K. Anton, *Geschichte der preussischen Fabrikgesetzgebung bis zu ihrer Aufnahme durch die Reichsgewerbeordnung*, pp. 58–59. On Prussian state policy toward child labor see esp. Klaus L. Hartmann, "Schule und 'Fabrikgeschäft.'"

CHAPTER 3

1. See the "Tabellen, 1814–15" at the end of Julius Heuser, "Karl Friedrich August Grashof als Reorganisator des Volksschulwesens am Niederrhein"; Natorp to the Landes-Direktor, Prignitz (July 1, 1811), GS 4803.

2. In early 1815 Governor General Sack called improvement of teaching incomes and reform of training "the two main pieces" without which "all instructions, all regulations, all methods of control . . . are sheer folly" (Erwin Schaaf, *Die niedere Schule im Raum Trier-Saarbrücken von der späten Aufklärung bis zu Restauration, 1780–1825*, pp. 274–75). See also Natorp to the Landes-Direktor, GS 4803.

3. See, e.g., Johann Anton Küpper, *Versuch, eine zweckmässige Verfassung für den protestantischen Prediger- und Schullehrerstand zu entwerfen*, 1:140–46.

4. On the Berlin seminar see Friedrich Herzberg, *Ueber einige wichtige Hindernisse, die der Verbesserung des Volksschulwesens überhaupt und des hiesigen Landküsterseminariums insbesondere im Wege stehen*, pp. 21–25. Herzberg was the last director. See also Friedrich Buchholz and Gerhard Buchwald, eds., *Die brandenburgischen Lehrerseminare und die ihnen angegliederten Präparandenanstalten*, pp. 15–18. In a report to the king in Feb. 1801, Massow had noted that "formal Seminar-Institutes" were too expensive to be established in sufficient numbers (Gunnar Thiele, *Allgemeine Voraussetzungen zur Geschichte der preussischen Lehrerseminare*, p. 203).

5. Seminar statistics in Victor Cousin, *Report on the State of Public In-*

struction in Prussia, pp. 150–62, 292–93; "Tabellarische Übersicht der in Königlichen Preussischen Staaten befindlichen Schullehrer-Seminare," RB, n.s. 9 (1834): 353–57.

6. The legislation was published in Cousin, *Report*, pp. 183–93.

7. Ibid., pp. 164–65. Since the late 1820s the Potsdam and Neuzelle seminars had introduced emergency one-year courses (Buchholz and Buchwald, *Die brandenburgischen Lehrerseminare*, pp. 90, 99). According to the report of the section in 1841 57 percent (895) of the 1,578 active teachers in the Frankfort district had completed a full seminar course (PR 6 [1843]: 173–74). In the Potsdam district 67 of the 73 new teachers in 1836, and all 56 in 1843, were seminar graduates. See the reports of the section in SPB 1 (1836): 505–6, and SPB 12 (1847): 195–98. In Province Prussia the sections estimated the percentages of seminar-trained teachers in the early 1840s; they ranged from 25 percent (Gumbinnen district) to 75 percent (Danzig district). See the summaries of their reports in CB 1865: 748–55. For a report on the shortage of seminar graduates by the early 1840s, with statistics on the ratio of graduates to active teachers, see PR 7 (1843): 373–75.

8. Küpper, *Versuch*, 1:136–46. Küpper became a school councillor in the Trier district in 1817. See Schaaf, *Die niedere Schule*, p. 267.

9. Küpper, *Versuch*, 1:137–38.

10. See esp. the discussion of Friedrich Gedike in Detlef K. Müller, *Sozialstruktur und Schulsystem*, pp. 98–109. For background see ibid., pp. 154–57; Karl-Ernst Jeismann, *Das preussische Gymnasium in Staat und Gesellschaft*, pp. 156–60.

11. Küpper, *Versuch*, 1:139. A "respectable" income, Küpper estimated, was at least 700 thaler.

12. Quoted in Buchholz and Buchwald, *Die brandenburgischen Lehrerseminare*, p. 139.

13. See esp. Rolf Engelsing, "Probleme der Lebenshaltung in Deutschland im 18. und 19. Jahrhundert," pp. 12–15. On student life see Hans Gerth, *Bürgerliche Intelligenz um 1800*, pp. 38–40; Konrad H. Jarausch, "The Sources of German Student Unrest, 1815–1848," 537–38.

14. Par. 58 of the draft law, in Lothar Schweim, ed., *Schulreform in Preussen, 1809–1819*, p. 176. For earlier comments on the advantages of rural settings for seminars see, e.g., W., "Über Schullehrerseminarien," DS 21 (1799): 64–69; Johann Georg Krünitz, *Landschule*, pp. 736–37; Manfred Heinemann and Wilhelm Rüter, *Landschulreform als Gesellschaftsinitiative*, p. 122.

15. Wilhelm Zimmermann, *Die Anfänge und der Aufbau des Lehrerbildungs- und Volksschulwesens am Rhein um die Wende des 18. Jahrhunderts*, 3:114–21.

16. See the notes on the facilities of the seminars in Cousin, *Report*, pp. 150–62. The relevant towns were Potsdam, Erfurt, Marienburg, Magdeburg, Halberstadt, Königsberg, Alt-Stettin, and Breslau (two seminars). The Berlin seminar, it should be noted, was removed to Potsdam in 1817 to avoid big-city life. See Müller, *Sozialstruktur und Schulsystem*, pp. 198 and 687.

17. Konsistorialrat and Oberdomprediger Streithorst, "Über die besondere

sittliche Vorbereitung künftiger Landschullehrer," DS 10 (1795): 3–15.

18. W., "Auch ein Wort über Seminarien . . . ," DS 22 (1800): 15–35. See also the reports on the Halberstadt and Wesel seminars in Krünitz, *Landschule*, pp. 693–711; the report on the Alt-Stettin seminar in DS 19 (1798): 142–66.

19. See par. 58 of the draft law, in Schweim, *Schulreform*, pp. 177–78. In 1809 Humboldt reported that the normal institute in Königsberg "aims, first, to accustom the children to a frugal life-style and deprivations," and that the "entire orientation . . . is to educate the children so that they will later gladly accept a teaching office under the most unfavorable conditions and lovingly persevere in it even in oppressive circumstances" (Gerhardt Giese, ed., *Quellen zur deutschen Schulgeschichte seit 1800*, p. 82).

20. Cousin, *Report*, p. 181. The founder of the Lastadie seminar, on the outskirts of Stettin, likened its *Internat* to "a village household of the simplest kind" (Ibid., p. 171).

21. Buchholz and Buchwald, *Die brandenburgischen Lehrerseminare*, p. 35. For descriptions of seminar life see ibid., pp. 96–98; Franz Flaskamp, *Die Anfänge westfälischer Lehrerbildung*, pp. 11–12; *Die Lehr- und Erziehungs-Anstalten der Provinz Westfalen*, pp. 91–93, 102–3.

22. Cousin, *Report*, p. 206. He added that "at the same time everything breathes liberality of thought and love of science and letters."

23. Schweim, *Schulreform*, p. 176.

24. Wilhelm Harnisch, *Der jetzige Standpunkt des gesammten preussischen Volksschulwesens*, pp. 209–16. See also Harnisch's "Einige Bemerkungen über Bildungsanstalten für Volksschullehrer in den preuss. Staaten," *Der Schulrat an der Oder* 10 (1817): 3, and "Welche Zöglinge zieht die schlesische Bildungsanstalt für protestantische Schullehrer in Breslau und wie zieht sie dieselben," *Der Schulrat an der Oder* 5 (1816): 63–64.

25. See, e.g., the director's report on the Bruhl seminar and the instruction for the Potsdam director in Cousin, *Report*, pp. 208–37.

26. See the statistics in "Tabellarische Übersicht."

27. The circular was published in Cousin, *Report*, pp. 194–98.

28. See esp. Krünitz, *Landschule*, pp. 693–71; DS 19 (1798): 142–66; Philip von der Reck's views on the small seminar near Overdyck, in Heinemann and Rüter, *Landschulreform*, pp. 121–38.

29. Quoted in Clemens Menze, *Die Bildungsreform Wilhelm von Humboldts*, p. 224. For an excellent appraisal of Humboldt's views see ibid., esp. pp. 121–37, 190–224.

30. *Johann Gottlieb Fichte*, esp. pp. 45–159.

31. Helmut König, ed., *Deutsche Nationalerziehungspläne aus der Zeit des Befreiungskrieges*, esp. pp. 55–57, 84–93. See also Karl-Ernst Jeismann, " 'Nationalerziehung,' " pp. 212–14.

32. Gunnar Thiele, *Die Organisation des Volksschul- und Seminarwesens in Preussen, 1809–19*, pp. 88–98. See also Menze, *Die Bildungsreform Wilhelm von Humboldts*, pp. 452–67; Fritz Fischer, *Ludwig Nicolovius*, pp. 277–92.

33. The plan is published in Thiele, *Die Organisation des Volksschul- und Seminarwesens*, pp. 162–75.

34. Quoted in ibid., p. 132.

35. On the gymnasium teachers see Menze, *Die Bildungsreform Wilhelm von Humboldts,* pp. 270–73, 384–404, 432–49; Jeismann, *Das preussische Gymnasium,* pp. 312–21, 352–54. For the new exemptions from military service see Müller, *Sozialstruktur und Schulsystem,* p. 84.

36. Friedrich Wilhelm Niedergesäs, *Das Elementarschulwesen in den königlichen preussischen Staaten,* p. 106.

37. Schweim, *Schulreform,* pp. 225–27, 233–34. See also pars. 17 and 58 of the draft law, in ibid., pp. 143, 177–78. In a letter to the *Kurmarkdeputation* in June 1810, Süvern had warned against overemphasizing "knowledge of pedagogical theory and literature" (Thiele, *Die Organisation des Volksschul- und Seminarwesens,* p. 133).

38. See esp. Thomas Nipperdey, "Volksschule und Revolution im Vormärz," pp. 126–32.

39. See esp. Diesterweg's "Bescheidene Bemerkungen über Seminarien und die Einrichtungen in denselben," RB 1 (1827): 58–68 and RB 2 (1827): 48–104. The most recent and thorough biography of Diesterweg is Hugo Gotthard Bloth, *Adolph Diesterweg.* For an excellent analysis of his concept of teacher training see Eberhard Gross, *Erziehung und Gesellschaft im Werk Adolph Diesterweg,* esp. pp. 26–74. Diesterweg's articles in the *Rheinische Blätter* have been reprinted in *Friedrich Adolph Wilhelm Diesterweg: Sämtliche Werke, I. Abteilung: Zeitschriftenbeiträge,* ed. Heinrich Deiters et al. (Berlin, 1956–).

40. Cousin, *Report,* pp. 208–36, 271–72; Flaskamp, *Die Anfänge westfälischer Lehrerbildung,* p. 21. On Zahn's appointment see Klaus Goebel, "Diesterwegs Nachfolger in Meurs."

41. See esp. Harnisch's "Die zweckmässigste Vorbereitung zum Eintritt in ein Schullehrerseminar," *Der Volksschullhrer* 1 (1824): 103 ff., and *Die Schullehrerbildung.* In January 1849 the ministry held a conference of seminar directors and teachers, but the handpicked group of twelve excluded Diesterweg, who had had to resign from the directorship of the Berlin seminar in 1847. The conference made no important changes in the cautious reform program that its chairman, Ferdinand Stiehl (see below), proposed. See SC 6 (1849): 5–7, 33–39, 76–80, 85–88, 154–60.

42. Landfermann's memorandum was later published in SC 5 (1848): 120–30. See also *Dietrich Wilhelm Landfermann.*

43. For an example of a devout, relatively contented Catholic graduate who accepted the pastor's authority see Adam Langer, *Erinnerungen aus dem Leben eines Dorfschullehrers.* But even Langer complained in retrospect about his low income and the bothersome duties of the sextonship.

44. See SM 756 (Protestant seminar in Soest, 1826–45); SM 1706 (Catholic seminar in Büren, 1825–35); GS 3806 (Protestant seminar in Potsdam, 1827–30, 1834–35, 1837, 1847); the table on the "Social Origin of *Seminaristen*" for the Protestant seminar in Alt-Döbern, 1819–49, in Buchholz and Buchwald, *Die brandenburgischen Lehrerseminare,* p. 51. On the Potsdam lists, it should be noted, the fathers' occupations for 16 of the 186 graduates were illegible. The remainder included a clergyman (*Visitator*), a town forester (*Stadtförster*), a judicial official (*Justiz-Kommissarius*), and three town

clerks (*Rathsdiener*). There were 13 pastors, 17 "lower officials," and 19 "middle officials" on the Alt-Döbern rolls. The Soest and Büren rolls included 2 "preachers" (*Prediger*), 1 "canon" (*Canonikus*), 6 tax officials, and 7 office clerks.

45. Some of the twelve cantors, organists, and sextons on the Potsdam lists may also have been teachers. Twelve teachers' sons applied to the Meurs seminar in 1826, but only two were accepted. See Diesterweg, "Zur Geschichte der Seminarien, mit besonderer Beziehung auf das Seminar in Meurs," RB, n.s. 3 (1831).

46. Lottmann, "Zur Geschichte des Westfälischen Schulwesens," RB, n.s. 9 (1834): 154. For similar views see Daniel Schürmann, "Beshreibung des Volksschulwesens und des Lehrerstandes, besonders im Bergischen, während meiner durchlebten Tage," RB, n.s. 6 (1832): 39 ff.; F. B. Gelderblom, *Wehrstand und Lehrstand.*

47. Karl Böhm, "Blicke rück- und vorwärts," PV 11 (1843): 21.

48. Louis Balster, "Schulwesen, namentlich Besoldung der Lehrer," *Der Sprecher* 1840: 1452.

49. Johann Wilhelm Nehm, *Darlegung einiger Übelstände, welche den Volksschullehrerstand noch drücken, nebst Angabe der Erfordnisse zur Hebung derselben*, p. 34. Nehm was a graduate of the Soest seminar. See Riepe, *Erinnerungen an Johann Wilhelm Nehm, nebst Andeutungen über Zustände des Lehrerlebens.*

50. Otto Hattermann, *Konservative und liberale Strömungen in der preussischen Volksschulpolitik, 1819 bis 1848*, pp. 22–44. For the same stereotype in Bavaria see Josef Neukum, *Schule und Politik*, pp. 32–53.

51. Wander's account was originally published in 1869 and reprinted in *Karl Friedrich Wilhelm Wander, 1803 bis 1879*, pp. 43–70.

52. The ministry began to press for Wander's removal in Oct. 1843, but the district government in Liegnitz was reluctant to proceed to that extreme. See Hattermann, *Konservative und liberale Strömungen*, pp. 101–2. See also Wander's *Pädagogische Briefe vom Rhein an den Verfasser der Volksschule als Staatsanstalt.*

53. This account is based on the documents in HD 3388. See esp. Kamphausen to section, March 24, 1828; church and school committee to section, Aug. 20, 1826; petition (signed by forty-two residents) to *Bürgermeister*, Aug. 16, 1826. Kamphausen allowed the Reformed pastor's tutor to attend the lessons with which he was preparing his brother for the seminar, and the Lutherans charged that he was betraying secrets to the enemy camp. In 1816 Velbert had 595 residents—419 Lutheran, 122 Reformed, and 54 Catholic (*Beschreibung des Regierungsbezirkes Düsseldorf nach seinem Umfange, seiner Verwaltungs-Eintheilung und Bevölkerung*, p. 45).

54. Kamphausen transferred to another village in 1830.

55. "Stellet den Lehrer den Gleichgebildeten gleich," PV 12 (1844): 149.

56. E., "Schreiben eines jungen Lehrers an den Herausgeber," SS 1 (1843): 114–17. Wander attributed teachers' dissatisfaction "primarily" to the contradiction between "the higher level of education in the seminars" and the low incomes, and denied both "overeducation" and the corruption of city life. See his *Pädagogische Briefe*, pp. 287–90.

CHAPTER 4

1. PV 12 (1844): 89–90. In Pre-March, it has been noted, "emancipation" became a slogan that signified either "loosening from the past" or "direction into the future." See Karl Martin Grass and Reinhart Koselleck, "Emanzipation," pp. 168–69. On teachers' use of the term see, e.g., A. Rohlfs, *Die Volksschule und ihre Lehrer*, pp. 21–23; "Ein Pommer über Emancipation der Lehrer," PV 10 (1842): 337–41. For background see Carl Jantke and Dietrich Hilger, eds., *Die Eigentumslosen*.

2. Of the 28,992 teachers in 1849, 6,063 were in *Städten* and 22,929, including 1,879 "assistants," in *Landgemeinde*. See *Tabellen und amtlichen Nachrichten über den preussischen Staat für das Jahr 1849*, pp. 409–531.

3. "Ein Pommer über Emancipation," p. 341.

4. On the guild masters see Theodore Hamerow, *Restoration, Revolution, Reaction;* P. H. Noyes, *Organization and Revolution*, esp. pp. 15–33, 155–91.

5. A. Breter, "Zahlen gelten!" PV 11 (1843): 97–100.

6. See esp. the discussion of a "standesgemässe bürgerliche Lebenshaltung" in Rolf Engelsing, "Probleme der Lebenshaltung in Deutschland im 18. und 19. Jahrhundert," pp. 17–19.

7. The 1820 figures are in Victor Cousin, *Report on the State of Public Instruction in Prussia*, pp. 266–68. For the Königsberg figures see CB, 1865, pp. 747–57. In 1857 the average rural incomes in the Düsseldorf district were 224 thaler for Protestant teachers and 209 thaler for Catholic teachers, but in the previous six years the 1,140 positions in the district had received an average improvement of 32 thaler. For the income averages (1857) and recent improvements (1852–57) in all districts see CB, 1859, pp. 48–49, 59–61, 122–25, 250–53, 314–17.

8. For the Trier figures see Erwin Schaaf, *Die niedere Schule im Raum Trier-Saarbrücken von der späten Aufklärung bis zu Restauration, 1789–1825*, pp. 338–39; the section's report (Oct. 1842) is to be found in PR 6 (1843): 73–74. The later figures did not include the rental value of teachers' lodgings or the value of their rights to use common lands. The Potsdam and Frankfort figures are from Carl von Schmieden, *Das Elementar- und Bürgerschulwesen in der Provinz Brandenburg in seiner Entwicklung und seinen Fortschritten*, pp. 41–85; "Einkommen der Geistlichen und Schullehrer im Regierungs-Bezirk Frankfort," SPB 8 (1843): 122–24; "Klassifications-Tabelle der öffentlichen Volks-Schullehrerstellen in den Städten und auf dem Lande in Regierungs-Bezirke Potsdam, 1841," in GS 3828.

9. See Fr. J. Neumann, "Zum Lehre von den Lohngesetzen," pp. 367–69. Both households and individuals were included as taxpayers. See also the income estimates for rural laborers and smallholders in Karl Obermann, "Zur Klassenstruktur und zur sozialen Lage der Bevölkerung in Preussen 1846 bis 1849," pp. 98–99; the estimates of incomes and living costs in Lothar Schneider, *Der Arbeiterhaushalt im 18. und 19. Jahrhundert, dargestellt am Beispiel des Heim- und Fabrikarbeiters*, esp. pp. 32–45.

10. See the *Instruktion* of Feb. 16, 1847, in BJ 3 (1847): 452–54; the *Circular-Verfügung* of Aug. 30, 1848, in SPB 13 (1848): 627.

11. See, e.g., Johann Wilhelm Nehm, *Darlegung einiger Übelstande, welche den Volksschullehrerstand noch drücken, nebst Angabe der Erfordnisse zur Hebung derselben*, pp. 12–15; *Die Denkschrift der märkischen Lehrer*, pp. 2–5.

12. *Die Denkschrift der märkischen Lehrer*, p. 5.

13. Karl Böhm, "Neujahrswünsche," PV 10 (1842): 18. Balster claimed that propertyless teachers who had to support families on 200 thaler per year (with free lodging) "have to be very economical and careful with their budget, and indeed must go without much entertainment that does not cost very much." See his "Schulwesen, namentlich Besoldung der Lehrer," *Der Sprecher*, 1840, pp. 413–15.

14. See, e.g., Nehm, *Darlegung*, pp. 7–14; *Die Denkschrift der märkischen Lehrer*, pp. 6–7; Balster, "Schulwesen," p. 435; W. Dyckerhoff, "Folgen der ungenügenden Besoldung der Elementarlehrer," PV 10 (1842): 227–29.

15. Dyckerhoff, "Folgen der ungenügenden Besoldung," pp. 230–31; P. G. Klein, "Höchst einfache Variationen über das beliebte, obgleich betrübte Thema: Besserung der äussern Stellung des Lehrerstandes," PV 7 (1839): 323. "We are human beings like everyone else," a group of Rhineland teachers submitted in 1847, "and we dare ask our church and state officials: who does not desire—in addition to God's inner reward, which lifts men above earthly sufferings and professional difficulties—a material reward corresponding to his circumstances?" (*Wünsche rheinischer Lehrer betreffend die Gestaltung der Schule und ihrer Verhältnisse, die Bildung, Stellung und Besoldung der Lehrer*, p. 19).

16. "Hauswirtschafts-Anschlag," PV 5 (1837): 329–32. "The teacher has to get used to being addressed as 'my dear fellow' [*Mein Lieber*] even by subaltern officials," Klein wrote, "and a glance at his coat, adorned with the pearl of humility, makes him as friendly in accepting this cordial greeting as another in accepting a more polite form of address" ("Höchst einfache Variationen," p. 339).

17. For the 1848 proposals see the detailed compilation of teachers' reform programs, including both the spring assemblies and later conferences in Prussia, in PJ 4 (1849): 14–103.

18. See esp. "Stellet den Lehrer den Gleichgebildeten gleich," PV 12 (1844): 137–40, 149–52, 156–59, 167–69; A. Breter, "Arbeits- und Besoldungsverhältnisse. Wer ist am schlimmsten daran?" PV 9 (1841): 382–83, 386–90; Riepe, "Volksschulwesen," *Der Sprecher*, 1839, pp. 108–11.

19. J. Eduard Hesse, *An Preussens Volksschullehrer! Grundzüge zu einer das ganze Volksschulwesen umfassenden Petition* (not paginated); "Stellet den Lehrer den Gleichgebildeten gleich," p. 139. To Nehm, "the profession of *Volksschullehrer* is not only more difficult but also more important than that of officials [*Beamten*]"; its task was "the habituation of the child to orderliness, cleanliness, patience, obedience, loyalty, etc." and "the ennobling of the child's mind, the development of his talents, the awakening of love for God and man" (Nehm, *Darlegung*, p. 17).

20. "Lehrerstand," *Der Sprecher*, 1839, p. 160.

21. Nehm, *Darlegung*, p. 64. See also PJ 4 (1849): 65–66; "Denkschrift

über die Wünsche und Anträge der Volksschullehrer Schlesiens," appended
to SS 6 (1848): 49.

22. GS 3686. See esp. Superintendent Graefe (Wittstock) to Potsdam section, Feb. 21, 1843; Schoolteacher Schröder (Steinhöfel) to Superintendent Albrecht (Angermünde), March 19, 1843; Albrecht to section, March 24, 1843; Councillor Meyer to Albrecht et al., April 30, 1843.

23. See, e.g., Osthoff, "Offenes Schreiben an Hrn. Dr. Diesterweg," *Der Sprecher*, 1839, pp. 758–59; Balster, "Schul- und Küsterwesen (Schluss)," *Der Sprecher*, 1839, pp. 987–91; Dorfschullehrer Modestus Senex, "Über den sogennannten Schulmeisterdünkel," PV 5 (1837): 305–9. Although sexton duties "do not deprive the teacher of moral worth," Westphalian teachers wrote, "they do determine his measure of respect and regard among the lower sort, who regard him as their equal because of these similar functions" (*Denkschrift der märkischen Lehrer*, p. 38).

24. *Denkschrift der märkischen Lehrer*, p. 37. See also Ein Schullehrerfreund, "Der Schullehrer und die Thurmuhr," PV 9 (1841): 343–44.

25. Klein, "Höchst einfache Variationen," pp. 333–38.

26. Karl Friedrich Wihelm Wander, *Die Volksschule als Staatsanstalt*, pp. 60–61. See also, e.g., "Oekonomische Stellung der Lehrer," PR 10 (1845): 84–86; Helbing, "Aufruf an Preussens Volksschullehrer," BJ 4 (1848): 422–25; *Wünsche rheinischer Lehrer*, p. 23; "Denkschrift über die Wünsche und Anträge der Volksschullehrer Schlesiens," pp. 43–45. Of the pensions for 131 retired teachers in the Potsdam district in 1846, 19 were over 100 thaler, 69 were between 60 and 100 thaler, and 43 were under 50 thaler (Otto Schulz, "Monatliche Schulnachrichten, No. 10 (Oct. 1846)," BJ 4 [1848]: 13).

27. Klein, "Höchst einfache Variationen," pp. 340–41. See also Karl Böhm, "Eine Phantasiereise durch das Land der Wahrheit," PV 9 (1841): 241–45.

28. "Denkschrift über die Wünsche und Anträge der Volksschullehrer Schlesiens," p. 45. The rector in Teltow, it was reported in 1848, abandoned his family and migrated to America. The homeless "widow" had to beg for her children and live in the poor house (*Gemeindehaus*) with three other destitute families. In this case the main fault lay with the teacher, but the reporter still felt that "we teachers cannot tolerate this kind of treatment for the wife of a colleague and cannot allow her and her children to end up in disgrace." See Bittkow, "Noth einer Lehrerwittwe. Dringende Bitte," RB, n.s. 38 (1848): 254–55.

29. PJ 4 (1849): 60–64.

30. On the advantages and disadvantages of land endowments see, e.g., Hesse, *An Preussens Volksschullehrer!*; "Zur Lehrerbesoldungsfrage," RB, n.s. 38 (1848): 247–48; Karl Böhm, "Zeitfragen, vorgelegt zur Besprechung," PV 8 (1840): 124. On the arrangements for firewood see the detailed income breakdowns (1847) for rural teachers in GS 82 (Superintendancy Bernau) and 411 (Superintendancy Angermünde). In 1838–39 the peasants in Biesdorf wanted recently settled day laborers to pay a fee for the wood, but the Potsdam section disapproved and the teacher had to manage with an inadequate supply (GS 4951). In the early 1840s several younger teachers in Westphalia requested that their communities provide a fixed annual sum for the wood

(Friedrich Laduga, *Beiträge zur Entwicklung des Volksschulwesens in der Provinz Westfalen, 1815–1848*, pp. 71–72).

31. GS 34. See esp. "Verhandelt Dobberzin," May 5, 1834; Albrecht to section, Jan. 6, 1842, and Nov. 25, 1845; "Verhandelt Dobberzin," Oct. 27, 1845. Albrecht reported that the church and school committees wanted Krause transferred and that he would agree so long as he was offered a position no worse than his present one; but he was still teaching in Dobberzin in 1861.

32. These statistics exclude Berlin. See F. W. C. Dieterici, "Statistische Übersicht des öffentlichen Unterrichts im Preussischen Staate im Jahre 1816 und im Jahre 1846," pp. 35–37.

33. See, e.g., *Die Denkschrift der märkischen Lehrer*, pp. 11–12; the report from *Kreis* Minden (Westphalia) in BJ 1 (1845): 691–97; "Denkschrift über die Wünsche und Anträge der Volksschullehrer Schlesiens," p. 42.

34. *Die Denkschrift der märkischen Lehrer*, pp. 14–16; P. G. Klein, "Einige Worte in Bezug auf den in No. 30 der vorjährigen P. V. Sch. Z . . . 'Die Volksschullehrer haben zum sterben zu viel . . . ,'" PV 6 (1838): 158–59. See also the report from Silesia in BJ 3 (1847): 147.

35. Laduga, *Beiträge*, p. 40; *Die Denkschrift der märkischen Lehrer*, p. 13.

36. The budgets, with inspectors' frequent references to local poverty in their accompanying reports, are in GS 586 (Superintendancy Angermünde), 629 (Superintendancy Zehdenick), and 920 (Superintendancy Kyritz). Striez's comments in his report to District President Bassewitz, Jan. 18, 1838, are in GS 3815. They were not included in the published version; see Schmieden, *Das Elementar- und Bürgerschulwesen*. For teachers' impressions of rural poverty in Brandenburg see Schleich, "Hebung der untern Volksklasse," PV 12 (1844): 259–60; "Der Zustand der Sommerschule in der Mark Brandenburg," SPB 13 (1848): 132–33, 160–65.

37. From the section's statistics in HD 2586. By 1849 there were 13,165 "factory children" under age fourteen (7.4 percent of the school-age population) in the Düsseldorf district. See *Tabellen und amtlichen Nachrichten*, p. 561. According to the regulation in 1839, children under nine could not work in factories and those from age nine to fifteen were limited to ten hours per day. But in 1845 the president of the Düsseldorf district government requested that the regulation be extended to children in domestic industry—noting that "precisely in this area the greatest and worst abuses occur, since the largest factories cannot escape supervision so easily" (Karl-Heinz Ludwig, "Die Fabrikarbeit von Kindern im 19. Jahrhundert," p. 85.

38. Grashof's comments from his memorandum to the provincial *Landtag* are reproduced in Nehm, "Schulgeld oder Schulsteuer?" *Der Sprecher*, 1839, pp. 1494–98, 1512–14. In 1832, Diesterweg had also reported teachers' troubles with fee arrears in the Rhineland. See his "Achtungswürdiges Benehmen der Lehrer in schwerer Zeit und hoffnungsreiche Aussichten für die Zukunft," RB, n.s. 5 (1832): 102–8.

39. Johann Peter Fasbender, *Beobachtungen und Erinnerungen aus meinem Leben*, p. 57. This is a vivid recollection of teachers' disputes with parents and local officials over the school fee and stresses the impact of population growth and poverty. The district government in Düsseldorf issued

detailed instructions to local officials on school attendance in 1839 and again in 1840. See Friedrich Wilhelm Niedergesäs, *Das Elementarschulwesen in den königlichen preussischen Staaten*, pp. 261–66.

40. Fasbender, *Beobachtungen*, p. 65.

41. Ibid., pp. 67–68. The petitioners went on to request a new law from the provincial *Landtag* in 1845. They were counting on the support of several sympathetic delegates, but these declined after soliciting a negative opinion from the district school councillor.

42. Balster, "Beaufsichtigung der Schule, betreffend die Ausschliessung des Lehrers vom Ortsschulvorstande," *Der Sprecher*, 1840, p. 463. See also Klein, "Höchst einfache Variationen," p. 325. Again, Diesterweg had anticipated teachers' complaints; see his "Das Amt des Schulvorstandes: Wie wichtig die Tätigkeit der Schulvorstande sei, und worin sie bestehe," RB 3 (1828): 79–86.

43. *Die Denkschrift der märkischen Lehrer*, pp. 25–26. See also *Wünsche rheinischer Lehrer*, pp. 14–15; the summary of the petition from teachers in the Bunzlau, Haynau, Goldberg, and Liegnitz regions of Silesia to the Silesian *Landtag*, Feb. 1845, in SS 4 (1846): 177–82; "Petition der unterzeichneten Lehrer Westfalens . . . betreffend: Aufnahme des Volksschullehers als Mitglied des Ortsschulvorstandes und des Presbyteriums," BJ 3 (1847): 633–36.

44. Dr. Werther, "Der Bakel. Eine Novelle für Schullehrer," PV 7 (1839): 135–38.

45. Bruno Sauer, *Aus dem Leben eines märkisch-pommerschen Dorfschullehrers um 1800.* See also Johann Anton Küpper, *Versuch, eine zweckmässige Verfassung für den protestantischen Prediger- und Schullehrerstand zu entwerfen*, 2:26–27.

46. See, e.g., the internal memoranda of the Lutheran High Consistory in 1768, and esp. Sadewasser to Teller (Dec. 16), GS 3822; Alfred Heubaum, "Die Geschichte des ersten preussischen Schulgesetzentwurfes (1798–1807)," pp. 217–18; Ferdinand Vollmer, *Die preussische Volksschulpolitik unter Friedrich dem Grossen*, pp. 270–71.

47. Schaaf, *Die niedere Schule*, pp. 210–12, 225–26.

48. Küpper, *Versuch*, pp. 17–18, 158–62.

49. See the ordinances for the Düsseldorf district in 1814 and 1817, in Niedergesäs, *Das Elementarschulwesen*, pp. 303–4, 543–52. The exception, at least in law, was the Trier district, where the section excluded the pastors and deprived the communities of their "right of presentation" (Schaaf, *Die niedere Schule*, p. 335).

50. PJ 4 (1849): 52–56. For earlier advancement schemes see, e.g., "Stellet den Lehrer den Gleichgebildeten gleich," pp. 158–59, 167–68; Wander, *Die Volksschule als Staatsanstalt*, pp. 23–29, 37–39, 58–59; *Wünsche rheinischer Lehrer*, p. 23.

51. In 1822 there were 1,231 assistants (including a few women who gave instruction in domestic skills) in Prussia, but in 1849 the *Land* alone had 1,879 male assistants. See Ernst Engel, "Beiträge zur Geschichte und Statistik des Unterrichts, insbesondere des Volksschulunterrichts, im preussis-

chen Staate," pp. 99–116; *Tabellen und amtlichen Nachrichten*, pp. 409–531.

52. Report from *Kreis* Minden, in BJ 1 (1845): 696.

53. "Denkschrift über die Wünsche und Anträge der Volksschullehrer Schlesiens," p. 54.

54. "Willkürliches Verfahren bei Besetzung der Schullehrerstellen," PV 11 (1843): 239.

55. "Die Lehrerwahl," PV 9 (1841): 183. In 1835 twenty-two candidates applied for the position in Ickten (Düsseldorf district). See HD 2970. There were twenty-one applicants for the position in Pattscheid, in the same district, in 1840; twenty of them were seminar graduates, and seven had been teaching for at least five years. See HD 3650. Neither position was particularly well endowed.

56. Report from the *Magdeburger Wochenblatt*, reprinted in PV 11 (1843): 384.

57. The provincial conferences in Brandenburg, Pomerania, Silesia, the Rhineland, and Westphalia proposed this procedure for appointments. PJ 4 (1849): 54–55.

58. PJ 4 (1849): 74–78.

59. SC 5 (1848): 244–46. The assembly in Bonn on April 30, 1848, was dominated by Catholic teachers; their petition repudiated the recent Köln-Deutz assembly and stated, "The *Volksschule* will remain in an intimate relationship [*innigen Verhältnisse*] with the family as well as the community, the state and the church" (SC 5 [1848]: 219–22). But see also the petition from twelve Catholic teachers in Breslau (July 25, 1848) in SC 5 (1848): 348–51.

60. At the Brandenburg provincial conference Schnell argued for a "general religious instruction" and condemned the confessions as "untruth, lies"; but other delegates warned against antagonizing the communities. The majority conclusion was that the school "paves the way" for confessional instruction. See the *Protokolle der Provincial-Lehrer-Conferenz zu Frankfort a.O.*; "Die Provincial-Lehrerconferenz zu Frankfort a.d.O.," SPB 13 (1848): 645–54. The assembly in Köln-Deutz (April 26, 1848) voted that "the *Volksschulen* are state institutions . . . without depriving the church of its rightful influence on the ethical-religious instruction of youth"; but a minority had wanted to elimate the latter phrase (SC 5 [1848]: 218). At the later Rhineland conference there was general agreement that exclusion of clergymen from the inspectorate was not intended as "an alienation of the school from the church," but simply "to prevent unfriendly relations with servants of the church, which bring harmful results to church and school" (SC 5 [1848]: 335). A Protestant teachers' assembly for the Koblenz district, held in Saint Goar on May 18–19, had included ten pastors as well as Councillor Landfermann. Probably under their guidance the resulting petition devoted considerable attention to the confessional issue and concluded "that it is impossible and inappropriate at the present time to free the *Volksschulen* from their confessional character, and that the attempt to do so would lead to harmful disorder in the elementary school system" (SC 5 [1848]: 257–80, and esp.

261–65). See also the reports on the Duisburg and Saarbrücken assemblies in SC 5 (1848): 313–15, 329–30.

61. W--g, "Der Lehrer als Presbyter," SC 2 (1845): 225. For requests that teachers be eligible for election to the *Presbyterium* see "Petition der unterzeichneten Lehrer Westfalens"; *Wünsche rheinischer Lehrer*, p. 16; SC 5 (1848): 220, 324.

62. *Protokolle der Provincial-Lehrer-Conferenz, Beilage* 1.

63. *Die Denkschrift der märkischen Lehrer*, pp. 37–38.

64. SM 460. See esp. Balster to Superintendent Consbruck, Dec. 4, 1845; Frahne to Consbruck, March 31, 1846; Consbruck to Balster, April 20, 1846.

65. *Die Denkschrift der märkischen Lehrer*, p. 31. "Of course the clergyman has a more scholarly training than the schoolteacher," the petitioners admitted, "but because it is training for a completely different profession it provides him with little qualification for the office of school inspector" (Ibid., p. 29).

66. Wander, *Die Volksschule als Staatsanstalt*, pp. 34–36.

67. SM 460. See esp. Frahne to Balster, Jan. 9, 1837; Balster to Düsseldorf section, Jan. 9, 1837.

68. Klein, "Höchst einfache Variationen," pp. 331–32.

69. Y., "Eine Schulerfahrung," PV 4 (1836): 61.

70. A. Wolff, "Eine ähnliche, aber dennoch in ihren Folgen erfreulichere Schulerfahrung . . . ," PV 4 (1836): 317. See also "Aus Pommern," pp. 137–38.

71. In 1848 every provincial conference condemned the secret reports (PJ 4 [1849]: 74). For other attacks on them see, e.g., Schulmeister Felix Jun., "Die Schulberichte sollten auch den Lehrern vorgelegt werden," PV 2 (1834): 61; "Denkschrift über die Wünsche und Anträge der Volksschullehrer Schlesiens," p. 51; the petition of the Tivoli assembly, Berlin (April 26, 1848), in Helmut König, ed., *Programme zur bürgerlichen Nationalerziehung in der Revolution von 1848–1849*, p. 117.

72. HD 2847. See esp. Hagen to Petersen, July 25, 1848; Petersen to section, July 31, 1848; school committee to Petersen, July 30, 1848; section to Hagen, Aug. 11 and Aug. 22, 1848.

73. Striez's report to District President Bassewitz (Jan. 18, 1838), GS 3815. See also Landfermann's criticisms in SC 5 (1848): 124–27; Franz Ludwig Zahn, "Eine Wort über die Leitung des Volksschulwesens," SC 2 (1845): 377–401.

74. *Wünsche rheinischer Lehrer*, pp. 9–10. For similar statements see, e.g., "Ein Pommer über Emancipation der Lehrer," pp. 239–40; Wilhelm Nehm, "Soll der Staat die Tochter der Kirche freien (Schluss)," *Der Sprecher*, 1838, pp. 87–90; König, *Programme*, pp. 116–17.

75. At the Silesian conference several delegates argued that the inclusion of clergymen would contradict "the principle, asserted repeatedly in the emancipation question, that each *Stand* should elect its immediate supervisory officials from its own ranks." The conference stipulated that the new *Kreis* inspectors be "freely elected" by the teachers, but accepted clergymen if they were "schoolmen" and resigned their clerical offices (SS 6 [1848]: 401–8). See also PJ 4 (1849): 74–78.

CHAPTER 5

1. On the Berlin seminar see Friedrich Buchholz and Gerhard Buchwald, eds., *Die brandenburgischen Lehrerseminare und die ihnen angegliederten Präparandenanstalten*, pp. 165–212. From 1835 to 1841 the Meurs seminar graduated 125 teachers; approximately 39 of them were working in towns in 1843. Of the 25 graduates in 1843, 12 were assigned to towns, all as assistants. See Franz Ludwig Zahn, "Verzeichniss der im Seminar zu Meurs gebildeten Lehrer, 1823–45," *Schul-Anzeiger für die Rheinprovinz und Westfalen* 2 (Jan. 1844): 6–12 (attached to SC 1, 1844).

2. See, e.g., Richard Boschan, *Das Bildungswesen in der Stadt Potsdam bis zur Wiederaufrichtung des preussischen Staates*, pp. 68–70; F. A. Block, *Geschichte des städtischen Schulwesens zu Merseburg*, pp. 40–57; Ferdinand Schnell, "Das Schulwesen der Stadt Prenzlau," SPB 12 (1847): 327–28.

3. Eduard Spranger, *Wilhelm von Humboldt und die Reform des Bildungswesens*, pp. 185–92; Emil Hollack and Friedrich Tromnau, *Geschichte des Schulwesens der königlichen Haupt- und Residenzstadt Königsberg i/Pr. mit besonderer Berücksichtigung der niederen Schulen*, pp. 457–64.

4. See the documents in *Die Stein'schestädteordnung in Breslau*, 2:322–26.

5. Helmut König, *Zur Geschichte der bürgerlichen Nationalerziehung in Deutschland zwischen 1807 und 1815*, 1:345. Süvern's draft law obligated the towns to introduce a school tax, but only to supplement existing endowments and municipal aid. See par. 49 in Lothar Schweim, ed., *Schulreform in Preussen, 1809–1819*.

6. Victor Cousin, *Report on the State of Public Instruction in Prussia*, pp. 134–38.

7. There is a convenient synopsis of population statistics for Prussia and other German states in Donald G. Rohr, *The Origins of Social Liberalism in Germany*, pp. 13–19. Detlef K. Müller, *Sozialstruktur und Schulsystem*, is an impressive attempt to relate Prussian urban education to social and demographic change in the nineteenth century. But Müller is concerned primarily with the development of high school systems, and his quantitative evidence is derived largely from Berlin.

8. The general pattern of growth and the shift from older, usually parish endowments to new cash salaries are well illustrated by the detailed income breakdowns for teaching positions in twenty-one of the eighty towns in the Potsdam district in 1847 (GS). For other examples see Block, *Geschichte des städtischen Schulwesens*, pp. 61–64, 71–81, 154–62; Albrecht Brinkmann, *Geschichte der Dortmunden Volksschulen*, pp. 98–100, 146–47, 154–62. This section, it should be stressed, is intended only to provide essential background on urban socioeconomic conditions and municipal government in Pre-March. There is an insightful discussion of the latter in Reinhart Koselleck, *Preussen zwischen Reform und Revolution*, pp. 561–85.

9. See, e.g., Hollack and Tromnau, *Geschichte des Schulwesens*, pp. 486–501; Block, *Geschichte des städtischen Schulwesens*, pp. 62–82.

10. Müller, *Sozialstruktur und Schulsystem*, pp. 190–92; Friedrich Herz-

berg, *Über das Berlinische Elementarschulwesen;* Dietrich Rittershausen, "Beiträge zur Geschichte des Berliner Elementarschulwesens von der Reformation bis 1836," pp. 178–317; Friedrich Wienecke, "Die Begründung der Berliner Schul-Kommission am September 1811."

11. The plan was published in *Jahrbücher des preussischen Volks-Schul-Wesens* 6(1827): 169–222.

12. Ibid., p. 170.

13. See the reports in SPB 7 (1842): 123; SPB 11 (1846): 1–2; SPB 12 (1847): 64, 279.

14. For background see Günter Liebchen, "Zu den Lebensbedingungen der untern Schichten im Berlin des Vormärz: Eine Betrachtung an Hand von Mietspreisentwicklung und Wohnverhältnisse," in Otto Büsch, ed., *Untersuchungen zur Geschichte der frühen Industrialisierung vornehmlich im Wirtschaftsraum Berlin/Brandenburg,* pp. 270–314; Dieter Bergmann, "Die Berliner Arbeiterschaft in Vormärz und Revolution, 1830–50; Eine Trägerschicht der beginnenden Industrialisierung als neue Kraft in der Politik," in ibid., pp. 455–511. On the relationship between industrial development and public education see Peter Lundgreen, "Schulbildung und Frühindustrialisierung in Berlin/Preussen: Eine Einführung in den historischen und systematischen Zusammenhang von Schule und Wirtschaft," in ibid., pp. 452–610.

15. The statistics on school attendance are from Otto Schulz's reports in SPB 3 (1838): 106–9 and SPB 13 (1848): 134–39. For the budget statistics see the reports in SPB 12 (1847): 575–77, 766–67; tables 82 and 86 in Müller, *Sozialstruktur und Schulsystem,* pp. 564, 572. The net expenditure on the debt service climbed from 666,242 thaler in 1835 to 1,001,145 thaler in 1840 and was still 667,410 thaler in 1845.

16. See Otto Schulz's reports in SPB 9 (1844): 147–58; the report in BJ 1 (1845): 56–57.

17. Böhme, "Über Gesang und Gesangunterricht in Volksschulen," RB, n.s. 12 (1835): 238–41. See also the managers' defense in "Über die Verhältnisse der Berlinischen Privatschulen," SPB 13 (1848): 335–44.

18. See the Brandenburg school college's warnings about illegal assistants in SPB 2 (1837): 227–29; SPB 5 (1840): 353–54.

19. Otto Schulz, "Der Noth des Schullehrerstandes," SPB 10 (1845): 147–63; the report in PV 11 (1843): 167–68; the report in BJ 1 (1845): 56–57.

20. "Statistische Uebersicht der Bevölkerung sämmtlicher Städte der Kurmark Brandenburg . . . ," pp. 265–77. For background see Büsch, *Untersuchungen.*

21. The section's report is in *Regierung Potsdam, Amtsblatt,* 1838, p. 55. Striez's remarks are in his report to District President Bassewitz (Jan. 18, 1839), GS 3815.

22. The Greiffenberg documents are in GS 603–5. See esp. GS 603: Pastor Hunger's report, Aug. 1815; Wedell-Parlow to section, April 11 and Aug. 21, 1825, May 30, Oct. 10, and Nov. 28, 1829. For the population statistics see "Statistische Uebersicht der Bevölkerung sämmtlicher Städte," p. 270.

23. GS 604. See esp. Albrecht to section, Oct. 10, 1833, and July 21, 1835;

Pastor Fittbogen to section, April 10, 1849; magistrate to section, May 14, 1849; section men to section, May 16, 1849; section to Greiffenberg, June 3, 1849. The new regime, it should be noted, complained that the owners of three new settlements of sharecroppers and hired hands in the Greiffenberg school district were not paying a fair share. One of the owners was the *Landrat*.

24. GS 764–65. See esp. GS 764: Striez's report, Sept. 4, 1834. GS 765: Councillor von Türk's report, Oct. 10, 1828; magistrate to section, Jan. 24, 1829; Wedell-Parlow to section, Feb. 27, 1829; Councillor Schulz's report, June 25, 1829. For the teaching incomes in 1847 see GS 322.

25. Carl von Schmieden, *Das Elementar- und Bürgerschulwesen in der Provinz Brandenburg in seiner Entwicklung und seinen Fortschritten*, p. 83; "Klassifications-Tabelle der öffentlichen Volksschullehrerstellen in den Städten und auf dem Lande in Regierungbezirke Potsdam, 1841," in GS 3826.

26. *Tabellen und amtlichen Nachrichten über den preussischen Staat für das Jahr 1849*, pp. 409–531. For background see Walter Schäfer, "Die ideengeschichtlichen Grundlagen der Reform des Volksschulwesens im Grossherzogtum Berg und in der Stadt Düsseldorf von 1799–1816," pp. 59–84.

27. HD 2892–98. There is a detailed account of the origins and development of this school dispute in the report of the section commission, Dec. 31, 1831 (HD 2894). See also HD 2892: *Landrat* Miquel to section, Sept. 10, 1830; HD 2893: *Oberbürgermeister* to section, Oct. 28, 1830. In 1828 silk workers in Crefeld had rioted, and in Aug. 1830 there was another disturbance among textile workers in Aachen. See Richard Tilly, "Popular Disorders in Nineteenth Century Germany: A Preliminary Survey," pp. 22–23, 33.

28. See esp. HD 2893: school committee meeting, Nov. 29, 1830, and teachers' response, Jan. 7, 1831; *Oberbürgermeister* to schoolteachers, Jan. 23, 1831. HD 2898: excerpt from meeting of city council and section commission, Nov. 24, 1831; school committee *Promemoria*, Nov. 25, 1831; meeting of city council, Nov. 28, 1831.

29. Johann Friedrich Wilberg, *Erinnerungen aus meinem Leben, nebst Bemerkungen über Erziehung, Unterricht, und verwandte Gegenstände*, pp. 180–89.

30. From the statistics of the section in HD 2586. According to a report in 1847, Elberfeld had seventeen regular teachers and thirty-two assistants (SPB 12 [1847]: 487–89).

31. Karl Böhm, "Neujahrswünsche," PV 10 (1842): 19.

32. Eduard Mücke, "Auch Etwas über Lehrer und deren äussere Verhältnisse." I have used a copy of the article in GS 3836.

33. Ferdinand Schnell, "Über das preussische Volksschulwesen. Bemerkungen in Bezug auf das städtische Schulwesen," PV 5 (1837): 188.

34. Otto Schulz, "Der Noth des Schullehrerstandes," p. 148.

35. —r, "Wie empfängt in manchen Schulen der Hülfslehrer sein Honorar," PV 4 (1836): 334–35.

36. "Die Hülfslehrer Berlins als Missionare," PV 4 (1836): 267–69; "Ant-

wortschreiben des Lehrers . . . an den . . . schen Knabenschulen zu Berlin . . . ," PV 4 (1836): 97–100.

37. The assistants' petitions were published in SPB 13 (1848): 348–49; "Materialien zur Geschichte des Berliner Schulwesens nach der Revolution von 1848," pp. 297–304.

38. Helmut König, ed., *Programme zur bürgerlichen Nationalerziehung in der Revolution von 1848–49*, pp. 122, 126–27. The composition of the fifteen-member Tivoli committee was reported in Bloch, "Die Wünsche der Lehrer an die neue Zeit," BJ 4 (1848): 310. In 1848 the managers were willing to forego a public subsidy, but only if they were guaranteed "state-sponsored equality" with the municipal schools. See "Über die Verhältnisse der Berlinischen Privatschulen."

39. See esp. John R. Gillis, *The Prussian Bureaucracy in Crisis, 1840–1860*, pp. 39–43, 58–66.

40. Wandelstern, "Ein Tag aus dem Leben eines Schullehrers," BJ 1 (1845): 561–70.

41. Striez to Potsdam section, June 4, 1842, GS 3836.

42. See, e.g., Böhm, "Neujahrswünsche," pp. 18–19; Ferdinand Schnell, "Über das preussische Volksschulwesen, und dessen Entwicklung in neuerer Zeit . . . ," PV 4 (1836): 327–28; "Die ungünstige Stellung der Stadtschullehrer im Verhältniss zu der Stellung der meisten Landschullehrer," PV 10 (1842): 318–19.

43. Ferdinand Schnell, "Einiges über die Verhältnisse der Volksschullehrer, nebst einigen Nachrichten über das Prenzlauer Stadtschulwesen," PV 10 (1842): 71–72. See also the report on Hirschberg (Silesia) in SPB 11 (1846): 4–5; Otto Schulz's comments on younger teachers in Berlin in SPB 11 (1846): 20–25.

44. PV 12 (1844): 353–54.

45. Block, *Geschichte des städtischen Schulwesens*, p. 65; J. Eduard Hesse, *An Preussens Volksschullehrer!*

46. Schneider, "Die Lage der Volksschullehrer," PV 10 (1842): 167–68.

47. See the reprint of articles from the *Vossische Zeitung* in PV 12 (1844): 171–78.

48. A. Breter, "Zahlen gelten!" PV 11 (1843): 97–100; "Wünsche und Anträge der Breslauer evang. Elementarlehrer," SS 6 (1848): 113–19. See also the report on teachers' salaries in Breslau in SS 4 (1846): 45–46.

49. See the copy of Mücke's article from the *Vossische Zeitung* (Feb. 18, 1843), in PV 11 (1843): 123. See also A. Rohlfs, *Die Volksschule und ihre Lehrer*, p. 22. "Denkschrift über die Wünsche und Anträge der Volksschullehrer Schlesiens," appended to SS 6 (1848): 37–38.

50. "Hab' ich Recht?" PV 9 (1841): 146–47. See also Karl Böhm, "Der Rüge Rüge," PV 5 (1837): 377–79; "Eine Paralelle," PV 9 (1841): 253–54. In 1848 the Silesian and Brandenburg conferences demanded that the theology candidates be excluded from the rectorates; three others would tolerate them "only if they have achieved the same level of pedagogical education as any other teacher and are subject to the same conditions and rules with respect to appointment and promotion" (PJ 4 [1849]: 54; "Die Provinzial-Lehrerconferenz zu Frankfurt a. d. O.," SPB 13 [1848]: 675).

51. König, *Programme*, p. 123.
52. Ibid., p. 124.
53. PJ 4 (1849): 56–57.

CHAPTER 6

1. For background on Altenstein and the post-1840 ministry see Otto Hattermann, *Konservative und liberale Strömungen in der preussischen Volksschulpolitik, 1819 bis 1848*; Bernhard Krueger, *Stiehl und seine Regulative*. Krueger rightly stresses that Eichhorn, Eilers, and Stiehl were committed to reform, but ignores their reaction to the Breslau incident (see below). See also Gerd Eilers, *Zur Beurtheilung des Ministeriums Eichhorn von einem Mitgliede desselben*, esp. pp. 107–18.

2. Heinrich Deinhardt, "Die Volksschule und ihre Nebenanstalten," in Helmut König, ed., *Gedanken zur Nationalerziehung aus dem Vormärz*, p. 315.

3. Quoted in Ludwig Clausnitzer, *Geschichte des preussischen Unterrichtsgesetzes*, p. 84.

4. Hattermann, *Konservative und liberale Stromüngen*, pp. 22–40; Thomas Nipperdey, "Volksschule und Revolution im Vormärz," pp. 123–25; Josef Neukum, *Schule und Politik*, esp. pp. 32–53.

5. See the ministry's *Promemoria* of 1841, in CB 1865: 748–55; Eichhorn's response to the Ministry of the Interior, April 21, 1847, in SPB 12 (1847): 437–40; Krueger, *Stiehl*, pp. 77–83.

6. Krueger, *Stiehl*, pp. 70, 75.

7. PR 6 (1843): 556–61. The article was originally published in the *Literarische Zeitung*, 1847, no. 17. The author was not identified, but there is an approving reference to Stiehl, whom Eilers recommended to Eichhorn in 1844.

8. PR 6 (1843): 558.

9. Ibid., p. 557.

10. Ibid., pp. 560–61.

11. SPB 12 (1847): 437–40.

12. Hattermann, *Konservative und liberale Strömungen*, pp. 95–96. Excerpts from the provincial law are in Clausnitzer, *Geschichte des preussischen Unterrichtsgesetzes*, pp. 126–31.

13. Friedrich Harkort, *Bemerkungen über die preussische Volksschule und ihre Lehrer*, esp. pp. 40–54, 72–75, 89–94. For background on Harkort see Gottfried Uhlig, *Bourgeoisie und Volksschule im Vormärz*, esp. pp. 118–27.

14. Robert M. Bigler, *The Politics of German Protestantism*, pp. 187–230.

15. Krueger, *Stiehl*, p. 71.

16. A sober, detailed account of the Breslau incident, using Stiehl's investigation and the ministry's reports, is Artur Heidrich, "Die Auflösung des evangelischen Schullehrerseminars zu Breslau am 29. 1. 1846." See esp. pp. 8–9, 17–19.

17. Ibid., pp. 20, 29. In his inaugural address Gerlach had called for a return

to the "ancient, solid, proven foundation of the Gospel" in rural education and had criticized modern instruction for conceding the existence of God only to exercise the children's "thinking power" and provide variety. For his ideal of the schoolteacher he cited a *Schulreglement* isued in the Duchy of Berg in 1764. See Gerlach, "Rede bei Einweihung des Breslauer Lehrer-Seminars," SC 2 (1845): 153–65.

18. (Haensel), *Die Keime zur Auflösung des Kgl. evang. Schullehrer-Seminars zu Breslau.* The author had been a pupil in the Breslau seminar during the first semester of Gerlach's directorship.

19. Heidrich, "Die Auflösung des evangelischen Schullehrerseminars," p. 25.

20. Ibid., pp. 10, 18.

21. Quoted in Hattermann, *Konservative und liberale Strömungen,* p. 103.

22. The cabinet order and Stiehl's draft published in Krueger, *Stiehl,* pp. 180–83. Stiehl had begun his draft with a tribute to "the quiet and beneficial effect of many schoolteachers." The ministry, it should be noted, sent the order to the provincial administrations, but did not publish it for the teachers' benefit.

23. Ibid., p. 182. "With the establishment of special educational institutions for the *Volksschullehrer,*" Stiehl had written, "the intention certainly was not to create a segregated *Stand* whose strivings and demands on life advance ruthlessly beyond the people whose children are entrusted to it" (Ibid., p. 181).

24. Quoted in Hattermann, *Konservative und liberale Strömungen,* pp. 37–39.

25. The response from the section was published in Riepe, *Erinnerungen an Johann Wilhelm Nehm, nebst Andeutungen über Zustände des Lehrerlebens,* p. 65. The Arnsberg section had informed Nehm that the teachers' "hard-pressed situation lies less in the insufficiency of their income than in their inability to limit their life-styles and needs to the means at their disposal" (Ibid., p. 69).

26. See the responses of the sections in ibid., pp. 64–69; SPB 7 (1842): 471–74; Johann Peter Fasbender, *Beobachtungen und Erinnerungen aus meinem Leben,* pp. 63–67.

27. A copy of the article and the official correspondence are to be found in GS 3836. Mücke, it should be noted, was not a seminar graduate; he had attended a gymnasium and had abandoned a military career as a lower officer (*Unter-Officer*). The retired *Landrat* was Heinrich Ludwig von Bornstedt. Mücke later claimed that Bornstedt had read and approved the article, but apparently he regretted his signature. He died while the section was considering a legal proceeding against him.

28. Ibid. In fact Mücke did not repent. In December 1842 he published another brash article, protesting secret procedures in the state bureaucracy, in the *Vossische Zeitung.* A few months later, in a published account of his dealings with the section, he denied that he had intended to attack higher officials, but also protested that he was not a "liar" (PV 11 [1843]: 114–16). The section again requested a formal disciplinary proceeding, and this time the ministry agreed, though still suggesting that a warning would suffice.

29. See esp. Reinhart Koselleck, *Preussen zwischen Reform und Revolution*, pp. 398–403.

30. Karl Mager, "Die Volksschule als Staatsanstalt," PR 6 (1843): 322–23.

31. Koselleck, *Preussen*, p. 404.

32. Wander, *Die Volksschule als Staatsanstalt*, pp. 13–14; *Die Denkschrift der märkischen Lehrer*, pp. 1–3; A. Rohlfs, *Die Volksschule und ihre Lehrer, II. Sendschreiben*, pp. 16–17. Rohlfs had argued that the schools could not remain "halfway" between community and state. "The control of the school . . . is as meticulous as possible, with the school considered a state institution and the teacher a state official [*Staatsbeamter*]; and yet the state makes no sacrifice to promote this intellectual sphere."

33. SS 6 (1848): 371. Lawyers faced a similar contradiction. One observer commented that after the Napoleonic Wars the state consistently tried "to keep the legal profession subordinate, its strength dispersed, to deny it the rights of state officials while simultaneously burdening it with all the duties of officials" (Lenore O'Boyle, "The Democratic Left in Germany, 1848," pp. 378–79).

34. PJ 4 (1849): 78–80.

35. GS 3836. See also Mücke's poetic tribute to "brave" Wander in PV 10 (1842): 378–79.

36. Karl Böhm, "Der Lehrer und seine Bedeutung," PV 5 (1837): 259.

37. Riepe, "Volksschulwesen," *Der Sprecher*, 1839, p. 109. In 1841 Riepe made another, more explicit appeal for corporate self-help and noted that the *Landrecht* recognized the right of petition. See his *Erinnerungen*, pp. 46, 55–56.

38. Böhm, "Zeitfragen, vorgelegt zur Besprechung," PV 8 (1840): 145.

39. Fasbender, *Beobachtungen*, p. 66. See also Riepe, *Erinnerungen*, pp. 52, 64–65; SPB 7 (1842): 474.

40. Diesterweg, "Über Lehrervereine," RB 4 (1829): 69–101; Fasbender, "Das 14te Lehrerfest von Berg und Mark . . . ," RB, n.s. 13 (1836): 94–100; "Zu dem Bericht 'Das 14te Lehrerfest von Berg und Mark . . . ,'" RB, n.s. 13 (1836): 110–21; Diesterweg's reports in RB, n.s. 20 (1839): 332–34 and RB, n.s. 21 (1840): 363–402. For background on the music festivals and the shift to associations in Westphalia see Uhlig, *Bourgeoisie und Volksschule*, pp. 18–19, 34–36, 118–20.

41. Diesterweg, "Über Lehrervereine," pp. 470–71, 474; A. Breter, "Vorschlag zur Stiftung eines Brandenburgischen Lehrervereins," PV 10 (1842): 185–88; Stiller, "Wo liegen die Ursachen der Kranken Verhältnisse des Volksschullehrerstandes . . . ?" PV 11 (1843): 49–54.

42. Böhm, "Aufruf zu einer Provinzial-Schullehrer-Vereine," PV 10 (1842): 197.

43. A. Breter, "Volksschullehrer-Versammlung der Mark Brandenburg," PV 10 (1842): 202–3; Dyckerhoff, "Folgen der ungenügenden Besoldung der Elementarlehrer," PV 10 (1842): 234. On Feb. 29, 1840, Diesterweg had called a group of younger teachers, most of them graduates of his Berlin seminar, to his home to found a "Younger Berlin Teachers' Association"; twenty-seven of them signed the statute he had already drafted. In 1841 this *Verein* voted to extend its discussions from pedagogical "knicknacks" to the teachers'

"dependent relationship" and "oppression," and to promote reform with publicity. See the account by Ludwig Rudolph in *Berliner Blätter für Schule und Erziehung* 6(1865): 25–26; "Zur Nachricht," PV 9 (1841): 152.

44. The ministerial decrees (Jan. 12 and May 22, 1835) are in Ludwig von Rönne, ed., *Allgemeiner Theil. Privat-Unterricht. Volksschulwesen*, pp. 525–26.

45. SPB 7 (1842): 376–78.

46. This report was originally published in the *Kölnische Zeitung* and reprinted in PR 7 (1843): 68–69.

47. According to instructions from the section (Feb. 16, 1844), the journal could no longer be purchased for teachers' libraries and reading circles (!), but individuals could not be forbidden to subscribe to "such a worthless paper, dangerous to their better convictions" (GS 3819). Five Berlin teachers who had written "provocative" articles for the journal were called to the town hall and given a warning by the school superintendent. The editor, Dr. Kobitz, had been warned a few days earlier. See the report in the *Leipziger Allgemeine Zeitung*, Sept. 1844, reprinted in PR 10 (1845): 87.

48. Diesterweg, "Schulwesen," *Der Sprecher*, 1839, pp. 861, 877. See also his report in RB, n.s. 21 (1840): 363–402. On the liberal ideal of association see esp. Friedrich Müller, *Korporation und Assoziation*.

49. Harkort, *Bemerkungen*, pp. 74, 90–94.

50. PR 5 (1842): 332–34; PR 7 (1843): 369–70.

51. See Heinrich Heffter, *Die deutsche Selbstverwaltung im neunzehnten Jahrhundert*, pp. 321–38; Bigler, *The Politics of German Protestantism*, pp. 187–230.

52. König, *Gedanken zur Nationalerziehung*, p. 177. See also Diesterweg, "Schulwesen," p. 861.

53. For the ministerial ordinance on the *Kreis* and provincal conferences see SPB 13 (1848): 355–58. Wander was not elected to the provincial conference in Silesia; since he did not attend the *Kreis* conference the *Landrat* declared him ineligible. He blamed clerical influence at the latter for the majority vote against the Breslau petition of April 25 on the issue of church-school relations. Later he declined a special invitation to the provincial conference, noting that his "un-Talleyrandish honesty in radical demands concerning the relationship of the school to the church" might do more harm than good. See "Offene Erklärung an Ein hohes Ministerium. . . ," RB, n.s. 38 (1848): 159–67; his letter to the provincial conference in SS 6 (1848): 310–11. At a session of the national assembly on July 1, 1848, Deputy Mätze protested that the *Kreis* assemblies had not been "entirely free," but three other deputies and the minister of culture contradicted him. Mätze's proposal that new conferences be called, without the *Landräte* and inspectors, was rejected by a vote of 200 to 145. The minister also objected to Harkort's compromise amendment (not voted on), which proposed that the results of free discussions at the provincial conferences be communicated to the national assembly (*Stenographische Bericht über die Verhandlungen der zu Vereinbarung der preussischen Staatsverfassung berufenen Versammlung*, pp. 325–30). There is a summary of the discussions of elementary school issues in the national assembly in PJ 4 (1849): 148–64.

54. PJ 4 (1849): 73.

55. For accounts of this *Verein* activity see ibid., pp. 230–39; Wilhelm Appens, "Die pädagogischen Bewegungen des Jahres 1848," p. 131.

56. "Aufruf an die rheinischen Lehrer," SC 6 (1849): 67.

57. PJ 4 (1849): 239.

58. Helmut König, ed., *Programme zur bürgerlichen Nationalerziehung in der Revolution von 1848–49*, p. 117. See also Theodor Hegener, "Die Unterrichtsfrage vom demokratischen und nationalen Gesichtspunkte aus erörtert," in ibid., pp. 142–43. For a general discussion of the differences between traditional corporatism and association see Thomas Nipperdey, "Verein als soziale Struktur in Deutschland im späten 18. und frühen 19. Jahrhundert."

CHAPTER 7

1. See esp. Diesterweg, "Schulwesen," *Der Sprecher*, 1839, pp. 861, 877; Diesterweg, "Die Allgemeine Bedingungen des Gedeihens der Lehrervereine," RB, n.s. 21 (1840): 363–402; Friedrich Müller, *Korporation und Assoziation*, pp. 256–91.

2. On this point see esp. James J. Sheehan's articles: "Liberalism and Society in Germany, 1815–1848," and "*Partei, Volk, and Staat.*"

3. Heinrich Deinhardt, "Die Volksschule und ihre Nebenanstalten," in Helmut König, ed., *Gedanken zur Nationalerziehung aus dem Vormärz*, pp. 172–73.

4. Ibid., p. 178.

5. See esp. Reinhart Koselleck, *Preussen zwischen Reform und Revolution*, pp. 560–85; Heinrich Heffter, *Die deutsche Selbstverwaltung im neunzehnten Jahrhundert*, pp. 246–67.

6. Mager, "Die Volksschule als Staatsanstalt," PR 6 (1843): 324–27, 333–34.

7. *Stenographische Berichte über die Verhandlungen der zu Vereinbarung der preussischen Staatsverfassung berufenen Versammlung*, pp. 87–88. Schwerin's remarks were directed primarily against the many proposals from teachers that the schools be "centralized" and "detached from the community."

8. There is a convenient table of the various drafts of school provisions in 1848 in Bernhard Krueger, *Stiehl und seine Regulative*, pp. 184–89.

9. See esp. Sheehan, "*Partei, Volk, and Staat*," pp. 167–70.

10. See esp. Diesterweg, "Über die Amtliche Stellung der Volksschullehrer," RB, n.s. 3 (1831): 259–82; Diesterweg, "Sind die Deutschen Volksschulen Staatsanstalten?" RB, n.s. 9 (1834): 53–72. In both articles Diesterweg was remarkably blunt in rejecting communal control over the school and teacher.

11. PJ 4 (1849): 159–62.

12. PJ 4 (1849): 15–19, 53–60. The major exception was the Westphalian provincial conference, which specified that the state should pay only teachers' raises. The petition commission of the national asembly, summarizing petitions from "1,400 teachers, various communities, and some private indi-

viduals," stressed the general consensus that the *Volksschule* be made a "state institution" with teachers salaried directly from the state treasury. The report was published in SC 5 (1848): 321 ff.

13. At the Brandenburg conference, Schnell had argued that "if it is determined that . . . the communities should participate in self-administration, they must also participate in the management of their schools. . . ." The compromise formula was that "the school is a state institution with the *Mitwirkung* of the communities." In the phrasing of the Silesian conference a "unified, independent *Volksschule*" would nonetheless secure "the natural rights of the family and the civil and ecclesiastical communities." Likewise the majority at the Rhineland conference voted that the school should enjoy an "independent position," but "on that basis a *Grundgesetz* should regulate its relationship to state, church, and community." But all three conferences proposed that the teacher receive a state salary and that the appointment right of the community be limited to a small number of state-proposed candidates (SPB 13 [1848]: 641–44; SS 6 [1848]: 370; SC 5 [1848]: 354–55).

14. "Von der Henneberger Kreiskonferenz in Suhl," RB, n.s. 39 (1849): 79.

15. SS 7 (1849): 376–77. See also the petition from teachers in *Kreis* Nimptsch (Oct. 1848) in SS 7 (1849): 356–58; the report on the *Kreis* conference in Custrin (Brandenburg) in BJ 4 (1848): 444.

16. Richard Baron, "Durch welches Mittel ist die Volksschule zur Volkssache zu machen?" SS 2 (1844): 105–9.

17. Böhm, "Der Lehrerstand und seine Bedeutung," PV 5 (1837): 259–60. See also his "Zeitfragen, vorgelegt zur Besprechung," PV 8 (1840): 123–24; Karl Friedrich Wilhelm Wander, *Die Volksschule als Staatsanstalt*, pp. 15–23; Fr. Horn, "Was will der Volksschullehrer unserer Tage hinsichtlich seines Berufsrechts . . . ?" PV 10 (1842): 146–52. To Horn "the *Volksschullehrer*, entrusted with responsibility for his own work and impact, must stand unchallenged [*unangefochten*] and untouchable [*unantastbar*] in all his functions." But in 1847 a Silesian teacher, echoing Deinhardt, warned that "as soon as we become state servants—i.e., as soon as we wear something other than the communal uniform—we will be required to harmonize our efforts with higher authorities [*nach Oben*] rather than with our immediate surroundings, and obviously that cannot be advantageous to our business" ("Die Schule als Staatsanstalt," SS 5 [1847]: 262).

18. Karl-Ernst Jeismann, "Die Eingabe eines Schwelmer Lehrers an das preussische Innenministerium, Sektion für Kultus u. Unterricht, aus dem Jahre 1814," pp. 130–31.

19. Theodor Hegener, "Die Unterrichtsfrage vom demokratischen und nationalen Gesichtspunkte aus erörtert," in Helmut König, ed., *Programme zur bürgerlichen Nationalerziehung in der Revolution von 1848–49*, pp. 129–44. Hegener, it should be noted, was willing to grant the communities the right to appoint their teachers and protect their interests with school committees.

20. SS 6 (1848): 371.

21. SS 6 (1848): 370. See also "Denkschrift über die Wünsche und Anträge der Volksschullehrer Schlesiens," appended to SS 6 (1848): 3–4. Hegener had

written that the priorities of the school must be high German and national geography and history; thus the individual would "be aware that he belongs to a large family of many millions of brothers who build a powerful *Reich,* bound together by their natural inclination as blood relations" (König, *Programme,* pp. 135–36).

22. "Von der Henneberger Kreiskonferenz," pp. 78, 81.

23. SS 6 (1848): 372.

24. SS 6 (1848): 375–76. See also "Denkschrift über die Wünsche und Anträge der Volksschullehrer Schlesiens," p. 6; "Von der Henneberger Kreiskonferenz," p. 81.

25. König, *Programme,* p. 150.

26. Krueger, *Stiehl,* pp. 187–89.

27. "Stellet den Lehrer den Gleichgebildeten gleich," PV 12 (1844): 139.

28. O. Z., "Ueber die persönliche Stellung des Lehrers vor Gericht," SS 4 (1846): 354–56. In 1837, Karl Böhm had also wanted the teaching office to include exemption from the lower courts. See his "Der Lehrerstand und seine Bedeutung."

29. E., "Schreiben eines jungen Lehrers an den Herausgeber," SS 1 (1843): 115.

30. Dyckerhoff, "Folgen der ungenügenden Besoldung der Elementarlehrer," PV 10 (1842): 228–29.

31. Baron, "Durch welches Mittel . . . ," p. 128.

32. *Wünsche rheinischer Lehrer betreffend die Gestaltung der Schule und ihrer Verhältnisse, die Bildung, Stellung und Besoldung der Lehrer,* pp. 11–12. In a letter to the "popular representatives" (Aug. 1848), Werner Herx, a teacher in Cologne, claimed to speak "in the name of the uneducated people, excluded from the highest goods of life" (quoted in Wilhelm Appens, "Die pädagogischen Bewegungen des Jahres 1848," p. 152). See also Balster, "Schulwesen, namentlich Besoldung der Lehrer," *Der Sprecher,* 1840, pp. 1432–36, 1452–54; Wander, *Die Volksschule als Staatsanstalt,* pp. 13–23.

33. C. Felde, "Ein Wort an Deutschlands Volksschullehrer und ihre Freunde," BJ 4 (1848): 387. See also König, *Programme,* pp. 129–44; Karl Friedrich Wilhelm Wander, *Die alte Volksschule und die neue.*

34. Hintze, "Von dem nothwendigen Unterschiede der Erziehung nach Zeiten und Ständen," PV 11 (1843): 85–87, 91–92.

35. Hintze's draft is published in König, *Programme,* pp. 101–11. The quotation is on p. 103. For background on Hintze see ibid., p. 34.

36. Ibid., pp. 103, 107–10.

37. Ibid., pp. 118–20, 123–24. In the committee that completed the Tivoli petition, Bloch argued that each community should determine its own mode of school support (with supplementary state funds), but found no support (BJ 4 [1848]: 372).

38. The proposals for teacher training are in PJ 4 (1849): 46–51.

39. SPB 13 (1848): 660–66, 672. Hintze defended the compromise on the grounds that it left open the possibility of a university education for teachers in a later reorganization of the entire school system. See his "Die Provincial-

Lehrerkonferenz für die Provinz Brandenburg a. d. O.," RB, n.s. 39 (1849): 245.

40. SS 6 (1848): 373–74.

41. In April 1849, Friedrich Harkort charged that many teachers had "allowed themselves to be stamped as underlings of anarchic democracy" (*Handlangern der zügellosen Demokratie*). The chairmen of the Dortmund *Kreis* conference, including Balster, protested that less than 3 percent of the teachers fit that description; in general the teaching corps had acted "in the truly patriotic spirit" and "predominantly in the Prussian dynastic interest," and indeed had been a "strong dam" against "anarchic democracy" in the countryside and small towns. See SC 6 (1849): 88; SS 7 (1849): 218–20.

CONCLUSION

1. See esp. Karl-Ernst Jeismann, "Die 'Stiehlschen Regulative.'"

2. Folkert Meyer, *Schule der Untertanen*, esp. pp. 201–2. Meyer's analysis of the teachers' associations is insightful; but in stressing their hostility to Social Democracy he may underestimate their commitment to political democracy and equality of opportunity. To some extent, I suspect, he describes a shift in the context of *Standespolitik* rather than in its ideological posture. Democratic and national ideals that were radical in Pre-March occupied a very different position in the ideological spectrum of the Second Empire. See also C. L. A. Pretzel, *Geschichte des deutschen Lehrervereins in den ersten 50 Jahren seines Bestehens*; Helmut Meyer, "Das Selbstverständnis des Volksschullehrers in der zweiten Hälfte des 19. Jahrhunderts"; Douglas R. Skopp, "The Mission of the *Volksschule*"; Andreas Möckel, "Schulpolitik und Einheitsschulgedanke im deutschen Lehrerverein, 1900–1920."

3. Peter V. Meyers, "Professionalization and Societal Change," pp. 551–53.

4. Wilhelm Heinrich Riehl, *Die bürgerliche Gesellschaft*, esp. pp. 66–112, 312–49. The book was originally published in 1851. Riehl generalized about Germany as a whole, but his focus was on the south and southwest.

5. Ibid., pp. 81–82, 346–49.

6. In this regard the teachers' social perspective may have been reflected in, and reinforced by, the ideology they adopted. See esp. Lothar Gall, "Liberalismus und 'bürgerliche Gesellschaft.'" Gall argues that the liberal ideal of a "klassenlosen Bürgergesellschaft 'mittlerer Existenzen,'" developed in the preindustrial and prerevolutionary environment of Pre-March, retained a traditional concept of *Stand* that was ill suited to the class society of the second half of the nineteenth century.

7. For a somewhat different perspective on the relationship between professional status, association, and bureaucracy see John R. Gillis, *The Prussian Bureaucracy in Crisis, 1840–1860*, esp. pp. 95–98. In 1848, Gillis argues, many younger officials in the higher state bureaucracy "viewed their professional discontents as a subordinate aspect of the broader political and social situation"; they did not bother to organize professional associations because "corporate interests had been displaced by civic concerns." In con-

trast subaltern officials organized voluntary associations that were "directed toward immediate economic and social goals" and "represented a direct challenge to both the traditional system of authority and the corporate ideal." But compare also Erich J. C. Hahn, "The Junior Faculty in 'Revolt'"; Lenore O'Boyle, "Klassische Bildung und soziale Struktur in Deutschland zwischen 1800 und 1848."

BIBLIOGRAPHY

The following list is limited to material cited in the text.

ARCHIVAL RECORDS

The archival records used in this study are in Hauptstaatsarchiv Düsseldorf, Abteilung Kalkum; Staatsarchiv Münster; Geheimes Staatsarchiv, Berlin-Dahlem. Numbers in the notes refer to individual folders, as classified in the archives. The local school files are classified under *Spezialakten*.
The full citations are:
Hauptstaatsarchiv Düsseldorf, Abt. Kalkum: Regierung Düsseldorf, Schulwesen.
Staatsarchiv Münster: Provinzialschulkollegium and II. B, Regierung Arnsberg, Volksschulen.
Geheimes Staatsarchiv, Berlin-Dahlem: Pr. Br. Rep. 2, Regierung Potsdam, II. Abteilung, Kirchen-und Schulwesen.

PRIMARY LITERATURE

Periodicals

Articles from these periodicals are cited in the notes, but are not listed individually in the bibliography.

Berliner Blätter für Schule und Erziehung.
Berliner Jahrbücher für Erziehung und Unterricht.
Centralblatt für die gesammte Unterrichts-Verwaltung in Preussen, edited by Ferdinand Stiehl.
Der deutsche Schulfreund. Ein nützliches Hand- und Lesebuch für Lehrer in Bürger-und Landschulen, edited by Heinrich Gottlieb Zerrenner.
Jahrbücher des preussischen Volks-Schul-Wesens, edited by Ludolph Beckedorff.
Pädagogischer Jahresbericht für Deutschlands Volksschullehrer, edited by Karl Nacke.
Pädagogische Revue. Centralorgan für Wissenschaft, Geschichte und Kunst der Erziehung, edited by Dr. Karl Mager.
Preussische Volks-Schul-Zeitung, edited by Dr. J. G. Kobitz.

Regierung Potsdam, Amtsblatt.
Rheinische Blätter für Erziehung und Unterricht mit besonderer Berücksichtigung des Volksschulwesens, edited by Adolph Diesterweg.
Schlesische Schullehrerzeitung, edited by Christian Gottlieb Scholz.
Schulblatt für die Provinz Brandenburg, edited by Otto Schulz and Ferdinand Striez.
Schul-Chronik, edited by Franz Ludwig Zahn.
Der Schulrat an der Oder, edited by Wilhelm Harnisch.
Der Sprecher (formerly *Rheinisch-Westfälischer Anzeiger*).
Der Volksschullehrer, edited by Wilhelm Harnisch.

Books and Articles

Allgemeines Landrecht für die Preussischen Staaten von 1794. Edited by Hans Hattenhauer and Günther Bernert. Frankfurt, 1970.
"Auszug eines Berichts an die Königliche Regierung zu Lingen, die Beschaffenheit des Landschulwesens in der Inspection Lienen (in der Grafschaft Tecklenburg) betreffend." *Jahrbücher der preussischen Monarchie,* Nov. 1799: 288–92.
Beschreibung des Regierungsbezirkes Düsseldorf nach seinem Umfange, seiner Verwaltungs-Eintheilung und Bevölkerung. Düsseldorf, 1817.
Cousin, Victor. *Report on the State of Public Instruction in Prussia.* Translated by Sarah Austin. London, 1834.
Die Denkschrift der märkischen Lehrer. Zustände der Volksschule und ihrer Lehrer im Rheinland und Westfalen, pt. 1. Iserlohn, 1843.
Diesterweg, Friedrich Adolph Wilhelm. *Friedrich Adolph Wilhelm Diesterweg: Sämtliche Werke, I. Abteilung: Zeitschriftenbeiträge.* Edited by Heinrich Deiters et al. Berlin, 1956– .
Dieterici, F. W. C. "Statistische Übersicht des öffentlichen Unterrichts im Preussischen Staate im Jahre 1816 und im Jahre 1846." *Mittheilungen des Statistischen Bureaus in Berlin* 1 (1848): 33–51.
Dietrich, Theo, and Klink, Job-Günter, eds. *Volksschulordnungen 16. bis 18. Jahrhundert.* Zur Geschichte der Volksschule, vol. 1. Bad Heilbrunn, 1964.
Eilers, Gerd. *Zur Beurtheilung des Ministeriums Eichhorn von einem Mitgliede desselben.* Berlin, 1849.
Einige patriotische Vorschläge zur Verbesserung des Schulwesens auf dem Lande. Leipzig, 1780.
Engel, Ernst. "Beiträge zur Geschichte und Statistik des Unterrichts, insbesondere des Volksschulunterrichts, im preussischen Staate." *Zeitschrift des königlichen Preussischen Statistischen Bureaus* 9(1869): 99–116.
Fasbender, Johann Peter. *Beobachtungen und Erinnerungen aus meinem Leben.* Wesel, 1862.
Felbiger, Johann Ignaz von. *Johann Ignaz von Felbiger.* Edited by Julius Scheveling. Paderborn, 1958.

Fichte, Johann Gottlieb. *Johann Gottlieb Fichte: Addresses to the German Nation.* Edited and translated by George Armstrong Kelly. New York, 1968.

Gelderblom, F. B. *Wehrstand und Lehrstand.* Düsseldorf, 1847.

Die Gesetzgebung auf dem Gebiete des Unterrichtswesens in Preussen, vom Jahre 1817 bis 1868. Berlin, 1869.

Giese, Gerhardt, ed. *Quellen zur deutschen Schulgeschichte seit 1800.* Quellensammlung zur Kulturgeschichte, vol. 15. Göttingen, 1961.

[*Haensel.*] *Die Keime zur Auflösung des Kgl. evang. Schullehrer-Seminars zu Breslau.* Leipzig, 1846.

Harkort, Friedrich. *Bemerkungen über die preussische Volksschule und ihre Lehrer.* Hagen, 1842.

Harnisch, Wilhelm. *Die Schullehrerbildung: Für die, welche sie suchen, und für die, welche sie befördern.* Eisleben, 1836.

———. *Der jetzige Standpunkt des gesammten preussischen Volksschulwesens.* Leipzig, 1844.

Herzberg, Friedrich. *Ueber einige wichtige Hindernisse, die der Verbesserung des Volksschulwesens überhaupt und des hiesigen Landküsterseminariums insbesondere im Wege stehen.* Berlin, 1801.

———. *Über das Berlinische Elementarschulwesen.* Berlin, 1819.

Hesse, J. Eduard. *An Preussens Volksschullehrer! Grundzüge zu einer das ganze Volksschulwesen umfassenden Petition.* Quedlinburg and Leipzig, 1848.

Jantke, Carl, and Hilger, Dietrich, eds. *Die Eigentumslosen. Der deutsche Pauperismus und die Emancipationskrise in Darstellungen und Deutungen der zeitgenössischen Literatur.* Freiburg, 1965.

König, Helmut, ed. *Deutsche Nationalerziehungspläne aus der Zeit des Befreiungskrieges.* Berlin, 1954.

———, ed. *Gedanken zur Nationalerziehung aus dem Vormärz.* Berlin, 1959.

———, ed. *Programme zur bürgerlichen Nationalerziehung in der Revolution von 1848–49.* Berlin, 1971.

Krünitz, Johann Georg. *Landschule.* Oekonomische-technologische Encyklopädie. Oder allgemeines System der Staats-Stadt-Haus-und Landwirtschaft, pt. 61. Berlin, 1793.

Küpper, Johann Anton. *Versuch, eine zweckmässige Verfassung für den protestantischen Prediger- und Schullehrerstand zu entwerfen; mit Rücksicht auf das Herzogtum Berg.* 2 vols. Düsseldorf, 1807.

Landfermann, Dietrich Wilhelm. *Dietrich Wilhelm Landfermann. Erinnerungen aus seinem Leben.* Leipzig, 1890.

Langer, Adam. *Erinnerungen aus dem Leben eines Dorfschullehrers.* Landeck in Silesia, 1900.

Die Lehr- und Erziehungs-Anstalten der Provinz Westfalen. Münster, 1830.

Lichtenstein, Ernst. "Aus dem Krisenjahr der Pestalozzi-Schulreform in Preussen. Ein unveröffentlichter Bericht von Bernh. Chr. Ludwig Natorp." *Zeitschrift für Pädagogik* 1 (1955): 83–108.

"Materialien zur Geschichte des Berliner Schulwesens nach der Revolution von 1848." *Jahrbuch für Erziehungs- und Schulgeschichte* 1 (1961): 279–304.

Nehm, Johann Wilhelm. *Darlegung einiger Übelstände, welche den Volksschullehrerstand noch drücken, nebst Angabe der Erfordnisse zur Hebung derselben.* Essen, 1839.

Neumann, K. H. *Über die jetzt eingeleitete Verbesserung des Elementarschulwesens.* Potsdam, 1811.

Niedergesäs, Friedrich Wilhelm. *Das Elementarschulwesen in den königlichen preussischen Staaten.* Crefeld, 1847.

Overberg, Bernhard. *Bernhard Overbergs Anweisung zum zweckmässigen Schulunterricht,* edited by J. Niessen. Breslau, 1905.

Prenninger, Johann Friedrich, ed. *Landschulbibliothek. Oder Handbuch für Schullehrer auf dem Lande.* Vols. 1–3. Berlin, 1779–83.

Protokolle der Provincial-Lehrer-Conferenz zu Frankfort a. O. Berlin, n.d.

Riehl, Wilhelm Heinrich. *Die bürgerliche Gesellschaft.* Die Naturgeschichte des Volkes als Grundlage einer deutschen Sozial-Politik, vol. 2, 9th ed. Stuttgart, 1897.

Riepe. *Erinnerungen an Johann Wilhelm Nehm, nebst Andeutungen über Zustände des Lehrerlebens.* Essen, 1841.

Rohlfs, A. *Die Volksschule und ihre Lehrer.* Berlin, 1842.

———. *Die Volksschule und ihre Lehrer, II. Sendschreiben.* Charlottenburg, 1843.

Rönne, Ludwig von, ed. *Allgemeiner Theil. Privat-Unterricht. Volksschulwesen.* Das Unterrichtswesen des preussischen Staates, vol. 1. Berlin, 1855.

Salzmann, Christian Gotthilf. *Christian Gotthilf Salzmanns Pädagogische Schriften.* Edited by Ernst Wagner. 2 vols. 2nd ed. Langensalza, 1890.

Schmieden, Carl von. *Das Elementar- und Bürgerschulwesen in der Provinz Brandenburg in seiner Entwicklung und seinen Fortschritten.* Leipzig, 1840.

Schram, Josef. *Die Verbesserung der Schulen in moralisch-politischer-pädagogischer und polizeilicher Hinsicht.* Dortmund, 1803.

Schweim, Lothar, ed. *Schulreform in Preussen, 1809–1819. Entwürfe und Gutachten.* Weinheim, 1966.

"Statistische Uebersicht der Bevölkerung sämmtlicher Städte der Kurmark Brandenburg. . . ." *Mittheilungen des Statistischen Bureaus in Berlin* 2 (1849): 265–77.

Steinbart, Gotthilf Samuel. *Vorschläge zu einer allgemeinen Schulverbesserung, insofern sie nicht Sache der Kirche sondern des Staates ist.* Zullichau, 1789.

Stenographische Berichte über die Verhandlungen der zu Vereinbarung der preussischen Staatsverfassung berufenen Versammlung. Beilage zu Preussischen Staats-Anzeiger, vol. 1. Berlin, 1848.

Stephani, Heinrich. *Heinrich Stephani, 1761–1850. Zur Schulpolitik und Pädagogik.* Edited by Günter Ulbricht. Berlin, 1961.

Tabellen und amtlichen Nachrichten über den preussischen Staat für das Jahr 1849. Vol. 2. Berlin, 1851.

Wander, Karl Friedrich Wilhelm. *Die Volksschule als Staatsanstalt. Ein*

Wort für Hebung des Volksschulwesens und bessere Stellung der Volksschullehrer. Leipzig, 1842.

——. *Pädagogische Briefe vom Rhein an den Verfasser der Volksschule als Staatsanstalt*. Mannheim, 1845.

——. *Die alte Volksschule und die neue. Ein Wort an die Vertreter des deutschen Volkes*. Breslau, 1848.

——. *Karl Friedrich Wilhelm Wander, 1803 bis 1879*. Edited by Pädagogische Fakultät der Karl-Marx-Universität, Leipzig. Berlin, 1954.

Wilberg, Johann Friedrich. *Erinnerungen aus meinem Leben, nebst Bemerkungen über Erziehung, Unterricht, und verwandte Gegenstände*. Essen, 1836.

Wünsche rheinischer Lehrer betreffend die Gestaltung der Schule und ihrer Verhältnisse, die Bildung, Stellung und Besoldung der Lehrer. Elberfeld and Iserlohn, 1847.

Zedlitz, Karl Abraham von. "Vorschläge zur Verbesserung des Schulwesens in den Königlichen Länden." *Berlinische Monatschrift* 10 (1787): 97–116.

SECONDARY LITERATURE

Anderson, Eugene N. "The Prussian *Volksschule* in the Nineteenth Century." In *Entstehung und Wandel der modernen Gesellschaft*, edited by Gerhard A. Ritter, pp. 261–79. Berlin, 1970.

Anton, G. K. *Geschichte der preussischen Fabrikgesetzgebung bis zu ihrer Aufnahme durch die Reichsgewerbeordnung*. Leipzig, 1891.

Appens, Wilhelm. "Die pädagogischen Bewegungen des Jahres 1848. Ein Beitrag zur Geschichte der Pädagogik des 19. Jahrhunderts." Dissertation, Jena, 1914.

Bigler, Robert M. *The Politics of German Protestantism: The Rise of the Protestant Church Elite in Prussia, 1815–1848*. Berkeley, 1972.

Block, F. A. *Geschichte des städtischen Schulwesens zu Merseburg*. Merseburg, 1885.

Bloth, Hugo Gotthard. *Adolph Diesterweg. Sein Leben und Wirken für Pädagogik und Schule*. Heidelberg, 1960.

Boschan, Richard. *Das Bildungswesen in der Stadt Potsdam bis zur Wiederaufrichtung des preussischen Staates*. Potsdam, 1912.

Braun, Gustav. *Geschichte des organisch vereinigten Kirchen- und Schulamtes in Schlesien*. Breslau, 1933.

Brinkmann, Albrecht. *Geschichte der Dortmunden Volksschulen*. Dortmund, 1954.

Buchholz, Friedrich, and Buchwald, Gerhard, eds. *Die brandenburgischen Lehrerseminare und die ihnen angegliederten Präparandenanstalten*. Berlin, 1961.

Büsch, Otto, ed. *Untersuchungen zur Geschichte der frühen Industrialisierung vornehmlich im Wirtschaftsraum Berlin/Brandenburg*. Berlin, 1971.

Busshoff, Heinrich. "Die preussische Volksschule als soziales Gebilde und politischer Bildungsfaktor in der ersten Hälfte des 19. Jahrhunderts. Ein Bericht." *Geschichte in Wissenschaft und Unterricht* 22 (1971): 385–96.

Clausnitzer, Ludwig. *Geschichte des preussischen Unterrichtsgesetzes. Mit besonderer Berücksichtigung der Volksschule.* 3rd. ed. Berlin, 1898.

Conze, Werner. "Vom 'Pöbel' zum 'Proletariat.' Sozialgeschichtliche Voraussetzungen für den Sozialismus in Deutschland." *Viertel-jahrsschrift für Sozial- und Wirtschaftsgeschichte* 41 (1954): 333–64.

——. "Beruf." In *Geschichtliche Grundbegriffe: Historisches Lexikon zur Politisch-Sozialen Sprache in Deutschland,* edited by Otto Brunner, Werner Conze, and Reinhart Koselleck, vol. 1, pp. 490–507. Stuttgart, 1972.

Daheim, Hansjürgen. *Der Beruf in der modernen Gesellschaft. Versuch einer soziologischen Theorie.* Beiträge zur Soziologie und Sozialphilosophie, vol. 13. Cologne, 1967.

Deutsches Wörterbuch. Vol. 10, sec. 2, pt. 1. Edited by M. Heyne et al. Leipzig, 1960.

Dohmen, Günther. *Die Entstehung des pädagogischen Bildungsbegriffs und seines Bezugs zum Schulunterricht.* Bildung und Schule. Die Entstehung des deutschen Bildungsbegriffs und die Entwicklung seines Verhältnisses zur Schule, vol. 2. Weinheim, 1965.

Engelsing, Rolf. "Probleme der Lebenshaltung in Deutschland im 18. und 19. Jahrhundert." In Rolf Engelsing, *Zur Sozialgeschichte deutscher Mittel- und Unterschichten,* pp. 11–25. Kritische Studien zur Geschichtswissenshaft, vol. 4. Göttingen, 1973.

Fischer, Fritz. *Ludwig Nicolovius: Rokoko, Reform, Restauration.* Stuttgart, 1939.

Fischer, Wolfram. "Der Volksschullehrer: Zur Sozialgeschichte eines Berufsstandes." *Soziale Welt* 12 (1961): 37–47.

Flaskamp, Franz. *Die Anfänge westfälischer Lehrerbildung. Das Seminar zu Büren.* Rheda, 1957.

Flitner, Andreas. *Die politische Erziehung in Deutschland. Geschichte und Probleme, 1750–1880.* Tübingen, 1957.

Fooken, Enno. *Die geistliche Schulaufsicht und ihre Kritiker im 18. Jahrhundert.* Probleme der Erziehung, vol. 5. Wiesbaden-Dotzheim, 1967.

Gagliardo, John G. *From Pariah to Patriot; The Changing Image of the German Peasant, 1770–1840.* Lexington, Ky., 1969.

Gall, Lothar. "Liberalismus und 'bürgerliche Gesellschaft': Zu Charakter und Entwicklung der liberalen Bewegung in Deutschland." *Historische Zeitschrift* 220 (1975): 324-56.

Gerth, Hans. *Bürgerliche Intelligenz um 1800. Zur Soziologie des deutschen Frühliberalismus.* Kritische Studien zur Geschichtswissenschaft, vol. 19. Göttingen, 1976.

Gillis, John R. *The Prussian Bureaucracy in Crisis, 1840–1860: Origins of an Administrative Ethos.* Stanford, 1971.

Goebel, Klaus. "Diesterwegs Nachfolger in Meurs. Die politische Vorgeschichte der Berufung Franz Ludwig Zahns zum Seminardirektor 1832." *Rheinische Vierteljahrsblätter* 36 (1972): 229–44.

Götze, Walter. *Die Begründung der Volksbildung in der Aufklärungsbewegung.* Langensalza, 1932.

Grass, Karl Martin, and Koselleck, Reinhart. "Emanzipation." In *Geschichtliche Grundbegriffe: Historisches Lexikon zur Politisch-Sozialen Sprache in Deutschland,* edited by Otto Brunner, Werner Conze, and Reinhart Koselleck, vol. 2, pp. 153–97. Stuttgart, 1972.

Gross, Eberhard. *Erziehung und Gesellschaft im Werk Adolph Diesterwegs. Die Antwort der Schule auf die Soziale Frage.* Weinheim, 1966.

Hahn, Erich J. C. "The Junior Faculty in 'Revolt': Reform Plans for Berlin University in 1848." *American Historical Review* 82 (1977): 875–95.

Hamerow, Theodore. *Restoration, Revolution, Reaction: Economics and Politics in Germany, 1815–1871.* Princeton, 1958.

Hartmann, Klaus L. "Schule und 'Fabrikgeschäft.' Zum historischen Zusammenhang von Kinderarbeit, Kinderschutzgesetz und allgemeiner Elementarbildung." In *Schule und Staat im 18. und 19. Jahrhundert: Zur Sozialgeschichte der Schule in Deutschland,* edited by K. Hartmann, F. Nyssen, and H. Waldeyer, pp. 171–253. Frankfurt, 1974.

Hattermann, Otto. *Konservative und liberale Strömungen in der preussischen Volksschulpolitik, 1819 bis 1848.* Volkstum und Erziehung, vol. 5. Hamburg, 1938.

Heffter, Heinrich. *Die deutsche Selbstverwaltung im neunzehnten Jahrhundert. Geschichte der Ideen und Institutionen.* Stuttgart, 1950.

Heidrich, Artur. "Die Auflösung des evangelischen Schullehrerseminars zu Breslau am 29. 1. 1846. Eine Episode aus dem Vormärz." Dissertation, Breslau, 1929.

Heinemann, Manfred. *Schule im Vorfeld der Verwaltung. Die Entwicklung der preussischen Unterrichtsverwaltung von 1771–1800.* Göttingen, 1974.

Heinemann, Manfred, and Rüter, Wilhelm. *Landschulreform als Gesellschaftsinitiative. Philip von der Reck, Johann Friedrich Wilberg und die Tätigkeit der 'Gesellschaft der Freunde der Lehrer- und Kinder in der Grafschaft Mark' (1789–1815).* Göttingen, 1975.

Hesse, Hans Albrecht. *Berufe im Wandel. Ein Beitrag zum Problem der Professionalisierung.* Soziologische Gegenwartsfragen, n.s. 25. Stuttgart, 1968.

Heubaum, Alfred. "Die Geschichte des ersten preussischen Schulgesetzentwurfs (1798–1807)." *Monatschrift für höhere Schulen* 1 (1902): 20–40, 111–22, 145–54, 209–20, 305–21.

Heuser, Julius. "Karl Friedrich August Grashof als Reorganisator des Volksschulwesens am Niederrhein 1814–1816. Ein Beitrag zur preussischen Schulgeschichte." Dissertation, Cologne, 1929.

Hillmann, Robert. "Lehrer- und Küstereinkommen vom 16. bis 18. Jahrhundert. Ein Beitrag zur Geschichte der wirtschaftlichen Lage der

Volksschullehrer." *Pädagogische Monatshefte* 8 (1902): 513–26, 569–79.

Höber, Kerrin. *Die merkantilistische Nationalerziehung.* Göttingen, 1936.

Hollack, Emil, and Tromnau, Friedrich. *Geschichte des Schulwesens der königlichen Haupt- und Residenzstadt Königsberg i/Pr. mit besonderer Berücksichtigung der niederen Schulen.* Königsberg, 1899.

Jarausch, Konrad H. "The Sources of German Student Unrest, 1815–1848." In *The University in Society,* vol. 2, edited by Lawrence Stone, pp. 533–69. Princeton, 1974.

Jeismann, Karl-Ernst. "Die 'Stiehlschen Regulative': Ein Beitrag zum Verhältnis von Politik und Pädagogik während der Reaktionszeit in Preussen." In *Dauer und Wandel der Geschichte: Aspekte europäischer Vergangenheit,* edited by Rudolf Vierhaus and Manfred Botzenhart, pp. 423–47. Münster, 1966.

———. "Die Eingabe eines Schwelmer Lehrers an das preussische Innenministerium, Sektion für Kultus u. Unterricht, aus dem Jahre 1814." *Westfälische Zeitschrift* 118 (1968): 115–33.

———. "'Nationalerziehung.' Bemerkungen zum Verhältnis von Politik und Pädagogik in der Zeit der preussischen Reform, 1806–1815." *Geschichte in Wissenschaft und Unterricht* 19 (1968): 201–18.

———. "Tendenzen zur Verbesserung des Schulwesens in der Grafschaft Mark, 1798–1848." *Westfälische Forschungen* 22 (1969–70): 78–97.

———. *Das preussische Gymnasium in Staat und Gesellschaft. Die Entstehung des Gymnasiums als Schule des Staates und der Gebildeten, 1787–1817.* Industrielle Welt, vol. 15. Stuttgart, 1974.

König, Helmut. *Zur Geschichte der Nationalerziehung in Deutschland im letzten Drittel des 18. Jahrhunderts.* Monumenta Paedagogica, vol. 1. Berlin, 1960.

———. *Zur Geschichte der bürgerlichen Nationalerziehung in Deutschland zwischen 1807 und 1815.* 2 vols. Monumenta Paedagogica, vols. 12–13. Berlin, 1972.

Koselleck, Reinhart. *Preussen zwischen Reform und Revolution. Allgemeines Landrecht, Verwaltung und soziale Bewegung von 1791 bis 1848.* Stuttgart, 1967.

Kosler, Alois M. *Die preussische Volksschulpolitik in Oberschlesien, 1742–1848.* Einzelschriften zur schlesischen Geschichte, vol. 3. Breslau, 1949.

Krueger, Bernhard. *Stiehl und seine Regulative. Ein Beitrag zur preussischen Schulgeschichte.* Weinheim, 1970.

Laduga, Friedrich. *Beiträge zur Entwicklung des Volksschulwesens in der Provinz Westfalen, 1815–1848.* Universitas. Archiv für wissenschaftliche Untersuchungen und Abhandlungen, vol. 2. Münster, 1927.

La Vopa, Anthony J. "Status and Ideology: Rural Schoolteachers in Pre-March and Revolutionary Prussia." *Journal of Social History* 12 (1979): 430–56.

Ludwig, Karl-Heinz. "Die Fabrikarbeit von Kindern im 19. Jahrhundert. Ein

Problem der Technikgeschichte." *Vierteljahrsschrift für Sozial- und Wirtschaftsgeschichte* 52 (1965): 63–85.

Meiners, Wilhelm. "Landschulwesen und Landschullehrer im Herzogtum Cleve vor hundert Jahren." *Archiv für Kulturgeschichte* 3 (1905): 345–61.

———. "Das Volksschulwesen in Mark und Cleve unter Steins Verwaltung (1787–1804)." *Mitteilungen der Gesellschaft für deutsche Erziehungs- und Schulgeschichte* 16 (1906): 114 ff.

Menze, Clemens. *Die Bildungsreform Wilhelm von Humboldts.* Das Bildungsproblem in der Geschichte des europäischen Erziehungsdenkens, vol. 3. Hannover, 1975.

Meyer, Folkert. *Schule der Untertanen. Lehrer und Politik in Preussen, 1848–1900.* Historische Perspektiven 4. Hamburg, 1976.

Meyer, Helmut. "Das Selbstverständnis des Volksschullehrers in der zweiten Hälfte des 19. Jahrhunderts." Dissertation, Münster, 1961.

Meyers, Peter V. "Professionalization and Societal Change: Rural Teachers in Nineteenth Century France." *Journal of Social History* 9 (1976): 542-58.

Möckel, Andreas. "Schulpolitik und Einheitsschulgedanke im deutschen Lehrerverein, 1900–1920." Dissertation, Tübingen, 1961.

Müller, Detlef K. *Sozialstruktur und Schulsystem: Aspekte zum Strukturwandel des Schulwesens im 19. Jahrhundert.* Studien zum Wandel von Gesellschaft und Bildung im Neunzehnten Jahrhundert, vol. 7. Göttingen, 1977.

Müller, Friedrich. *Korporation und Assoziation. Eine Problemgeschichte der Vereinigungsfreiheit im deutschen Vormärz.* Schriften zum Öffentlichen Recht, vol. 21. Berlin, 1965.

Nell-Breuning, Oswald v. "Standischer Gesellschaftsaufbau." In *Handwörterbuch der Sozialwissenschaften*, vol. 10, edited by Erwin v. Beckerath et al., pp. 6–11. Stuttgart, 1959.

Neukum, Josef. *Schule und Politik. Politische Geschichte der bayerischen Volksschule, 1818–1848.* Munich, 1969.

Neumann, Fr. J. "Zum Lehre von den Lohngesetzen." *Jahrbücher für Nationalökonomie und Statistik*, 3rd. ser., 4 (1892): 219–37, 366–97.

Nipperdey, Thomas. "Volksschule und Revolution im Vormärz." In *Politische Ideologien und nationalstaatliche Ordnung: Studien zur Geschichte des 19. und 20. Jahrhunderts*, edited by Kurt Kluxen and Wolfgang J. Mommsen, pp. 117–42. Munich, 1968.

———. "Verein als soziale Struktur in Deutschland im späten 18. und frühen 19. Jahrhundert." In *Geschichtswissenschaft und Vereinswesen im 19. Jahrhundert. Beiträge zur Geschichte historischer Forschung in Deutschland*, edited by Hartmut Boockmann et al., pp. 1–44. Göttingen, 1972.

Notbohm, Hartwig. *Das evangelische Kirchen- und Schulwesen in Ostpreussen während der Regierung Friedrich dem Grossen.* Studien zur Geschichte Preussens, vol. 5. Heidelberg, 1959.

Noyes, P. H. *Organization and Revolution: Working Class Associations in the German Revolutions of 1848–1849*. Princeton, 1966.

Obermann, Karl. "Zur Klassenstruktur und zur sozialen Lage der Bevölkerung in Preussen 1846 bis 1849." *Jahrbuch für Wirtschaftsgeschichte* 1973, pt. 2, pp. 79–120.

O'Boyle, Lenore. "The Democratic Left in Germany, 1848." *Journal of Modern History* 33 (1961): 374–83.

———. "The Middle Class in Western Europe, 1815–48." *American Historical Review* 71 (1966): 826–45.

———. "Klassische Bildung und soziale Struktur in Deutschland zwischen 1800 und 1848." *Historische Zeitschrift* 207 (1968): 584–608.

Paulsen, Friedrich. *Der gelehrte Unterricht im Zeichen des Neuhumanismus, 1740–1892*. Geschichte des gelehrten Unterrichts auf den deutschen Schulen und Universitäten vom Ausgang des Mittelalters bis zur Gegenwart. Mit besonderer Rücksicht auf den Klassischen Unterricht, vol. 2. 3rd enl. ed. Berlin, 1921.

Pretzel, C. L. A. *Geschichte des deutschen Lehrervereins in den ersten 50 Jahren seines Bestehens*. Leipzig, 1921.

Ringer, Fritz K. *Education and Society in Modern Europe*. Bloomington, Ind., 1979.

Rittershausen, Dietrich. "Beiträge zur Geschichte des Berliner Elementarschulwesens von der Reformation bis 1836." *Märkische Forschungen* 9 (1865): 178–317.

Rohr, Donald G. *The Origins of Social Liberalism in Germany*. Chicago, 1963.

Rosenbaum, Margaret. "Untersuchungen zur Veränderung der Lage und des Selbstverständnisses des Lehrers während der Aufklärung in Deutschland; Ein Beitrag zur Geschichte des Volksschullehrerberufes." Dissertation, Cologne, 1970.

Sauer, Bruno. *Aus dem Leben eines märkisch-pommerschen Dorfschullehrers um 1800. Ein Beitrag zur Schul- und Kulturgeschichte*. Wissenschaftliche Beiträge zur Geschichte und Landeskunde Ost-Mitteleuropas, no. 89. Marburg, 1970.

Schaaf, Erwin. *Die niedere Schule im Raum Trier-Saarbrücken von der späten Aufklärung bis zu Restauration, 1780–1825*. Trier, 1966.

Schäfer, Walter. "Die ideengeschichtlichen Grundlagen der Reform des Volksschulwesens im Grossherzogtum Berg und in der Stadt Düsseldorf von 1799–1816." Dissertation, Cologne, 1929.

Schagen, Alfons. *Josef Görres und die Anfänge der preussischen Volksschule*. Studien zur rheinischen Geschichte, vol. 7. Bonn, 1913.

Schneider, Lothar. *Der Arbeiterhaushalt im 18. und 19. Jahrhundert, dargestellt am Beispiel des Heim- und Fabrikarbeiters*. Beiträge zur Ökonomie von Haushalt und Verbrauch, vol. 4. Berlin, 1967.

Schneider, K., and Petersilie, A., eds. *Die Volks- und Mittelschulen sowie die sonstigen niederen Schulen im preussischen Staate im Jahre 1891*. Berlin, 1893.

Schwartz, Paul. *Die neumärkischen Schulen am Ausgang des 18. und am Anfang des 19. Jahrhunderts.* Schriften des Vereins für Geschichte der Neumark, vol. 17. Landsberg, 1905.

———. "Die Schulen der Provinz Westpreussen unter dem Oberschulkollegium, 1787–1806." *Zeitschrift für Geschichte der Erziehung und des Unterrichts* 16 (1926): 51–123.

———. "Die Schulen der Provinz Ostpreussen unter dem Oberschulkollegium, 1787–1806." *Zeitschrift für Geschichte der Erziehung und des Unterrichts* 21 (1931): 54–78, 280–307.

Schwarz, Willi. "Die bergische Schule und ihre Wurzeln in der Vikarie- und Küsterschule: Beitrag zu Schulrechtsgeschichte (1700–1825) im Gebiet des heutigen Rheinisch-Bergischen Kreises." Dissertation, Cologne, 1966.

Sheehan, James J. "Liberalism and Society in Germany, 1815–1848." *Journal of Modern History* 45 (1973): 583–604.

———. "*Partei, Volk* and *Staat.* Some Reflections on the Relationship between Liberal Thought and Action in Vormärz." In *Sozialgeschichte Heute,* edited by Hans Ulrich Wehler, pp. 162–74. Göttingen, 1974.

Singer, Barnett. "The Teacher as a Notable in Brittany, 1880–1914." *French Historical Studies* 9 (1976): 635–59.

Skopp, Douglas R. "The Mission of the *Volksschule:* Political Tendencies in German Primary Education, 1840 to 1870." Ph.D. dissertation, Brown University, 1974.

Spranger, Eduard. *Wilhelm von Humboldt und die Reform des Bildungswesens.* Berlin, 1910.

Die Stein'schestädteordnung in Breslau. 2 vols. Breslau, 1909.

Thiele, Gunnar. *Die Organisation des Volksschul- und Seminarwesens in Preussen 1809–19. Mit besonderer Berücksichtigung der Wirksamkeit Ludwig Natorps.* Leipzig, 1912.

———. *Allgemeine Voraussetzungen zur Geschichte der preussischen Lehrerseminare.* Geschichte der preussischen Lehrerseminare, vol. 1. Berlin, 1938.

Tilly, Richard. "Popular Disorders in Nineteenth Century Germany: A Preliminary Survey." *Journal of Social History* 4 (1970–71): 1–40.

Uhlig, Gottfried. *Bourgeoisie und Volksschule im Vormärz. Schulpolitische Kämpfe in Westfalen, 1838–1848.* Berlin, 1960.

van de Kamp, Max. "Das niedere Schulwesen in Stadt und Stift Essen bis 1815." *Beiträge zur Geschichte von Stadt und Stift Essen* 47 (1930): 122–225.

Vollmer, Ferdinand. *Friedrich Wilhelm I und die Volksschule.* Göttingen, 1909.

———. *Die preussische Volksschulpolitik unter Friedrich dem Grossen.* Berlin, 1918.

von Hippel, Olga. *Die pädagogische Dorfutopie der Aufklärung.* Göttinger Studien zur Pädagogik, vol. 31. Langensalza, 1939.

Werres, Walter. "Die sozialgeschichtliche Begründung der modernen

Landschule in Deutschland." Dissertation, Münster, 1966.

Wienecke, Friedrich. "Die Landgnadenschulen der Kurmark." *Brandenburgia* 14 (1905–6): 312–17.

———. "Statistik des Schulwesens der Kurmark im Jahre 1806." *Brandenburgia* 18 (1909–10): 103–5.

———. "Die Begründung der Berliner Schul-Kommission am September 1811." *Brandenburgia* 20 (1911–12): 49–71.

Willemsen, Heinrich. "Das bergische Schulwesen unter der französischen Herrschaft (1806–1813)." *Mitteilungen der Gesellschaft für deutsche Erziehungs- und Schulgeschichte* 18 (1908): 65–95, 153–209.

Zimmermann, Wilhelm. *Die Anfänge und der Aufbau des Lehrerbildungs- und Volksschulwesens am Rhein um die Wende des 18. Jahrhunderts.* 3 vols. Cologne, 1953–65.

INDEX